# Housing Options for Disabled People

*of related interest*

An A–Z of Community Care Law
*Michael Mandelstam*
ISBN 185302 560 7 pb

Handbook for Assessing and Managing Care in the Community
*Philip Seed and Gillian Kaye*
ISBN 1 85302 227 6 pb

Community Care Practice and the Law, Second Edition
*Michael Mandelstam*
ISBN 1 85302 647 6 pb

Equipment for Older or Disabled People and the Law
*Michael Mandelstam*
ISBN 1 85302 352 3 pb

Multicultural Issues in Occupational Therapy
*Edited by Zeenat Meghani-Wise*
ISBN 1 85302 474 0 pb

Home at Last
How Two Young Women with Profound Intellectual
and Multiple Disabilities Achieved Their Own Home
*Pat Fitton, Carol O'Brien and Jean Willson*
ISBN 1 85302 254 3 pb

# Housing Options for Disabled People

*Edited by Ruth Bull*

Foreword by Baroness Masham

Jessica Kingsley Publishers
London and Philadelphia

The right of the contributors to be identified as authors of this work has been asserted by them in accordance with the Copyright, Designs and Patents Act 1988.

First published in the United Kingdom in 1998 by
Jessica Kingsley Publishers Ltd
116 Pentonville Road
London N1 9JB, England
and
325 Chestnut Street
Philadelphia, PA 19106, U S A

Second impression 2000

**Library of Congress Cataloging in Publication Data**
A CIP catalogue record for this book is available from the Library of Congress

**British Library Cataloguing in Publication Data**
Housing options for disabled people
1.Handicapped – Housing 2.Architecture and the handicapped
I.Bull, Ruth
720.8'7

ISBN 1-85302-454-6

Printed and Bound in Great Britain by
Athenaeum Press, Gateshead, Tyne & Wear

# Contents

# Preface

This book is about the availability of solutions to problems met by the disabled person in need of specifically designed or adapted housing.

It places within an historical context a policy and legislative background in need of continual updating and improvement for it to be in line with a need to resolve the scarcity of suitable housing for disabled people. Difficulties that exist can most effectively be overcome only by policies that are realistic both for users and for providers, the kind of difficulties that, especially for those with limited resources, can appear as formidable hurdles when first encountered. This book highlights the need for ongoing action.

It is now more possible than ever before to pool the resources of professionals to resolve problems in housing that face the disabled person.

If a disabled person seeks to live at home in the community the blocks that exist through lack of availability of resources, through the real limitations of buildings or through the non-accessibility of information, need to be removed. Joint working becomes essential, together with a collective response to problem solving. Assessing a situation is the first stage of a full procedure that culminates in a need for financing. There are a number of sources of help available and in particular the housing renewal grant system.

A creative approach to provision is needed for the translation of need to be converted into concrete assistance. Systems and networks must come to exist that make possible the harnessing of public and private sector resources made effective through a national programme.

The realisation of housing provision goals can only be achieved by linking directly the disabled person with the providers. Not only are the analytical and practical skills of the occupational therapist crucial in this link, but also the desire of the provider to be furnished with specific and relevant information, whether the needs are to be met with new-build housing or by adapting existing property. Careful planning at the right time can avoid frustrating and expensive mistakes.

Current limitations of provision for the housing of a disabled person or group stand in need of redress. For example, the absence of legislation that guarantees equal opportunity for disabled people in their living environment inevitably inclines housing organisations to allot low priority to the matter of housing disabled people. A need for reform is further underlined by the continual contestation in law by judicial review of social services authorities' responsibilities towards disabled people. This book points to the value of recommended standards and regulations that, once implemented by law, can set broad design requirements and design guides with a view to attaining suitable solutions for both general and individual needs in housing. Economic problems can be eased by good housing design and this needs emphasising when building homes accessible to all but that can be adapted to special needs with minimal cost and disruption. Good design can only emerge from consultations linked through each stage of the design process and between all parties.

Discussion about the practical housing needs of a disabled person leaving hospital, or an institution, or parental care focuses the need of the disabled person for improved lines of communication towards day to day independence in control of personal assistance requirements. For those who need. help, there are resource   centres to provide help. What needs to happen is that for those who seek information, the information becomes more readily available through standardised systems, so that the path of a disabled person with assessed and recognisable needs leads to the goal of that barrier-free environment that is integral to civil right.

I hope very much that this book will help make many people aware of the essential need for suitable housing for disabled people.

When people with serious disabilities find they need information about various housing schemes, they do find difficulty in obtaining the right solution. Local information services can be parochial and disabled people very often need to move to a different part of the country. If there was a service which could cover the country with the vital housing information, this would save worry and time.

*Baroness Masham*

# Introduction

*Ruth Bull*

This book is written for individuals or groups of disabled people who aspire to a barrier free environment, and for those who have the opportunity to uphold this ideal in the course of professional practice. Access and planning officers, managers of local government and social housing provision, architects and design-and-build teams, environmental health officers and agencies progressing housing grant works, all need to be familiar with the subjects covered here. Social workers helping disabled people and their carers to plan for their desired level of independence and control over their lives are encouraged to consider the advantages to the removal of barriers which block social interaction, and occupational therapists will find their role in housing for disabled people promoted through progression from undergraduate to masters level.

This book is written by members of the College of Occupational Therapists Specialist Section in Housing (COTSSIH). Each chapter stands alone, but together they progress the theme of the social, environmental and practical shifts which offer opportunities for a co-operative approach to better housing for people of all abilities.

The authors are at times providing information or expressing views based on their own practical experience or that of professional colleagues. All authors have worked in a housing related field for some considerable time, and examples given often derive from local practices, applicable nationally.

The development of housing options for disabled people, and the associated application of the principles and practice of occupational therapy, has developed differentially throughout Great Britain. This book offers one reference point for the spectrum of concepts and applications in this field. Little formal research has been completed on the occupational therapy contribution in housing: readers who are members of this profession may be stimulated to carry out research to enhance knowledge upon which better practice may be based.

Where examples are given, pseudonyms are used and situations and details are changed to protect confidentiality for individuals or authorities.

'Disability refers to a loss or limitation of opportunity owing to social, physical or attitudinal barriers' such as an inability to enter a building because of the siting of the entrance up a flight of steps (Morris 1993, p.21). This social model of disability challenges the assumptions made by people who may perceive disability as a medical problem; the independent living movement assumes that all human life is of value, anyone is capable of exerting choices and exerting control over their lives, and that 'disabled people have the right to participate fully in society' (Morris 1993, p.21). The authors of this book do not seek to uphold one model as against another, but anticipate that readers will develop their own understanding of disability by keeping abreast of current literature and thinking, and through their own experience.

Since the Housing Act 1985 shifted the role of housing authorities from major providers to a more strategic role (see Chapter 2) housing associations have been the growth area for rented social housing, attracting both public and charitable money and taking a prominent position in building accessible and convenient housing for successive generations. This is seen in developments of 'mobility' and 'visitability' standards of general needs housing, built alongside specialist accommodation convenient for people with different abilities, including indoor wheelchair users. Councils who once owned most of the public sector rented housing can transfer their housing to local housing companies. This followed a trend already established in several boroughs.

The introduction of the right to buy housing association dwellings under the Housing Act 1996 has allowed a higher number of accessible properties onto the housing market. At the same time privately owned properties are being made accessible through disabled facilities grants. Some private house builders see the advantage of building accessible housing, recognising that this is convenient for people with children, older people, disabled people and those who wish to be able to entertain their disabled friends.

Disabled people expect to be able to make their own decisions in response to housing options before them. Professionals are constrained by legislation and guidance, local policies, and ethical considerations, yet often hold the key to unlocking resources. This book offers opportunities to use that key. 'The distinctive nature of management in the public domain lie in the dilemmas to be faced ... the dilemmas are never finally resolved' (Stewart and Ranson 1988). In housing, the dilemmas are in the desire both to build marketable private dwellings and to meet the needs of disabled people; to control and monitor public service levels yet to facilitate, enable and promote choice.

# References

*Housing Act 1996.* London: HMSO.

Morris, J. (1993) *Independent Lives – Community Care and Disabled People.* Basingstoke: Macmillan.

Stewart, J. and Ranson, S. (1998) *Management in the Public Domain.* London: Sage Publications.

# CHAPTER I

# The Legislative and Policy Context

## Ruth Bull and Veronica Watts

## Introduction

The current legislative and policy framework for housing services for disabled people has evolved in an incremental fashion since the introduction of Britain's welfare state. The result may be perceived to be untidy; instead of one law vested in one primary agency, responsibility rests with different statutory authorities and efficient service delivery demands collaboration and co-operation between them, both at a strategic and operational level. Occupational therapists and other professionals working in the field of disability housing need to understand this maze if they are to make best use of the different options available and act as informed advisors and 'enabling partners' to the disabled people they serve. Understanding the legal and policy context is not an option; it is an essential foundation for good practice. This first chapter aims to introduce readers to that context and to provide the foundation for subsequent chapters which develop different subjects and specialist aspects in more detail. It does not set out to provide a definitive text on relevant law; that would take a book in its own right. Rather it aims to provide a broad understanding for those new to the subject and points readers to sources of further detailed guidance. For brevity, hereafter the term 'disabled person' will apply to those of all ages unless otherwise stated, including elderly people who may not consider themselves disabled in the conventional sense but who present in need of services. This approach also reflects the reality that disabled people also age, and for the purposes of this chapter the distinction between the two groups is relatively arbitrary and possibly unhelpful.

We are grateful for the considerable and generous assistance of Sheelagh Richards, Occupational Therapy Advisor to the Department of Health, in compiling this chapter and for her continuing endeavours towards high professional standards for the occupational therapy profession in general and in the housing field in particular.

*Scope of the chapter's content*

Unfortunately space does not permit inclusion of the detail of separate legislation in the field of housing and welfare provision in Scotland; neither does the text reflect the integrated nature of health and social services organisations in Northern Ireland, or separate guidance issued by the Welsh Office, for instance. However, reference is included to major areas of difference in Scotland and readers pointed to the relevant guidance.

*The housing needs of disabled people*

The following vignettes illustrate the daily challenges presented to occupational therapists and other professionals in social services and housing agencies who are charged with the responsibility of meeting the housing needs of people with a chronic illness or disability.

---

### Example: Leonard Williams

As an agricultural worker, Leonard Williams had lived in the countryside all his life. He inherited his small, thatched cottage from his mother and lived a contented though impoverished life with the company of several cats and dogs. Being unable to drive, he relied on a kindly neighbour to do his shopping but otherwise survived well until hospital investigations revealed advanced and inoperable cancer. Leonard refused to accept advice from professionals whom he saw to be 'interfering busy-bodies'. He rejected all mention of residential care but agreed to the district nursing service calling regularly. They provided a commode to avoid him having to use the outside toilet at night and arranged for a home improvement agency to deal with some essential home repairs to keep him 'wind and water tight'.

Leonard was quite satisfied with these arrangements until his son came to visit. He immediately lodged a complaint that inadequate provision had been made for his father's welfare and demanded that an extension with bathroom and toilet facilities be provided. At the age of 90, Leonard did not wish the disruption this would involve and, given his rapidly failing health, the statutory agencies were not optimistic that building work could be completed sufficiently quickly, even if the necessary expenditure were to be approved. Moreover, Leonard's son had never visited his father regularly, appeared unwilling to listen to his wishes and, somewhat inevitably, his motivation was in question.

## Example: Ashok Rao

Ashok and Bharati Rao were a young couple living in a three-bedroom, semi-detached council property with their two young children. Ashok worked as a stock controller for a local builders' merchant, the premises being conveniently located less than a mile from the family's home. At the age of 30 Ashok was told he had multiple sclerosis but he remained largely problem free for three years until an acute episode resulted in a sudden loss of mobility. A referral to the social services department suggested the family required rehousing as Ashok was unable to climb the stairs and was struggling up and down on his bottom with his wife's assistance. Space on the upper landing was limited for wheelchair access and there were steps at both the front and rear doors to the property. Rehousing might have seemed the obvious solution, particularly in view of the progressive nature of multiple sclerosis. However, Ashok and Bharati were far from reaching such a conclusion themselves. Living on a single income, the couple had no savings to finance a house move and believing his condition was likely to go into remission and his mobility would improve, Ashok was determined that ease of access to both his employment and the children's school were more immediate priorities. The family wished to stay put. The design and accommodation layout of the home permitted only one solution; the installation of a stair lift.

Some housing agencies and professionals might consider this an unwise provision for a client with a deteriorating condition, or an unsatisfactory solution with children in the home, despite the fact that the electrical control could be readily immobilised. But Ashok was not ready to contemplate life with a severe disability and he and Bharati wanted a solution which would enable them to cope with their immediate crisis, continue to live in their comfortable home and maintain the important friendships and support they enjoyed in their immediate community.

## Example: James Walters

Helen and Michael Walters had a family of four including James, a nine-year-old with severe athetoid cerebral palsy. With three older sisters and brothers devoted to his every need, James was a gregarious child at the centre of a busy and socially active family. They had all coped well with James' needs, sharing the tasks involved in his daily care. In their large spacious home there was plenty of space for James' wheelchair, but as he grew and became heavier, carrying him up and down stairs and lifting him in and out of the bath was becoming a strain for his mother.

---

### Example: James Walters (continued)

Michael Walters had established his own small company and was beginning to travel overseas to develop an export trade. The older children were busy doing what teenagers do and could no longer be relied upon. Helen decided it was time to adapt the home to make it easier for her to cope and sought social services' help to build a ground-floor extension with a bedroom, bathroom and play facilities for James' personal use.

The existing upstairs bathroom was sufficiently spacious to allow a number of acceptable options including the provision of a bath-lifter, adaptation of the shower to enable level access and replacement of the pedestal wash-basin to provide James with a closer approach. A wheelchair lift could have been fitted to the wide, straight flight of stairs. Alternatively, a through-ceiling lift could have been installed in the downstairs cloakroom space, although this would have required some reconfiguration of the upstairs accommodation.

Helen and Michael had, however, engaged a private architect and had plans prepared for the extension they believed James required. As they did a great deal of business entertaining, they did not wish the appearance of the hallway to be diminished by a lift installation. Neither did they wish to lose the use of the cloakroom or have the upstairs layout altered, and considered that their older children should not be inconvenienced by disability equipment in the bathroom.

They argued that James should be enabled to have his friends to visit, some of whom were also wheelchair users, and that dedicated ground-floor facilities would better promote his independence and dignity. An extension would represent a better investment in his personal autonomy as he grew towards adulthood.

---

Current social policy calls for services to be provided, and therefore resources to be expended, on a 'needs led' basis but these cases illustrate the complexities of discriminating between needs, wants, wishes and demands. Ensuring that resources are spent on those in greatest need requires that professional practice is guided by explicit policies and procedures which are known to both service users and professionals alike and which guard against practice which is either inequitable, discriminatory or driven by individual attitudes and values. In the course of this chapter, readers might consider how these clients could, or should, be assisted within the current scope of statutory provision. The law confers *powers* and *duties* – what statutory authorities *may do* or what they *must do*. There is a wealth of guidance to draw upon but no blueprint or prescribed solutions to individual needs. Subsequent authors lay the foundations for good practice; ultimately the aim should be to meet the service user's needs and expressed preferences after an objective, well-informed assessment and decision making process in which the elderly or disabled person, and his or her carers, participate fully as equal partners.

Much disability is a consequence not of the 'impairment' experienced by the individual but by the environment in which they, and we, all live. Internal or household environments can be as disabling as the external or public environment. In terms of daily survival and ease of living, having a home which is enabling and not 'dis-abling' is the immediate concern of many people addressing the effects of a temporary or permanent restriction of their functional abilities. The Office of Population, Censuses and Surveys (OPCS) surveys of disability in Great Britain estimated that there are just over six million adults with one or more disabilities, of whom around 4000 (or 7%) live in some kind of communal establishment. Almost 14 per cent of adults living in private households have at least one disability. Almost 70 per cent of disabled adults were aged 60 or over and nearly half were aged 70 or over. Locomotor problems are the most common source of disability, affecting over four million adults (Martin, Meltzer and Elliot 1988). The increasing proportion of elderly people in the British population is a well-known trend; 16 per cent of the population are now over retirement age and the proportion of the very elderly is increasing. It is estimated that by the year 2031 over six million people in England and Wales will be over 75 years of age. Home ownership is also increasing so that a greater proportion of elderly people in particular will be faced not only with limitations imposed by the style of their housing but by the concerns of affording the costs of maintenance and repair. According to the 1986 English House Conditions survey, elderly people over 75 occupy nearly one-third of houses lacking basic amenities such as an indoor toilet and an adequate hot water supply and almost 20 per cent of houses considered unfit for human habitation. The issues then are not only about those with severe disabilities who require more spacious housing, possibly with sophisticated technical aids such as environmental control systems, they are also about large numbers of elderly people who might not consider themselves disabled but experience problems owing to loss of safe mobility and advancing frailty. Many of them will be living in adverse environments which compound their difficulties.

Some homes are immediately adaptable, others are not, or would involve expenditure disproportionate to the gains. Urban and rural settings offer different constraints and opportunities for alternative housing. Elderly and disabled people living in private, public or social housing have different choices available to them; some have very poor choice when architectural, environmental, social and economic factors collectively conspire against both their needs and wishes. Government policy has evolved from regarding disabled peoples' housing needs as essentially 'special' or 'different' to recognising that, given the choice, most people would prefer to continue living in their familiar, established home, even if practical arrangements are less than ideal. When disabled people need to find a first home, or when rehousing is necessary, social considerations will be as important as bricks and mortar – but there will be more opportunity to pursue the ideal for each individual and their family or carers. Colleagues develop these themes in later chapters.

## Historical policy development

### The foundations of welfare provision

Two pieces of legislation remain as landmarks in the development of social welfare provision for disabled people: the National Assistance Act 1948, whose definition of 'disabled persons' stands in all subsequent legislation related to disabled people, and the Chronically Sick and Disabled Persons Act 1970 (CSDP Act) which requires local authorities to inform themselves of the numbers and needs of disabled people (as defined in the National Assistance Act) in their areas and, in Section 2, lays out a range of services including 'assistance with home adaptations, or the provision of any additional facilities designed to secure greater safety, comfort or convenience' which authorities should provide.

The National Assistance Act (Section 29) definition of disabled persons, viz:

> persons aged eighteen or over who are blind, deaf or dumb or who suffer from mental disorder of any description and other persons aged eighteen and over, who are substantially and permanently handicapped by illness, injury or congenital deformity or such other disabilities as may be prescribed by the Minister

remained largely unchallenged until a debate in the House of Lords in April 1996 during the passage, of the Housing Grants, Construction and Regeneration Bill, when their Lordships drew attention to the outdated terminology of this definition. The government consented to some immediate tidying up of the wording (although the spirit remains unchanged) and agreed that a modern alternative should be sought. Apart from the insensitivity of the terminology, the interpretations of *permanent* and *substantial* and the subtleties between a *chronic illness* and a *disability* have long been the focus of dissent between local authorities and service users who have found themselves on the losing side of local interpretations. The wording of a new definition promises to provoke a lively debate; suffice to say here that readers should be aware of the commitment to future change.

The CSDP Act is significant because it enables local authorities to assess the needs of people whom it considers to be 'registerable' within the National Assistance Act definition and if it is satisfied that it is necessary to arrange services to meet those needs, the authority has a duty to do so. Whereas the major responsibility for meeting housing needs (including grant aid to adapt properties) is now contained within housing legislation, ultimate responsibility still defaults to the 'welfare' authority, i.e. to local authority social services departments, under the terms of this Act. Their responsibilities are reinforced in other legislation, such as the Disabled Persons (Services, Consultation and Representation) Act 1986 and the Children Act 1989, which will be dealt with later. Although the provisions of the CSDP Act now sit within the wider scope of the new community care arrangements arising from the NHS and Community Care Act 1990, it is important to stress that the CSDP Act remains important because of the strong duties it imposes on authorities. Its relationship to community care is discussed later in the chapter.

(*Scotland*: Most of the provisions of the CSDP Act were deemed to be incorporated in the Social Work (Scotland) Act 1968. The Chronically Sick and Disabled Persons (Scotland) Act 1972 amended Section 29(2) of the CSDP Act so that Sections 1 and 2 would also apply to Scotland. References to Section 29 of the National Assistance Act should be read as Section 12 of the Social Work (Scotland) Act 1968.)

*The foundations of disability housing provision*

Prior to 1978 the housing needs of disabled people were primarily met through two discrete spheres of provision:

- by public sector housing provision, in the form of suitable housing for rent, or
- by welfare authorities, through the provision of adaptations to housing occupied by individual disabled people.

Integrated social services departments, which drew together the previously separate health and welfare, and children's departments, had been created by the Social Work (Scotland) Act 1968 and the Local Authority Social Services Act 1970. Their formerly general and permissive responsibilities to promote the welfare of disabled people were enhanced by the CSDP Act when 'arrangements' were translated into identifiable services; thus local authority social services departments (social work in Scotland) became the major providers of housing adaptation services for disabled people in both public and private sector housing.

The Public Sector Housing Act of 1957 had required housing authorities to consider the housing conditions and needs of their districts, but that they should have regard to the special needs of disabled people was made explicit in Section 3 of the CSDP Act:

> Every local authority … in discharging their duty … shall have regard to the special needs of chronically sick or disabled persons; and any proposals prepared and submitted to the Minister … for the provision of new houses shall distinguish any houses which the authority propose to provide which make special provision for the needs of such persons.

Local authorities therefore became responsible for ensuring that their own housing stock was designed to be accessible to disabled people. But what did 'accessible' mean? Ambulant disabled people had different needs from wheelchair users, for example, and those with sensory impairments had needs which might be even more difficult to define. To assist implementation of Section 3, the Department of the Environment (DoE) sought to produce templates for good housing design and subsequently published *Mobility Housing* and *Wheelchair Housing* in 1974 and 1975 respectively (Department of the Environment 1974, 1975).

Trevor Dodd deals with the detail in Chapter 5 but essentially this approach was based on the notion that *mobility housing* incorporated basic design criteria which were simply a development from normal standards which would make housing convenient to the majority of users and could be adapted conveniently at little additional costs, whereas *wheelchair housing* incorporated extra space and design standards which would be required by permanent wheelchair users. Housing authorities during the 1970s then embarked upon providing a proportion of mobility or wheelchair units in new housing stock or through renovation schemes where this proved practicable. The same standards were adapted by housing associations; an emergent source of social and 'special needs' housing provision.

Mobility housing proved revolutionary and popular; it met the needs of the majority of elderly people most commonly affected by loss of mobility and became the normative approach to the design of accommodation, including sheltered housing, for elderly people. Wheelchair housing, however, proved more problematic and contentious. Provision of small clusters of 'disabled houses' followed a pattern which had become popular in Europe, principally in the Netherlands, and whereas these houses were initially welcomed by disabled people who had previously struggled in hostile environments, they inevitably reinforced the notion of social difference. That permanent wheelchair users needed extra space and facilities designed for their safety and convenience was not in dispute, but by the 1980s the social stigma of 'ghetto' development was being challenged by a developing disability movement. Housing authorities and professionals were challenged by a more practical reality – the 'sods law' of matching needs and availability; of having a wheelchair house available but no identified tenant wanting it in that location at that precise point in time, or of having a tenant with an urgent need but no acceptable property available (see Chapter 4 for details of matching people to properties).

Bringing organisation to matching needs and resources was recognised in the 1978 Circular *Adaptations of Housing for People who are Physically Disabled* (Department of the Environment 1978). Whereas it recommended that the responsibility for identifying, assessing and advising on the housing needs of individual people, including the need for adaptations, should remain with social services authorities, it required that housing authorities assume clearer responsibilities for their own tenants by:

- providing structural adaptations of their own housing
- establishing registers to identify specially designed or adapted housing and tenants with unmet needs (which might be met by such housing)
- the allocation of wheelchair and mobility housing.

In the Housing Act 1974 (Section 56) the government had included additional financial provisions to support housing services for disabled people, namely discretionary improvement grants for works required for making a dwelling suitable for the accommodation, welfare or employment of a disabled occupant, and mandatory intermediate grants for installing standard amenities (toilet, fixed bath or shower etc.) which were lacking or for installing suitable alternative facilities where existing amenities were inaccessible to a disabled person. Guidance required local authorities to take advantage of the 'broad discretion' available to them and in an appendix, listed the 'structural' features which should be accepted as eligible for grant aid. This provision signalled the shift of emphasis in the provision of housing adaptations from social services to housing authorities; a trend which has been the subject of much debate but which has been further consolidated since 1990.

The majority of housing authorities responded positively to both these new responsibilities, at least in terms of developing effective adaptations services for their own tenants. Coupled with their responsibilities to assess the housing needs of their communities and plan provision accordingly, the 1978 directive paved the way for them to develop integrated policies which achieved a relevant mix of types of housing and management procedures which better ensured that available housing could be matched to the needs of tenants, including those with special needs. Social services departments welcomed this separation and clarification of responsibility; apart from being relieved of the necessity to negotiate between housing authorities and their disabled tenants, social services departments now had access to the additional grant aid which, coupled with their own Section 2 (CSDP Act) resources, enabled them to concentrate their funding on adaptations for private sector home-owners. It is important to note that improvement and intermediate grants were not subject to means testing whereas social services departments had traditionally means tested disabled clients using their powers under the Health and Social Services and Social Security Adjudications Act 1983. Social services departments and their clients would therefore only be responsible for costs in excess of grant aid.

As with so many areas of complex policy where responsibilities are divided between different statutory agencies, progress on one front brings concomitant disadvantages – in this instance, different arrangements for occupiers of public and private sector housing; the potential for inequity; and resultant confusion for disabled people in understanding the respective responsibilities of housing and social services agencies. The fact that current government guidance continues to highlight the need for greater strategic and operational collaboration between agencies simply serves to reinforce the complexity which persists.


## Legal and policy developments

During the 1980s, a number of pieces of legislation were enacted which have a direct bearing on disabled peoples' entitlements and the legal framework which underpins current community care and housing services. The following summaries include only main sections and provisions relevant to our considerations; readers are recommended to refer to the actual legislation or accompanying guidance for a more detailed understanding. The text will lead up to implementation of the NHS and Community Care Act 1990 and current community care policy.


*Social services' powers and duties towards disabled people*

DISABLED PERSONS (SERVICES, CONSULTATION AND REPRESENTATION) ACT 1986

This aimed to give substance to the CSDP Act by giving disabled people additional rights of representation. Only certain sections were implemented, including:

> Section 4 – duty on local authorities to assess need
>
> Sections 5 and 6 – identification and assessment of disabled
> school leavers

Section 8 – duty to have regard to abilities of carers

Section 9 – provision of information

Disability organisations lobbied the government to implement Sections 1–3 which are concerned with the appointment of 'authorised representatives' to make representations on behalf of disabled people, that is, to formalise the concept of personal advocacy. Ministers have taken the view that the requirements of these sections are to a large extent reflected in the new arrangements arising from implementation of the NHS and Community Care Act 1990 but have stated that the situation will be reviewed following several years' experience of community care. Local authorities were therefore encouraged, when implementing community care, to develop local advocacy schemes to meet particular needs.

Section 4 extends the duty of local authorities to consider the needs of disabled persons under Section 2 of the CSDP Act when requested to do so by a disabled person or his carer and decide whether the needs of the disabled person call for the provision by the authority of any services provided under Section 2. However, if when carrying out an assessment under the NHS and Community Care Act, it appears to a local authority that the person is disabled, the authority has a duty to proceed to making a decision on the services required under Section 4 and must inform the disabled person that they will be doing so.

Sections 5 and 6 require local education authorities to notify social services authorities of young people leaving full-time education who may be deemed to be disabled and entitled to services, and requires social services departments (in collaboration with education departments and local health services) to arrange an assessment of their needs and plan the support they will require to assist their transition to adult services. These 'transition' services may be an important trigger to begin consideration of young people's independent housing needs.

Section 8 requires an authority, when assessing the needs of a disabled person for welfare services, to 'have regard' to whether a carer can continue to give substantial amounts of care on a regular basis. Section 8 does not apply if the authority is already assessing a carer under the Carers (Recognition and Services) Act 1995 (see below).

CHILDREN ACT 1989

The Children Act 1989 defines disabled children as 'children in need' and emphasises the importance of their needs being met within the context of their family.

Section 17 states that the local authority has a general duty to 'safeguard and promote the welfare of children within their area who are in need ... by providing a range and level of services appropriate to those children's needs'. This includes disabled children.

Schedule 2 Part I sets out what types of services can be provided. Paragraph 6 requires that the local authority shall provide services designed to 'minimise the effect on disabled children ... of their disabilities ...' and give them the opportunity to lead lives which are as normal as possible. Paragraph 3 allows them to assess their needs at the same time as an assessment of their needs is made under any other relevant enactment.

Section 27 enables the local authority to request help from another authority or person in order to meet the needs of children in need and this authority must comply with the request if it is compatible with their own statutory duties and obligations.

(It is important to note that the provisions of the CSDP Act still apply to disabled children. The original definition of the CSDP Act was amended to include the age rule (over 18) to reflect the over-arching authority of the Children Act.)

The consequence of these arrangements means that where a local authority declines to make adequate arrangements for a disabled child under the terms of the CSDP Act (possibly where the family is ineligible for grant aid from the housing authority – see subsequent text on the Housing Grants, Construction and Regeneration Act 1996 – and social services are unable to fund the works under the CSDP Act Section 2 provisions) the authority continues to have a duty under the terms of the Children Act.

Further guidance in relation to children with disabilities is provided in *Child Health in the Community: A Guide to Good Practice* (Department of Health 1996).

(**Scotland:** In Scotland, Part II of the Children (Scotland) Act 1995 deals with the promotion of children's welfare and the duties of local authorities towards children in need, including disabled children or a child who is affected adversely by the disability of a member of the family. See *Scotland's Children: A Brief Guide to the Children (Scotland) Act 1995* (Scottish Office 1995).)

CARERS (RECOGNITION AND SERVICES) ACT 1995
This Act gives carers who are providing or intend to provide substantial care on a regular basis the right on request to a separate assessment of their ability to care or continue caring and requires local authority social services departments to take into account the results of that assessment when determining what, if any, services shall be provided to the user.

Detailed guidance is provided in *Carers (Recognition and Services) Act 1995: Policy and Practice Guide* (Department of Health 1996).

COMMUNITY CARE (DIRECT PAYMENTS) ACT 1996

This enables local authorities to give disabled people under the age of 65 direct cash payments in lieu of the community care services they have been assessed as needing to enable them to appoint carers of their own choosing and manage this important aspect of their lives. The Act also allows local authorities to include the value of aids and adaptations which might have been provided by the social services department. The draft guidance does however point to the merits of disabled people receiving (particularly expensive) equipment from social services and continuing to benefit from the maintenance and follow-up service which would be provided when their needs change – when they require equipment replacing, for example. Nevertheless, the technical provision exists for disabled people to seek a direct payment for the equipment which might be provided and installed in association with any minor works or an adaptation, or in respect of any adaptation it may have provided. The government brought this legislation into force from 1 April 1997 with a commitment to review the age limit after one year.

Further guidance is provided in *Community Care (Direct Payments) Act 1996: Policy and Practice Guidance* (Department of Health 1997).

MANUAL HANDLING OPERATIONS REGULATIONS 1992 (MHOR)

This came into force on 1 January 1993 in order to meet the European Community Directive (90/269/EEC) on the minimum health and safety requirements for the manual handling of loads where there is a risk particularly of back injury to workers. These regulations demand inclusion because they have introduced an entirely new debate into the realms of community care. They place a responsibility upon all employers to:

- avoid the need for hazardous manual handling so far as is reasonably practicable
- where such handling cannot be avoided, to assess the risk in advance to staff and patients/clients through their manual handling operations, and take into account all the relevant factors
- reduce any risk of injury to the lowest level reasonably practicable, using the assessment as a basis for action.

The regulations therefore have major implications for both health and social services authorities and many have developed protocols which lay out the conditions under which mechanical (or electrical) lifting devices must be employed. Whereas portable lifting devices were primarily provided by social services authorities as 'equipment to daily living' and fixed systems incorporated in housing adaptations where necessary, there is now a rife debate about whether the authority providing the care service – a health authority or private agency employing the nurse who is doing the lifting, for example – should have a *prima facie* responsibility to make provision under its health and safety arrangements.

Local policies will prevail but those involved in designing new build special needs housing would be sensible to consider internal layouts able to accommodate fixed and portable lifting systems and this must be a prime consideration in the design of housing adaptations.

## The legal framework for housing services

### HOUSING ACT 1985

This Act changed the role of housing authorities from major providers of public housing to a more strategic role which recognised that the contributions of housing associations and private sector developers needed drawing together in a more cohesive planning and collaborative framework. They are responsible for developing housing strategies which address the range of housing needs in their area (including the needs of elderly, disabled and vulnerable people) and ensuring that best use is made of private, public and voluntary sector housing stock (Department of the Environment 1995).

### LOCAL GOVERNMENT AND HOUSING ACT 1989 (PART VIII)

Through this legislation the government introduced a suite of renovation grants essentially focused on the regeneration and repair of housing in a poor standard of repair This range of grants included:

- *disabled facilities grants* – for the provision of facilities for a disabled person (mandatory for access features and discretionary for additional features; see later), and

- *assistance for the provision of minor works to dwellings* – for the provision of minor works including improvement of thermal insulation; small works of repair, improvement or adaptation required by an elderly person (often called 'staying put' grants); or works to adapt a dwelling to enable an elderly person to be cared for.

Renovation grants were also introduced for the improvement or repair of properties over ten years old (mandatory for housing found to be unfit) and grants for houses in multiple occupation (HMO).

Disabled facilities grants (DFGs) replaced the discretionary improvement and mandatory intermediate grants introduced in 1974 and after 1990 became the major source of statutory support for the adaptation of properties for disabled people in both private and public sector housing. The level of grant to be awarded is dependent upon a test of resources (ToR) designed centrally to ensure that resources are devoted to those in greatest need.

As a result of reviews, limits have been imposed on these grants; in January 1994 all mandatory grant limits, including DFGs, were reduced from £50,000 to £20,000 (£24,000 in Wales) and central exchequer subsidies were reduced to 60 per cent, except in Wales where they remain at 75 per cent. It is for housing authorities to determine whether they adapt their own properties through the use of DFGs or their own resources for capital works.

HOUSING GRANTS, CONSTRUCTION AND REGENERATION ACT 1996, PART I

Further change emerged from this Act which came into force on 17 December 1996. It is therefore convenient to move from any further detail of the original provisions of the 1989 Act to incorporate the 1996 revisions and describe the arrangements which now apply. The main features of the 1996 Act relevant to elderly and disabled people are:

- mandatory DFGs are retained, discretionary DFGs may be paid above the grant maximum of £20,000 for mandatory DFG purposes
- minor works assistance has been replaced by home repair assistance with wider scope, including the eligibility of disabled people, and higher grant limits
- with the exception of mandatory DFGs, grants to landlords will be available at the local authorities' discretion
- mandatory renovation grants, common parts grants and HMO (houses in multiple occupation) grants have been replaced by discretionary grants
- removal of the requirement for dwellings to be made fit on completion of DFG work.

*Disabled facilities grants.* When introduced, DFGs were designed to fund works to remove or help overcome any obstacles which prevented a disabled person from moving freely into and around the dwelling and enjoying the use of the dwelling and the facilities or amenities within it. In particular 'facilitating access to ...' or 'providing for the disabled occupant ...'

- ... and from the dwelling or the building in which the dwelling or ... flat is situated
- ... a room used or usable as the principal family room
- ... a room used or usable for sleeping, or alternatively providing such a room for the disabled occupant

- ... a room in which there is a lavatory, a bath or shower (or both) and a washhand basin or providing a room in which there is such a facility or facilities
- ... the preparation and cooking of food.

In essence the disabled occupant should have access to, and the ability to use, the main habitable rooms within the home. These provisions remain largely unchanged in the 1996 Act but Section 23(1) includes additional provisions which may be required on the grounds of safety:

> making a dwelling or building safe for the disabled person or other persons residing with him e.g. the provision of lighting where safety is an issue, or works which minimise the risks to people with behavioural problems; or for those with hearing difficulties, the provision of enhanced alarm systems to detect fire, or the means to escape from fire.

The above works are all eligible for mandatory grants. DFGs can also be used in 'common parts' of buildings (where a disabled person occupies a flat for example) to facilitate access or enable the disabled person to have the use of power or lighting; facilities to charge a powered wheelchair might be a good example. Discretionary DFGs may be awarded under Section 23(2) to make a dwelling or building suitable for the accommodation, welfare or employment of the disabled occupant in any other respect. Discretionary features may include, for example, access to a garden area; a safe play area for a disabled child; providing or adapting a room to enable a disabled person to work from home.

All owner-occupiers, private tenants (including those who occupy their homes under a licence) and housing association tenants are eligible for DFGs, as are landlords applying on behalf of a disabled tenant. Council tenants are also eligible to apply but it will be for the housing authority to decide whether to carry out the works using its own capital resources or advise the tenant to apply for a DFG.

The 1996 Act, like its predecessor, requires the housing authority to satisfy itself that works proposed for a disabled person are 'reasonable and practicable' in terms of the age and condition of a property; in other words, this is the final 'technical' hurdle where responsibility rests with the housing authority. First, it is required to ensure that the works are 'necessary and appropriate' to meet the needs of the disabled applicant and, in doing so, to consult the social services or welfare authority, usually its occupational therapy service. Working relationships between the agencies are therefore vital to the entire process; a principle which will be illustrated throughout this book.

*Home repair assistance* (HRA) replaces minor works assistance and is intended to complement the mainstream assistance available through the house renovation grant system. Assistance is discretionary and can be given in the form of either grant or materials for small scale works of repair, improvement or adaptation to a dwelling. Houseboats and mobile homes are included in this provision. HRA is available to owner occupiers, private tenants and those who occupy accommodation associated with their employment, but not to landlords (unless they are wholly or mainly resident in the dwelling), or to tenants of public sector bodies. All elderly and disabled people are eligible to apply.

If major works are required and a DFG or renovation grant might otherwise be appropriate, authorities may use HRA as an interim measure to do small but essential works. This flexibility may be particularly helpful to facilitate hospital discharges, or to deal with urgent needs when the full range of work required to bring a property up the desired standard will take a longer period of time.

Unlike DFGs, HRA is not mandatory and individual local authorities have the discretion to establish guidelines which prioritise the targeting of HRA, e.g. towards care in the community, energy efficiency or lead pipe replacement.

As with their predecessors, both DFGs and HRA are subject to specified expenditure limits; currently £20,000 for a mandatory DFG with discretionary grant being available for eligible works above this limit and £2000 per application and a maximum limit of up to £4000 in HRA for any one dwelling in any three year period. DFGs remain subject to the test of resources but the 1989 arrangements have been modified in the favour of disabled people; relevant persons whose income may be taken into account is now limited to the disabled occupant, for whose benefit the works are to be carried out; his spouse or partner; or the parent(s) of a disabled occupant who is less than 18 years of age.

The requirement that properties subject to a DFC application should also be brought up to 'fitness' standards has been waived in recognition of the additional stress this frequently caused disabled people. However, this is not to imply that the occupation of unfit housing by disabled people should be condoned; it simply gives councils the flexibility to consider each case on its merits. There will be instances where it is unreasonable and impractical to complete adaptations to an unfit property and housing authorities will wish to work with social services departments to consider what other solutions may be suggested to their client. Clearly where a disabled person is living in unfit housing, is unable to move and likely to remain in the property for some time, achieving the fitness standard should be an objective in the interests of their general health and well-being.

Further details on the provisions of the Act is provided in DoE Circular 17/96 *Private Sector Renewal: A Strategic Approach*; guidance on home repair assistance in Annex H, disabled facilities grants in Annex I, and on the operation of the means testing in Annex J2 (Department of the Environment 1996).

*Discussion*

In terms of entitlement, adaptations legislation has moved from the generally permissive approach of the 1970s to more positive legislation which prescribes in greater detail the facilities which disabled and elderly people have a right to enjoy. Nevertheless, successful implementation depends on authorities taking an enabling approach to their responsibilities; looking to see if they 'can do' something, rather than whether the law says they 'have to', which usually suggests they would rather not. In *Adaptations – Finding ways to say Yes* (Heywood 1994), Heywood has provided a seminal text which is recommended to both planners and professionals who are concerned to deliver efficient and effective adaptations services. However, as her subsequent research illustrates, resources come into this important equation (Heywood and Smart 1996). The DFG test of resources takes only income into account and, when set against the reduced maximum grant limits, service users can find themselves assessed to make a significant contribution which some may be unable to afford. As outlined earlier, service users have recourse to request additional help from social services departments through Section 2 of the CSDP Act or, in the case of children, under the terms of the Children Act. Means tests applied by local authority social services take both income and expenditure into account and where service users are unable to afford their contribution, social services departments have the facility to agree loan repayments or fix legal charges on a dwelling so that costs may be recouped as and when a property is sold. Since grants were introduced in 1989, local authorities have allowed their social services adaptations budgets to diminish in favour of increased expenditure on other aspects of community care. Although responsibility might 'default' to them, the extent to which they are able and willing to pick up work not funded by DFGs or HRA, or award 'top up' grants to clients who are unable to afford their contribution, will depend on their community care policies and on the eligibility and priority criteria which they apply in their decision making.

*Homelessness: The Housing Act 1996*

Finally in the field of housing provision, reference needs to be made to issue of homelessness since people with disabilities will not be immune from this unfortunate event. Under the provisions of the Housing Act 1996, people requiring settled accommodation (such as those with physical disabilities or mental illness) are expected to be afforded priority in the allocation of social housing if they cannot reasonably be expected to find accommodation for themselves. Local authorities have a duty to ensure that accommodation is available to people with disabilities who are unintentionally homeless as they are deemed to be in priority need (Department of the Environment/ Department of Health 1996).

## Community care

The provision of grant aid awarded by housing authorities is firmly placed within the government's commitment to community care:

> It is the main aim of the Government's policy for housing and community care that, wherever possible, care and support should be provided to people in their existing homes. Suitably designed or adapted housing along with appropriate health and social care services will be key components in enabling frail, elderly and disabled people to remain living in their own homes as comfortably and as independently as possible. (Department of the Environment 1996, p.46)

This principle was first enshrined in the 1989 White Paper *Caring for People – Community Care in the Next Decade and Beyond* (Cm 849) which set out a new framework for community care and complemented proposals in the 1989 NHS White Paper *Working for Patients* (Cm 555) Together they prefaced implementation of The NHS and Community Care Act 1990.

Community care as a concept is not new; local authority social services have been collaborating with health, housing and other agencies for many years to enable elderly, disabled and vulnerable people to remain in their own homes in the community. The CSDP Act and housing statute have been a primary source of such assistance. However, the Government had a number of objectives to achieve, not least of which was the need to provide an improved mechanism for controlling public expenditure on elderly people seeking residential care. The 'new' community care proposals had six key objectives:

- to promote the development of domiciliary, day and respite services to enable people to live in their own homes wherever feasible and sensible

- to ensure that service providers make practical support for carers a high priority
- to make proper assessment of need and good case management the cornerstone of high quality care
- to promote the development of a flourishing independent sector alongside good quality public services
- to clarify the responsibility of agencies and so make it easier to hold them to account for their performance
- to secure better value for taxpayers' money by introducing a new funding structure for social care.

As lead agencies for community care, local authority social services departments were set on the course of becoming 'enabling agencies'; arrangers and purchasers of care services rather than monopolistic providers. In order to safeguard private and voluntary providers of residential care and promote the development of alternative domiciliary services, local authorities were initially required to spend at least 85 per cent of their new resources, the special transitional grant (STG), in the independent sector.

### Community care planning

Promoting choice and independence, and giving both communities and individuals a greater say in the design and delivery of services, were fundamental aims of the reforms. Since 1992 local authorities have been required to develop and publish community care plans (CCPs) setting out how they intended to develop community care services for different groups of consumers and, in the course of doing so, to consult with health, housing and other interested agencies. These CCPs have now become the main framework for consultation with user interests. As housing authorities also have to plan and publish their proposals for meeting the housing needs of their local communities, common principles and mutually supportive proposals ought to be found in each document.

### Care management

Moving from a service provider model to an enabling function has had major implications for professional practice. Of greatest importance was the recognition that service users frequently felt that their needs and wishes were not listened to, or if they were, they were modified to fit the status quo of services available. New arrangements therefore introduced the concepts of 'needs-led' assessment, 'user-led' service provision and care management. For those requiring a straightforward or single service provision this would be provided much as before, but where service users had needs requiring a range of service responses, which may need to be co-ordinated between different agencies, a single care manager would be responsible for:

- ensuring that all components of the assessment were drawn together, including contributions as appropriate from other agencies
- designing and agreeing with service users a package of care designed to meet their needs
- arranging and monitoring the provision of these services (within the level of resources available)
- reviewing their quality and appropriateness and making adjustments as service users' needs changed.

Local authorities have adopted different approaches to the practice of care management; in some it is a service system or organisational process, in others care managers are emerging as a new breed of professional workers. (The majority of occupational therapists are now undertaking care management functions either on a full-time basis or with split purchaser/provider roles. (Local Government Management Board 1995) Whatever the model, care management is meant to deliver to the service user:

- genuine partnership in the identification of their own needs
- full participation in determining the type and level of services appropriate to meet those needs
- choice of services and flexibility in their provision
- co-ordination of the range of services provided.

Care management ought therefore to be the vehicle for building on the legal provisions and on the concepts outlined by colleagues elsewhere, such as advocacy and providing information to empower service users. It is the process through which the Community Care (Direct Payments) Act 1996 provides further opportunity for disabled people to take more control of the decisions which affect their autonomy and quality of life.

ASSESSMENT

Section 47 requires the local authority to assess any person who may be in need of community care services and then decide whether those needs call for them to provide any such services. Consequently, as mentioned earlier, assessment now takes place within the framework of this legislation although the provision of the CSDP and the Disabled Persons Act 1986 continue to stand. Not all clients in need of community care services will necessarily receive a full and comprehensive assessment; the intention is that the level of assessment is appropriate to the nature of the expressed need and is no more intrusive than it needs to be.

### Eligibility and priority criteria

In the pursuit of the efficient and effective use of resources and managing within limited budgets, 'eligibility and priority' criteria have entered the social services lexicon to define who is eligible to receive a service and the priority to be accorded to their needs in comparison with those of others. Social services departments are required to develop criteria for individual services, including access to an assessment, and make these known to referral agencies and to potential applicants. In doing so, eligibility and priority criteria signal to the community who may or may not receive a service.

### Implications for practice

The relationships between the conduct of assessments and the application of eligibility and priority criteria for the provision of services may present professional conflicts for the occupational therapist when assessments reveal needs which cannot subsequently be met, either in the best way or perhaps at all. In the context of housing adaptations and giving advice to housing authorities, the ethics of good practice demand that the assessment, conducted in open collaboration with the client, should result in an objective decision which holds good, whatever the source of funding. Indeed such objectivity will be crucial in gaining the confidence and co-operation of housing authorities and their grants officers. As indicated earlier, social services authorities' responsibilities under Section 2 of the CSDP Act to make arrangements for home adaptations are not affected by the legislation for the award of DFGs; where the housing authority either refuse or are unable to approve an application on 'reasonable and practical' grounds, it remains the social services' or welfare authorities' duty to assist. There may be instances when neither the housing or welfare authority can provide for the assessed needs in the present accommodation. Then an alternative solution needs to be explored (see CSDP Act 1970 Part 4 para.58).

### Collaboration in community care

The White Paper *Caring for People* recognised that housing is a vital component of community care and that it is often the key to independent living. It stated:

Social services authorities will need to work closely with housing authorities, housing associations and other providers of housing of all types in developing plans for a full and flexible range of housing. Where necessary, housing needs should form part of the assessment of care needs and the occupational therapist may have a key role here.

Other authors will expand on types of housing and the occupational therapist's role; here the intention is to round off on the importance of inter-agency collaboration in meeting the housing needs of elderly and disabled people.

As illustrated earlier, social services and housing authorities have a long tradition of working together and they ought to have policies and procedures in place which enable staff to carry out their authority's legislative responsibilities efficiently and effectively. Unfortunately, there is much evidence that high quality services are not yet universal (Heywood 1994, Heywood and Smart 1996, Department of the Environment 1996). Progress needs to be made at many levels:

- influencing housing developers in principles of good design to prevent future service demand created by lack of knowledge or foresight
- sharing knowledge and expertise in the identification of elderly and disabled peoples' housing needs within individual communities
- developing joint databases between the housing authority and other social housing providers and methods of matching housing to peoples' needs (see Chapter 4)
- developing inter-agency practice on housing allocations policies
- agreeing policies and procedures for the efficient management of housing authority grant aid.

The Department of the Environment's guidance on the revised grants scheme (DoE 1996a) provides examples of good practice and proposes improved working arrangements which local authorities may consider. On the broader front of community care policy, the Departments of Health and the Environment have more recently issued joint guidance on a framework for the development of joint housing, health and social services strategies to address the essential link between housing and community care (DoH/DoE 1997).

(*Scotland*: Comprehensive guidance is provided in *Community Care – The Housing Dimension*, Scottish Office Circular SWSG 7/94 (Scottish Office 1994).)

Legislation during this decade has transformed health, social services and housing authorities, in varying degrees, from planners and providers into purchasing or enabling agencies with a more distinct role in strategic policy development and a reduced role in direct service delivery. With a common purpose to meet the needs of their local communities, and recognising that their individual strategies, policies and procedures will have consequences for each other, it is evident that sound mechanisms are needed to ensure cohesion between their respective activities. As the mixed market develops and the range of service providers expands in the independent sector, the need for closer integration, at both strategic and operational levels, becomes even more important.

JOINT COMMISSIONING

This method where two or more authorities jointly plan and commission a service, is being promoted as one way of ensuring that services are effectively integrated, or 'seamless', in meeting users needs. The Department of Health's guidance, *An Introduction to Joint Commissioning* gives an overview of the principles but the *Practical Guidance on Joint Commissioning for Project Leaders* illustrates in detail how a range of services, and consequently their users, have benefited from this approach. (DoH 1995a and b.)

Occupational therapy services, which have historically spanned both health and social care and had a major interface with housing authorities, are identified as potential beneficiaries of a joint commissioning approach. If the respective authorities are unready to sign up to a comprehensive and collective approach, the efficiency of occupational therapy services would certainly be enhanced by the joint commissioning of aids and equipment services. The joint commissioning of housing adaptations services would require the participation of a wider set of players, registered social landlords for example. In Chapter 4 Jackie Parsons highlights current trends which illustrate both the need for, and benefits of, integrated approaches.

*Home improvement agencies*

In the field of housing and disability, the developing role of home improvement agencies (HIAs) provides an ideal example for the conceptualisation of cross-agency interests. HIAs came into existence as part of the DoEs housing renewal policy to provide practical support to vulnerable members of the community who were living in the country's poorest housing and needed financial and technical help to improve their properties. Since their inception in 1987, over 200 HIAs have been established and their national co-ordinating body, Care and Repair, aims to establish an agency in every local authority area by the turn of the century. HIAs became major facilitators of the renovation and minor works assistance schemes, enabling householders to access these funds and managing the repair process on their behalf. As they developed it became clear to HIAs that they had difficulty responding to the demand for very small repairs so trial handyperson schemes were developed to employ direct labour and carry out such work (Appleton 1996).

HIAs have sought to work closely with social services and in many authorities have become invaluable partners in housing adaptations services, relieving occupational therapists of many aspects of project management and progress chasing (Social Services Inspectorate/Department of Health 1994). Agencies have also played a major role in carrying out essential repairs or minor works speedily to facilitate effective hospital discharges. Both health and social services now have a major interest in the contribution which HIAs can make to the efficiency of their operations and there is clearly scope for services to be extended to support more people with mental health problems. Those with severe and enduring mental health problems may lack the motivation to care for the structural fabric of their homes, or the ability to organise and pay for works of repair. Occupational therapists and other members of community mental health teams need to be alert to these needs and informed about potential sources of help, including HIAs. (see Chapter 7.)

As independent providers, HIAs typify the potential for new agencies to diversify across the range of user needs and develop services which plug gaps or enable high cost professional resources to be used to greater effect. There is every likelihood that such developments will continue to challenge and change traditional ways of working.

## Conclusion

A short chapter on such a wide-ranging subject can only introduce readers to essential information; its brevity may serve to confuse rather than to clarify for the subject is indeed complex. At the time of writing, the complexities of social services authorities' responsibilities towards disabled people are being contested in law by a judicial review but inclusion of such detail is quite beyond the limited space available. Those new to practice in this interesting field are urged to read the relevant guidance and obtain a fuller understanding of the framework for local policies. Additional sources are provided in recommended reading. Those who may be enthused towards legal understanding will greatly benefit from reading Michael Mandelstam's *Equipment for Older or Disabled People and the Law* which, despite its more limited title, includes a sound critique on housing adaptations legislation (Mandelstam 1997).

# References

Appleton, N. (1996) *Handyperson Schemes: Making Them Work*. York: Joseph Rowntree Foundation.

*Carers (Recognition and Services) Act 1995*. London: HMSO.

*Caring for People: Community Care in the Next Decade and Beyond*. Cm 849 (1989). London: HMSO.

*Children Act 1989*. London: HMSO.

*Children (Scotland) Act 1995*. London: HMSO.

*Chronically Sick and Disabled Persons Act 1970*. London: HMSO.

*Community Care (Direct Payments) Act 1996*. London: HMSO.

Department of the Environment (1974) 'Mobility housing.' *Housing Development Directorate Occasional Paper* (HDD OP) 2/74. London: HMSO.

Department of the Environment (1975) 'Wheelchair housing.' *Housing Development Directorate Occasional Paper* (HDD OP) 2/75. London: HMSO.

Department of the Environment (1978) *Adaptations of Housing for People who are Physically Disabled* (DoE 59/78) (WO 104/87). London: HMSO.

Department of the Environment (1995) *Housing Strategies: The Preparation of Guidance for Local Authorities on Housing Strategies*. London: DoE.

Department of the Environment (1996a) 'Private sector renewal: a strategic approach.' *Circular 17/96*. London: DoE.

Department of the Environment (1996b) *An Evaluation of the Disabled Facilities Grant System*. London: HMSO.

Department of the Environment/Department of Health (1996) *Code of Guidance on Parts VI and VII of the Housing Act 1996: Allocation of Housing Accommodation: Homelessness*. London: DoE.

Department of Health (1995a) *An Introduction to Joint Commissioning*. Heywood: Health Publications Unit. London: DOH.

Department of Health (1995b) *Practical Guidance on Joint Commissioning for Project Leaders*. Heywood: Health Publications Unit.

Department of Health (1996) *Carers (Recognition and Services) Act 1995: Policy and Practice Guide*. London: Department of Health.

Department of Health (1996) *Child Health in the Community: A Guide to Good Practice*. London: Health Literature Line.

Department of Health (1997) *Community Care (Direct Payments) Act 1996: Policy and Practice Guidance*. London: Department of Health.

Department of Health/Department of the Environment (1997) *Housing and Community Care: Establishing a Strategic Framework*. London: Department of Health.

*Disabled Persons (Services, Consultation and Representation) Act 1986*. London: HMSO.

European Community (1990) 'Council directive on minimum health and safety requirements for manual handling of loads' (Ref. 90/269/EEC) *Official Journal of the European Communities*, 21.6.90, 33(L156)9–13.

*Health and Social Services and Social Security Adjudications Act 1983*.London: HMSO.

Heywood, F. (1994) *Adaptations: Finding Ways to Say Yes*. Bristol: SAUS Publications.

Heywood, F. and Smart, G. (1996) *Funding Adaptations: The Need to Cooperate*. Bristol: Policy Press.

*Housing Act 1974*. London: HMSO.

*Housing Grants, Construction and Regeneration Act 1996*. London: HMSO.

*Local Authority Social Services Act 1970*. London: HMSO.

*Local Government and Housing Act 1989*. London: HMSO.

Local Government Management Board (1995) *Occupational Therapy: Recruitment and Retention Survey*. London: LGMB.

Mandelstam, M. (1997) *Equipment for Older or Disabled People and the Law.* London: Jessica Kingsley Publishers.

*Manual Handling Operations Regulations* (1992). London: HMSO.

Martin, J., Meltzer, H. and Elliot, D. (1988) *OPCS Surveys of Disability in Great Britain: Report 1.* London. HMSO.

*National Assistance Act 1948.* London: HMSO.

*NHS and Community Care Act 1990.* London: HMSO.

*Public Sector Housing Act 1957.* London: HMSO.

Social Services Inspectorate/Department of Health (1994) *Occupational Therapy: The Community Contribution.* Heywood: Health Publications Unit.

The Scottish Office (1994) *Community Care: The Housing Dimension.* Circular SWSG 7/94, ENV 27/1 994, NHS MEL (1994)79. Edinburgh: The Scottish Office.

The Scottish Office (1995) *Scotland's Children: A Brief Guide to The Children (Scotland) Act 1995.* Edinburgh: The Scottish Office.

*Social Work (Scotland) Act 1968.* London: HMSO.

*Working for Patients.* Cm 555 (1989). London: HMSO.

## Further reading

Bradford, I. Mares and Wilkins (1994) *Home for Good: Making Homes Fit for Community Care.* Nottingham: Care and Repair.

Care and Repair (1994) *Poor Housing – Who Cares? The Housing Circumstances of Home Improvement Agency Clients.* Nottingham: Care and Repair.

Health and Safety Commission, Health Services Advisory Committee (1992) *Guidance on the Manual Handling of Loads in the Health Services.* London: HSE Books.

Health and Safety Executive (1992) *Manual Handling Operations Regulations 1992: Guidance on the Regulations* (Ref. L23). London: HSE Books.

Heywood, F. (1994) *Adaptations – Finding Ways to Say Yes.* Bristol: Policy Press.

Heywood, F. (1996) *Managing Adaptations: Positive Ideas for Social Services.* Bristol: Policy Press.

Morris, J. (1990) *Our Homes, Our Rights.* London: Shelter.

Morris, J. (1994) *The Shape of Things to Come? – User Led Social Services.* London: National Institute for Social Work.

National Institute for Social Work (1993) *Empowerment, Assessment, Care Management and the Skilled Worker.* London: HMSO.

Social Services Inspectorate (1991) *Care Management and Assessment: Practitioners' Guide.* London: HMSO.

Social Services Inspectorate (1991) *Getting the Message Across: A Guide to Developing and Communicating Policies, Principles and Procedures on Assessment.* London: HMSO.

Social Services Inspectorate (1991) *Assessment System and Community Care.* London: HMSO.

# CHAPTER 2

# Making the Most of an Occupational Therapist's Skills in Housing for People with Disabilities

*Ruth Bull*

This chapter considers the need for, and scope of, involvement of occupational therapists in all aspects of housing in the community.

### Different approaches to housing for disabled people

People living in the community occupy accommodation in which and from which they carry out their daily living activities and interactions. From this perspective, housing is a general requirement and, with properties developed over time, offers a varying degree of convenience.

Any individuals may find their accommodation physically or socially unsuitable for their chosen lifestyle. This experience is enhanced for people who are confronted by a degree of social marginalisation, or by barriers in the built environment which inhibit physical access within or beyond the home. People in this situation may find it convenient to consider themselves as disabled, or may acquire this label from others.

Where the limitations of the dwelling or neighbourhood severely frustrate attempts at everyday living, some people require outside help to resolve these difficulties. The approach will vary, based on every individual's knowledge and preference. 'Disabled people are frequently at a severe disadvantage

I am most grateful to staff of the College of Occupational Therapists and members of Specialist Section in Housing, for their contributions and support; and to my family for their patience and goodwill. My particular thanks to Joanna Buckle of Redbridge Independent Living Group for appraising and commenting upon this chapter.

in obtaining housing that meets their basic needs. The disadvantage may be economic, political, social/attitudinal or physical due to the inaccessibility of the majority of housing and the wider environment' (RADAR 1994).

### Considering the situation as technical

If the limitation is considered to be technical, the response is to arrange to resolve this mismatch between property and occupant by, for instance, building a ground-floor toilet or seeking to move to a more convenient dwelling.

Primary technical advice is available from architects, surveyors, people in the building trades and other technical advisors working for local authority, private, or not-for-profit agencies such as Care and Repair. This is supported by regulatory advice from local authorities regarding planning constraints, building regulations, environmental health and public safety. Occupational therapists can advise on practical features of buildings and adaptations, related to functional and ergonomic suitability for occupants.

### Considering the situation as financial

If the limitation is considered to be financial, the response is to consider personal resources and seek private or public funding as necessary.

Primary advice is available from sources of private funding such as banks, building societies or loan companies. This approach will only be helpful if the applicant is clearly seeking to pursue a private solution.

Contact with the local authority or its designated advice agency is preferable for anyone who seeks financial assistance for carrying out home repairs for elderly or disabled people, or adding disabled facilities for a disabled household member. These are usually means tested. Disabled facilities grants (DFGs) are available for certain works assessed by the 'welfare authority', (usually through its occupational therapy service) as being 'necessary and appropriate' (Department of the Environment 1996).

### Considering the situation as related to disability

If the limitation is considered to be related to a person's disability, the response is to seek help to resolve problems of personal care, access and independence in the community. Primary advice is likely to be sought in a number of ways.

PERSONAL CONTACTS

Disabled people may rely on their family resources and networks when facing the difficulties experienced at home because of the physical environment. They may look to 'experts' known to themselves, recommended or advertised.

Some people in the estate agency, surveying and building trades are competent and may have access to appropriate expertise, for example occupational therapist advisors, for provision of a wide range of suitable private housing or adaptation services. Others, well meaning, will give advice based on limited experience. The remainder will offer a low-price quick solution without the knowledge or understanding of design principles for housing which includes people of all abilities.

PUBLICLY SUPPORTED AGENCIES

Disabled or elderly people often turn first for advice to local agencies part-funded by national or local government or supported by housing associations. These may be part of a national network such as Care and Repair. Such agencies offer advice, can help the applicant make contact with the local authority and suggest ways of finding reputable surveyors and builders. For further information, see Chapter 3.

THE LOCAL AUTHORITY

In the United Kingdom local authorities hold the key to accessing public resources which have been allocated from taxes collected from, and invested on behalf of, the people of Great Britain. Scotland, Northern Ireland, England and Wales each have their own systems of administering their public duties, but each have responsibility for local assessment and provision of services for people with permanent disabilities which substantially affect their ability to manage at home. These responsibilities have developed through duties and powers given in post war legislation, which is covered in detail in Chapter 1.

The local authority has a duty to inform disabled people of the services relevant to their needs, and to publish information as to the nature of the services (Chronically Sick and Disabled Persons Act 1970, Section 1). Each person's situation being unique, even an authority with a proliferation of leaflets may fail to assist an applicant to understand their rights and opportunities. It is vital that all relevant local authority officers can guide disabled enquirers towards the range of available services.

## Exploring the place of occupational therapists in housing

*Historical Perspective*

When the profession was established in the 1930s, occupational therapists worked primarily to occupy and retrain chronically ill people in institutions.

The young profession matured quickly post war, focusing on analysis of functional disorder arising from a medical or surgical episode, and using a range of practical techniques for physical rehabilitation.

Occupational therapists harnessed both medical knowledge and practical skills in the retraining of people in daily living activities. Members of the profession followed on their hospital-based rehabilitation with home visits to ensure that patients would be safe and confident in managing at home, following hospital discharge.

The evolving profession subsequently had practitioners based in the community, employed by health authorities or social services departments. During the 1970s, following implementation of the Chronically Sick and Disabled Persons Act (CSDP Act), they became established in local authorities in significant numbers, assessing disabled people's needs for equipment and adaptations at home.

By the 1980s, adults of all ages and abilities were expressing preference for a self-determined lifestyle and integration into the community. Here, intention, determination and information was ahead of bricks and mortar. Much of the housing in Britain was built in an era where disabled people were in institutions or hidden away. Properties were designed within limitations of contemporary technology and fashion, posing a challenge to adapt and redesign with all abilities in mind.

*Practice areas for occupational therapists in housing*

In whatever setting disabled people encounter their first occupational therapists, these professionals should be equipped to advise on making the best match between the person and their home environment, if a disabled person chooses to use this service. Skill is developed through ongoing acquisition of legislative, technical and ergonomic knowledge about the challenges of the built environment, and the application of that knowledge in the range of clinical and social settings where occupational therapists encounter disabled people whose housing inhibits, for example, their chosen lifestyle. This range of settings includes the following.

- In a *general hospital*. A pre-discharge visit at home provides opportunity for an initial assessment of that person in his/her home environment. Here it is important to identify features inconvenient for access, mobility and safety, and for the disabled person's desired level of independence in household activities.

- In *elderly care*. An older person with limited mobility can *exist* in one room with a commode and expensive support services, but a creative occupational therapist will encourage the occupant to consider whether he/she would prefer a home with accessible features and access into the community, promoting dignity in retirement years. Skill is required to find out about and meet needs. These may not be easily expressed by an older person in a fast changing society.

- *Working with children.* Children, often encountered at school or clinic, require sensitive assessment at home with their family, to help plan a housing situation fit for the changes anticipated as they grow and as they take their place as young adults in the community. Duties towards children in need who are disabled include 'as far as possible securing accommodation that is suitable for their needs' (Children Act 1989).

- *Working with people with learning difficulties or mental health problems.* Such people, in inconvenient housing, may be frustrated in their attempts to participate in the community. Housing does not merely imply constructional limitations, but the location of the property to avoid social isolation arising from poor local transport, hilly location or hostile neighbourhood culture. In a full assessment involving families, friends and professionals, the occupational therapist is a specialist in the effects of the built environment.

**In local authorities**, different approaches develop. The following is an example of practice focusing on environmental modification.

---

### Example: Community occupational therapist, Chester County Council, Social Services

The occupational therapist worked with adult clients with *learning difficulties* both in the community and in small residential homes for over seven years. The particular physical and intellectual challenges for this client group were as follows:

1. *Poor balance and mobility* meant that both height and depth of features in any adaptation required careful consideration. All mirrors, door handles, windows and so on had to be checked minutely for height, either to help the client towards independence or to ensure the client's safety. Quite often, depth had to be marked by differentiating colours on walls, floors and work surfaces.

2. *Behavioural problems.* Some people experienced episodes of aggression or hyperactivity. A safe environment was provided by specifying padded walls, sound-proof walls and specialised intercom systems. Often telephones and televisions in the home had to be placed beyond reach to avoid risk to the client.

---

### Example: Community occupational therapist, Chester County Council, Social Services (continued)

---

3.  *People with Attention Deficit* and limited concentration span were often assisted by an occupational therapist allowing sufficient time over the analysis of each piece of equipment, or adaptation required, to arrive at the most appropriate environmental solution.

4.  *Colours, sound* and *touch* were considered, as they have been found to be of specific assistance to aid clients' memory, sight and perception.

---

*Community occupational therapists*

Although the major employee is the local authority social services department, Table 2.1 indicates the wider picture by detailing the distribution of members of the College of Occupational Therapists Specialist Section in Housing (COTSSIH), the majority of whom are occupational therapists.

The highest proportion of community occupational therapists involved in housing are frontline workers who see the challenge of the built environment as part of their everyday practice. Essential to good practice is an understanding that service users wish to participate in community care 'to negotiate involvement on our terms rather than be compromised by professional assumption' (Social Services Inspectorate 1994).

The College of Occupational Therapists promotes and supports specialist sections, considering that it is highly desirable that occupational therapists join the sections that are most relevant to their work. This will maximise their training opportunities and enable them to have a wider forum in which to exchange information and experience. It will also give greater lobbying power where there are aspects of legislation that appear to be unjust and to need change.

COTSSIH was formed in 1994 to address the need to link all British occupational therapists working with both purpose built housing and the adaptation of existing properties.

> ## Example: Community occupational therapist, The London Borough of Sutton (LBS)
>
> The occupational therapy service has strong links with public and private housing. The service, when appropriate, will carry out an assessment with a view to environmental restructuring (adaptation), or new design, relating to the housing needs of people with disabilities. Each assessment and subsequent recommendations is unique to the individual, their home and specific requirements. Examples of work include ramp access, lifts and shower room extensions. All work is carried out in close liaison with the client, carer and family. It relies on multi-disciplinary contact with LBS housing management for public housing. Private housing calls for liaison with environmental health and an independent agency, such as Staying Put, which is part of the national organisation Care and Repair (see Chapter 3).

## Occupational therapy core and specialist skills in housing

### Core skills

Occupational therapists are a profession trained in a unique combination of subjects which include medical, psychological, social and technical knowledge integrated into a problem-solving approach ideal for teasing out the tricky problems encountered by disabled people in an uncompromising environment. Basic undergraduate experience establishes the foundation for multi-disciplinary networking, with recognition of the place of a disabled person as central to the whole range of professional, technical and financial advisers whose expertise may be required.

Occupational therapists are concerned with human occupation, and have unique core skills in:

- using purposeful activity and meaningful occupation to promote health and well-being

- enabling people to explore, achieve and maintain balance in their daily lives

- assessing the effects of, and facilitating changes in, the environment to promote choice in lifestyle and social opportunities

- the selection and application of appropriate activities for people who have difficulty in carrying out daily living tasks, interaction and everyday occupation (College of Occupational Therapists 1995)

HOW CORE OCCUPATIONAL THERAPY KNOWLEDGE AND SKILLS RELATE
TO HOUSING

An understanding of how nerves and muscles work is little help without knowing how individuals prefer to live their daily lives. Yet that awareness is inadequate without specific and detailed analysis of function and situations, to work out together how to tackle the problems which people experience. 'The only tool which therapists have at their disposal is to change the environment to support or precipitate a change in the human system' (Kielhofner 1995).

---

### Example

---

Mrs Charles had pain and limited movement, worse in the mornings, typical of rheumatoid arthritis. She liked to sleep upstairs with her husband, but climbing the stairs was increasingly difficult. Planning for the future, her occupational therapist helped the couple design a level-access shower and bidet–toilet for Mrs Charles' independence in personal hygiene. These were provided downstairs, and involved resiting and redesigning the kitchen. When Mrs Charles was revisited some years later, she was widowed, used a wheelchair indoors, and had the lounge as her bedroom with the convenience of an accessible bathroom and kitchen nearby.

---

Suitable housing is the key to living in the community. Relating principals of occupational therapy to assessment of housing needs is part of good practice, whatever current level of skill and experience has been achieved. In professional practice, this may be analysed through considering these levels: basic; middle; higher. This relates to work being progressed with COTSSIH by the College of Occupational Therapists at the time of writing, in preparation for production of an accredited Master of Science module for occupational therapy in housing.

*Specialist skills*

The following lists of specialist skills at the basic, middle and higher levels are for guidance, and are not prescriptive.

BASIC LEVEL OCCUPATIONAL THERAPISTS IN HOUSING

The following skills are acquired at undergraduate level or within the first two or three years of practice in the community:

- daily living assessment skills within the home environment, taking into account physical and mental ability, cultural background, age, and needs of carers
- the ability to demonstrate awareness of health and safety issues, for example level pathways, floor coverings, electrical wiring, ventilation and general fire risks
- knowledge of how to assess for home adaptations, equipment and services available for modifying housing to meet assessed needs
- an understanding of the issues in advising on adaptations versus rehousing, reflecting local policies, practices and resources, and an ability to carry out specialist holistic assessments leading to appropriate recommendation
- knowledge and understanding of all relevant established and emerging legislation, national and local policies and guidelines
- knowledge of different tenures of housing and range of funding/ grant systems
- the ability to produce basic working sketch plans and to interpret and contribute to architects/surveyors specifications and drawings, having an awareness of the legal implications of practice, (e.g. neither occupational therapist's sketches nor their computer-assisted drawings are for building, but to assist professional analysis and inform technical specialists)
- the acquiring of further knowledge. Many occupational therapists enhance their skills by taking short courses in building design, construction and planning, for example courses run by the College of Occupational Therapists and the Centre for Accessible Environments. This enables them to work closely with architects, surveyors and builders in considering the feasibility of creating the right ergonomic and accessible environment for people with a range of abilities.

MIDDLE LEVEL OCCUPATIONAL THERAPISTS IN HOUSING

Practitioners established in a community setting who have achieved a basic level of competence will be able to:

- contribute to local housing policies, identifying and demonstrating the occupational therapists role and contribution
- work with housing officers, architects, planners, service users and the voluntary sector to analyse local housing needs for people with

different abilities/disabilities; participate in producing inter-departmental and inter-agency service specifications and policies; understand local government and housing association structure and funding

- draw scale plans and make comments on complex design schemes for adaptations or new build properties, understanding conventions used in drawings, architecture and building construction

- keep abreast of developments in client services and disability equality working practices, research and knowledge in the housing field

- show competence in training occupational therapists who need to acquire basic level skills in housing.

HIGH LEVEL OCCUPATIONAL THERAPISTS IN HOUSING

Practitioners working at specialist level in the housing field, or as managers or lecturers where housing is a key issue, will:

- keep abreast of current medical, therapeutic and social research and knowledge and its application in community practice

- input at consultation level on voluntary sector/user consultation forums

- have responsibility for input into major redevelopment or new build schemes and applications for local planning or partnerships between local authorities and housing associations, often with significant resource implications

- make informed comments on national policies, for example building regulations, disabled facilities grants or occupational therapy service development

- demonstrate a wide knowledge of national and local housing issues, sufficient to participate in, or convene meetings between senior officers in the local area, for example health, housing, planning, voluntary sector and social services, in order to contribute to strategic developments

- demonstrate specialist skills to contribute to the development of aspects of housing such as disabled persons housing services (DPHS, e.g. Walbrook DPHS, Derby) disabled persons accommodation agencies (DPAA, e.g. Kent DPAA) or learning disabilities reprovision, and to show practical knowledge and innovative ways of meeting general and individual housing needs deriving from disability, at a high level as part of a team

- show knowledge and presentation skills to represent the profession at a national level and contribute to professional development, guidance and literature
- show competence in training occupational therapists who need to acquire middle level skills in housing
- seek opportunities for enhancing personal developments and undertaking research in this specialist field, which may be through accredited study at Masters Level.

## To adapt or rehouse: The occupational therapist's contribution

---

### Example: Mrs Adams

Mrs Adams had multiple sclerosis, early stages. She, her husband and young family were keen to live a conventional lifestyle. They persuaded the local authority housing department that an occupational therapy assessment was unnecessary and accepted the tenancy of a council house on a new estate close to Mrs Adams' sister and family. The house, on a hillside and accessed down a steep verge, had one lounge and kitchen on the ground floor and all other facilities on the first floor.

Two years later came the referral to the local occupational therapy team. Mrs Adams could not use a wheelchair at home because of the restricted space and was dragging herself about holding furniture, her husband carrying her upstairs to bed and bathroom. Assessment indicated a need to provide access to the front door using a steplift and to the first floor using a vertical home lift. Statutory and local financial restrictions imposed a ceiling on the amount which could reasonably be spent on adapting the property. This was compounded by technical constraints on the practicability of achieving wheelchair accessible facilities for Mrs Adams' personal care of herself and her dependent children.

Their social worker, local team occupational therapist, housing officer and housing occupational therapist all participated in helping the family to face the limitations and lack of potential of this dwelling in this location.

In the neighbourhood, a housing association was developing a small estate built to the local authority's standards, (as influenced by the housing occupational therapist) with 10 per cent of properties built to wheelchair standard and general needs properties built to mobility standard. Mrs Adams

---

### Example: Mrs Adams (continued)

---

was offered a wheelchair accessible family flat finished to her specific requirements, with her sister also transferring to a new, four-bedroom house on the same site. Mrs Adams' standard of living was maintained by offering new build property again, and all family members are now settled onto the development and active within the community.

---

### Example: Mr Bhatti

---

Mr Bhatti, a young man hoping to leave residential care, expressed a strong preference to seek a rented flat in the private sector, fit for his independent lifestyle in a semi-reclining electric wheelchair. His plan was to have the flat adapted to his specifications. His occupational therapy manager, social worker and GP helped him to consider the legal, financial and practical barriers to achieving such a plan and encouraged him to accept an offer by a housing association of a purpose built wheelchair-user flat currently under construction. His occupational therapist discussed with him his required specification, which included electronic door and window openers and socket outlets for all his electronic equipment.

---

*A summary of considerations relating to adaptation versus rehousing*

- The choice to adapt or move is always the householder's, with exceptions where the disabled householder is not legally responsible for his or her own affairs, or where a property is scheduled for demolition.

- Choice does not mean that all options are open. Everyone is limited by legal, financial and practical constraints when considering tenure, location and size of property. Disabled people are no different.

- When someone wishes to leave residential care, the social worker and occupational therapist can make a significant contribution to generating realistic options.

- For those already in the community, the occupational therapist's role is to assess the needs of the disabled family member(s). This will take into account aspirations, prognosis and predicted ability, lifestyle, culture and how the household use their accommodation, with analysis of its limitations.

- Ideal housing is rare: there are disadvantages in pursuing adaptations to existing unsuitable property in a preferred location, and upheaval in moving to accommodation with more convenient design features. The occupational therapist should be prepared to advise on compromise.

- Team working is essential. The disabled person, family members, advocates, social workers, occupational therapists, doctors and advisors from the voluntary sector will each contribute to the assessment from a different perspective. It should not be underestimated how stressful this may prove for the disabled person and the importance of the disabled person being central to the process.

*How occupational therapy input is achieved in housing*

There are a number of different ways in which services are structured for the effective use of occupational therapy skills in housing. The following example of the role of an occupational therapist illustrates a current model of good practice.

---

### Example: Occupational therapy in housing, City of Salford, Community Occupational Therapy

The link occupational therapist is the deputy manager of the occupational therapy service for the city (an integrated service staffed by health and social services employed occupational therapists working from a central base).

The link occupational therapist meets regularly with the officer in housing who co-ordinates major adaptations at the housing department's headquarters, and also views all applications for transfer on medical grounds. Any that need occupational therapy input/information are forwarded to the occupational therapy service for assessment.

A client may prefer to opt for an adaptation, having applied to move, on realising that adaptations are available.

A database is kept by housing, with the facility to transfer information to the link occupational therapist. This identifies properties that have been adapted significantly and also lists people on the medical transfer list, indicating the type of property they require. From a shortlist of applicants, the link occupational therapist is asked to place the prospective tenants in priority order.

---

## The assessment process

### Information gathering

Before starting a housing assessment the occupational therapist will need:

- the disabled person's self-referral, self-assessment or request for occupational therapy services;
- details of the housing request if the applicant is initially requesting rehousing;
- relevant information from earlier professional, medical, physiotherapy, or social work assessments where available to complement and avoid duplication.

### Personal assessment

This takes the form of an initial interview with the service user, the carer and household members involved as appropriate. This should cover the following questions:

- You have asked for help: what do you think you need?
- What does 'independence' mean to you?
- Are you a carer? Do you have/need a carer?
- How would you describe your lifestyle? (Work, leisure, social etc.)
- What do you see as the problem with your housing?
- What sort of housing do you consider you require?
- Are you planning any changes?
- Do you have need for any features which are not in traditional local housing? (e.g. level entrance, wide doorways, access to facilities, turning space, braille signing, individually designed kitchens, bathrooms, windows, door openers, visual smoke detectors for deaf people.)

### General considerations in the assessment

- A housing assessment will follow the same principals as any other occupational therapy assessment. The whole picture is seen when ability is considered alongside social need, (e.g. moving to be near relatives) and housing need, (e.g. bedroom deficiency).

- Where all parties agree there is not a need for rehousing, the occupational therapy focus will be on seeking solutions in the existing property.

- The occupant may be deaf, or partially hearing, or blind, or partially sighted or deafblind or use walking equipment or a wheelchair. The occupational therapist needs to be aware of whether this is likely to change, given the stability, fluctuation or progressive nature of the disability, and to be sensitive to the way the disabled person chooses to face the future.

- The age and physical build of a disabled person and carer influence their ability to manage, as does the quality of their relationship and their respective views of dependence. This should be viewed in conjunction with activities which cause pain, breathlessness or heart stress for disabled person or carer. Obvious limitations of mobility, strength and range of movement should be assessed alongside less obvious problems such as incontinence or poor sensation.

- The occupational therapist has a personal store of knowledge and experience about function, disability, techniques, processes, models of good practice and recent research. These should be drawn upon appropriately and sensitively with each individual.

*Functional assessment at home*

This is a practical demonstration of the limitation of the property as it affects the disabled occupant(s) and carers and should take into account:

- how the applicant currently spends time in daily living, work, social and leisure activities

- how that person would prefer to spend the time

- what is stopping this.

In a hospital setting the occupational therapist will support rehabilitation by analysing specific functions, for example by teaching adaptive techniques following a stroke. Where problems in managing at home are temporary, the healthcare occupational therapist will arrange for the supply of equipment, such as toilet and bath equipment for use after a hip replacement operation.

The local authority occupational therapist is responsible for fulfilling the local authority's statutory function to assess and meet the needs of people whose disability is permanent and substantial, whatever the cause. This means that by the time an occupational therapist sees someone at home, problems experienced with their property are likely to be enduring, requiring a long-term solution.

A standard format or checklist such as that which follows helps focus on likely areas for improvement for the disabled person and household.

THE LOCALITY

- Is it hilly or level?
- Is it near shops, services, transport?
- Is there adequate parking nearby?
- Are there good neighbours?
- What else is important?

ACCESS

- Is the access or entrance communal or shared?
- What is the gradient of the front path?
- Is there a level or stepped threshold?
- How does the disabled person enter?
- Are shallower steps, rails, ramp and platform or steplift needed?
- Can they be provided in this location?
- Can the door be opened/closed from outside/inside?
- Is any entryphone/intercom useable by person with physical/sensory disability?

GENERAL INDOOR SPACE

- What are the distances, e.g. living room to front door?
- Is there space in the entrance hall?
- What are the widths of the corridors? Are there changes of corridor direction?
- Are there internal steps at ground level? Stairs?
- What restricts lifestyle and mobility?
- Can changes be made? (E.g. using the space differently)
- Is storage space adequate?
- Is there sufficient light for partially sighted people or deaf people who are signing or lip reading?

LOUNGE

- How is the space used?
- Is the use of walking equipment or wheelchair restricted?
- Can furniture be moved around? Can the door be rehung?
- Are electric light and socket outlets within reach?
- What is the room used for?
- Is anything preventing this use?

KITCHEN

- Where is the kitchen in relation to the dining area?
- Who uses the kitchen?
- Do people with different abilities use the one kitchen?
- Is there enough space to get to everything?
- Is it the route to the rear garden?
- Is the layout safe and convenient (e.g. sink on same side as cooker to avoid lifting hot pans across the room)
- What domestic appliances, large and small, are there?
- Are sinks, taps, windows, work surfaces and cupboard/shelf spaces within reach?
- What is important to the disabled user?

BEDROOMS

- Where do disabled person(s) sleep?
- Can this be changed?
- Is a bedroom at ground floor level necessary? Possible?
- Can access be improved to suit the individual? (E.g. stair rail, stairlift, vertical lift)
- Is the bedroom of adequate size, taking into account any wheelchair or walking equipment, necessary furniture, turning space, hoist, room for carer to assist, partner to sleep?
- Does room have other uses? (E.g. student's bedsitter)
- Is is near enough to bathroom/toilet?
- Are there socket outlets for any specialist equipment, and bedside light?

TOILET

- Where is it ... upstairs, downstairs, outside, in the family bathroom?
- Is it needed urgently/frequently?
- Are special features required? (E.g. space beside or in front for wheelchair or assistant?) Height? Distance from walls?
- Is a bidet–toilet needed for personal hygiene?
- What is the location of flush handle?
- It is useable with specialist mobile toileting chair?
- Is an inward opening door obstructing space?
- Can the toilet be reached conveniently, day or night?

BATHROOM / SHOWER ROOM

- Where is it? Is it combined with the toilet?
- Is there any difficulty reaching it? (E.g. steps, stairs)
- If a bath is there, is it useable safely with specialist equipment?
- Is a hoist required? Mobile or with overhead track?
- Is a shower needed?
- If you are contemplating any step into a shower, will this meet future needs? Can a level-access floor or tray be provided?
- Who will operate the shower? Where are controls needed?
- What is the height of the shower head? Is it fixed or hand held?
- Has anti-scald/thermostatically controlled model been specified?
- Are any grabrails needed?
- What turning/attendant space is required?
- Where are the heating, lighting, ventilation systems and controls?
- Are there any features or cultural preferences important to the user/carer?

IS HEATING ADEQUATE?

- Can it be controlled by the disabled person?

ARE THERE OTHER SAFETY HAZARDS?

- Is there lighting at entrance for partially sighted people?

- Are there safe facilities for the care of people with learning disabilities and challenging behaviour?

NEEDS OF DISABLED CARERS

- Can they fulfil their caring role safely?
- Do they have other personal needs and responsibilities?

This checklist is a useful starting point. Each occupational therapy service is likely to develop its own assessment format, standardised for easy recording on a computerised system. Criteria evolve to meet local needs and constraints based on legal parameters, for example criteria for disabled facilities grants.

### Outcome of the assessment

The occupational therapist works with the user and carer to develop an action plan based on a logical sequence of complexity and cost. This might include one or more of the following.

1.  *Advice only* where this fully meets the need – for example, suggesting different use of rooms, arrangement of furniture or practical techniques – or where a course of action is discussed and people decide to make arrangements privately.

2.  *Minor solutions,* for example specialist equipment such as bath seats or kitchen gadgets, or minor adaptations such as stair rails or convenient socket outlets.

3.  *Major solutions,* such as adding a ground floor internal toilet, installing a stairlift or vertical lift, turning a bathroom into a shower room or, where no existing space is available to meet the needs, constructing an extension. (For details of the adaptation process, see Chapter 3).

4.  *Alternative housing* where design features or access to facilities are not achievable within the technical limitations of the property and of the statutory, discretionary and personal finances available; or where the household choose to move privately or are accepted for a move within the public sector. (For details of options for moving house, see Chapter 4).

## Design matters

### Poor design

There are currently no national building regulations enforcing house design features which disabled people consider to be generally convenient and, legally, local planning guidance may only be advisory. Standards vary, often based on accepted practices rather than live research.

The following example shows how a failure to achieve good design standards had long-term consequences.

---

### Example

The housing occupational therapist helped to identify the need for a three-bedroom, wheelchair-user's flat in a new development of smaller dwellings. The architect amended plans, without fully consulting the occupational therapist. On site, it emerged that the extra room was created by reducing the corridor width from 1200m to 1000m and restricting access to the two smaller bedrooms. The property is unsuitable either for a wheelchair-user parent to care for the children, or for a disabled child to manage independently in a wheelchair: over a 15-year period successive tenants have moved on when requiring a wheelchair indoors.

---

*Improving design*

Arising from the above example, the occupational therapist, borough architect and rehousing manager recognised the need to research and produce a design guide. The following programme took place:

1. A visit by the occupational therapist, architect and housing officer took place to six people in the borough occupying purpose built accommodation for wheelchair users, with an age, race and gender mix. They asked open-ended questions, to encourage people to say everything they liked and disliked about their homes.

2. All the comments were included in a draft design guide, which also incorporated established and tested design principals.

3. The occupational therapist shared this with the local group of disabled people, and amended it in the light of their comments.

4. The occupational therapist worked with an access development worker (herself a wheelchair user) to analyse the comments received and establish principals of good practice.

5. The occupational therapist worked with an access design officer to compile the *Design Guide for People who Use Wheelchairs Indoors*.

6. The occupational therapist explored with planners the implications of the guide becoming a borough policy.

7. Their findings were taken to the council's planning, housing and social services committees to establish that they would form the borough standard to which 10 per cent of all developments of over 20 dwellings should be built; this being essential for council or housing associations, and strongly encouraged in the private sector.

It is necessary to keep accepted design principles under review. Technological changes include wheelchair design, communications systems and domestic cooking appliances. Challenging problems are overcome, such as the ingress of damp at level thresholds to the outside. Building and adapting is always for the future, to meet both current and predicted requirements. New building is an opportunity for the occupational therapist to influence standards not only for indoor wheelchair user's housing, but for general needs housing convenient for people to live, visit neighbours and participate in the community.

---

### Example

Walbrook housing association, DPHS Derby, employs occupational therapists as housing advisors. They work very closely with the association's architect, and have developed a very high level of skill in design work, reading and interpreting plans. They assess the disabled person's needs and work with architects and builders of new properties to ensure that the property is well designed and tailor made to meet the needs of the individual. They also provide a service of specialist assessment to the local authority social services and other housing associations, applying consistent standards of good design and adaptations across Derby based on their book *Cracking Housing Problems* (Walbrook Housing Association 1994).

---

*Good practice in relation to design*

DESIGN STANDARDS

Where local authority policies uphold good design standards (see Chapter 5) it is easier to expect or encourage developers in all housing sectors to consider building for people with a whole spectrum of different ages, cultures and abilities. This requires a 'managerial focus on occupational therapy' for guidance on policies and procedures (Social Services Inspectorate/Department of Health 1994).

Design standards, whether deriving from local authority policies or the design specifications of developers such as specialist housing associations, are only the basis of good design. Each general needs scheme, each specialist property, requires analysis of site, plan and elevation to ensure that convenient access and flexibility for successive occupants is achieved as fully as possible.

---

### Example

For deaf people: 'There is a myth that if, when you are designing a building for deaf people it does not matter if the building is noisy. Very few deaf people have no hearing at all' (Harrowell 1993). Good acoustics are essential to enable people to make use of any residual hearing they have.

---

APPLICATION

Design guides and standards, researched and accepted nationally or locally as policy, promote consistently high standards for people of *all* abilities in:

- new build or rehabilitation schemes
- major adaptations
- residential accommodation/day care
- sheltered housing for disabled and/or elderly people, where ease of access to communal facilities is essential.

## Moving house

The government emphasis on home ownership in the 1980/90s ran parallel with a decline in financial incentives for local authorities to build, a trend with potential to change in response to political initiatives in the late 1990s. While good policies had developed for building council houses to accessible standards through local political and social incentives to work with service users and social services (including their occupational therapists), no such incentives influenced the private sector. 'Wheelchair users rely on public sector housing to a greater extent than other people, not only because of their relative economic disadvantage, but because most housing stock is inaccessible', according to the 1993 Housing Organisations Mobility and Exchange Services report (HOMES 1993).

*Moving in the private sector*

---

### Example: Miss Gupta

---

Miss Gupta took early retirement from teaching due to increasing weakness as her disability progressed. Wishing to leave the adapted family home, she decided against an offer of council wheelchair-user housing and chose to buy a house nearby which was affordable, attractive and situated near shops. Aspects of the plan to adapt fell outside the statutory disabled facilities grant criteria. An occupational therapist helped her to modify the scheme, seeking a user-led solution. Miss Gupta had used a stairlift previously and wished to take the responsibility for its installation and use. The occupational therapy assessment indicated a potential risk of falling on transfer at the top landing.

---

ANALYSIS

- No national, and no known local schemes actively seek to develop, buy or sell property on the open market convenient for disabled people.

- House design features convenient for disabled people are rarely mentioned in advertisements.

- Private rented accessible homes are very rare except for some holiday accommodation.

- Many private houses, particularly those with internal steps, narrow corridors or small landings are unsuitable to adapt.

- Involving occupational therapists before renting or buying a property can save time and money.

- Where a disabled person's preferred adaptation plan may be potentially unsafe and inappropriate for an occupational therapist to recommend for public expenditure, a risk assessment or higher level professional opinion is often required. Each situation is different – there is no prescriptive solution.

*Moving in the public sector*

---

### Example: Mr and Mrs Ellis

Mr and Mrs Ellis had three children, one using a wheelchair. Homeless, they were in temporary accommodation. After reading in the local community care plan of proposals for disabled people's family housing, they contacted the social services department. A housing application was made, and assessment by the Healthcare Trust children's occupational therapist was arranged in consultation with the local authority occupational therapy service. The family needs were matched to a four-bedroom wheelchair users's house being built by a housing association in partnership with the local authority. The house completion was planned to the family's requirements.

---

ANALYSIS

- Local authorities may provide access to appropriate or adaptable housing from their own stock or through a housing association (see Chapter 4).

- A network of council and housing association officers is needed to ensure swift and smooth co-ordination of the allocation or transfer process.

- The occupational therapist may be seen as the pivot in the balance between the disabled person and their family needs, and the housing officers and their available properties.


## Ethical issues for occupational therapists

Occupational therapists are one of the professions supplementary to medicine. In the United Kingdom they are only permitted to be state registered if they have a diploma or degree in occupational therapy from an approved course of academic and practical study. The Occupational Therapists Board of the Council for Professions Supplementary to Medicine is responsible for the protection of the public. To this end the Board registers occupational therapists, regulates and monitors their professional education, and cancels registration in cases of misconduct.

The College of Occupational Therapists is the professional body which promotes and supports occupational therapists and which publishes the profession's Code of Ethics and Professional Conduct, through its Ethics Committee. The British Association of Occupational Therapists is the professional organisation for occupational therapists and their support staff in the United Kingdom. Acting through the College of Occupational Therapists, it seeks to 'promote honourable practice, and to repress malpractice'.

### Clinical reasoning

Members of the profession are expected to apply very clear clinical reasoning, underpinned by knowledge, experience and research. An occupational therapist who undertakes work that is beyond his or her experience and current knowledge and skills may find himself or herself open to allegations of professional incompetence (British Journal of Occupational Therapy (BJOT) 1996b). For example, an occupational therapist who reports to his/her manager that a disabled person 'deserves' to have an extension to the property under a grant system because that person has always worked hard for the community will be asked for further analysis of the need and limitations of access within the existing property, through application of practical, reflective and pragmatic reasoning (BJOT 1996a).

Under community care legislation local authorities are required to have published eligibility criteria, that is, guidance on how to match a certain level or type of social or environmental disadvantage to a corresponding level of help to alleviate the problem. The level of need is determined through assessment. The response to that need should be determined through a fair and consistent interpretation of the legal requirement to provide or arrange services for that level of need.

Occupational therapists must know the aspects of legislation which relate to their work in order to raise concerns if the authority's policies appear to fall short of their statutory obligations or to expect staff to practice below acceptable standards. Professional support may be sought from The College of Occupational Therapists (for individuals who are members of the professional organisation), or from the Occupational Therapy Officer at the Department of Health.

Where professionals are unhappy with restrictive, albeit legal criteria, it is good practice to analyse the effects upon clients, based on sound clinical reasoning and ethical considerations. Professional colleagues in other authorities may be called on, often via formal networks such as the London Boroughs Occupational Therapy Managers Group, to collaborate in research into practice and its effects. The ill-effects of weak criteria should then be reported to managers with proposals for improvements, to shift from resource-led to user-led criteria.

---

## Example

The accepted practice in one local authority was to offer adaptations in council property rather than rehousing, because of scarcity of suitable properties. The principal occupational therapist implemented liaison with the housing department to analyse and redress housing shortfall. Clinical reasoning was applied at management level when analysing the needs of inappropriately housed people and the advantages which would be offered by development of a comprehensive housing strategy which offered an opportunity for disabled people to exercise choice in the decisions between adaptation and rehousing.

---

### Standards of assessments

From the code of ethics it is understood that 'the occupational therapist is expected to act as an advocate for the client ... occupational therapists have a duty of care to clients.... Every client should have a clearly recorded assessment of need' and 'normally clients should be given sufficient information to make informed decisions about their health and social care' (College of Occupational Therapists 1996a).

The occupational therapist in the housing situation acts as the 'interpreter' of the needs of an individual, indicating why that person requires certain facilities. This is not to say that the occupational therapist advocates in favour of one individual as against another, but uses professional skills to represent need and individual circumstances.

---

## Example: Mrs Fernandez

Mrs Fernandez lived with her husband and teenage son and daughter in a small, three-bedroom council house with first-floor bathroom and one lounge and kitchen on the ground floor. They enjoyed the support and friendship of neighbours, which was an important aspect of the holistic assessment. Mrs Fernandez's heart and respiratory problems restricted her ability to manage stairs, which were unsuitable for a stairlift Their occupational therapist acted as her 'advocate', presenting her need for a ground-floor extension for a bedroom and toilet/shower room, although this would be at a higher cost than her authority's normal financial ceiling for housing adaptations. The occupational therapist's professional panel agreed to support the case and advocate to the housing services department the need for adaptation, not rehousing.

ETHICAL POLICIES

For Mrs Fernandez the housing policy was helpful. Joint working between the housing and welfare authorities promoted flexible provision of services. Where policies are too prescriptive, the applicant may feel trapped by financial limitations or by the constraints applied by the professional person allocated to assist them.

Policies safeguard both the way public money is spent and the way service users are treated. For instance, in order to facilitate access to bedroom, bathing and toilet facilities within a house, the most economic practice within current legal guidance is generally to provide a stairlift. An occupational therapist would expect, therefore, to bear this in mind when assessing need. However, a stairlift may be unsuitable for someone with a deteriorating neurological condition. The professional should fully involve the disabled person, and any informal carers, in considering the person's ability to manage a stairlift. A medical opinion may be helpful, indicating how the condition is affecting that individual. This will contribute to the assessment of actual and anticipated risk to the health and safety of those concerned, if this equipment is installed in this particular site.

Michael Mandelstam (1997) offers the following legal advice:

> An authority should not take over-rigid decision; if it does so it may be fettering its discretion. For example, the occupational therapy managers group issued some years ago guidelines on criteria for provision of home adaptations. It helpfully lists a number of contra-indications in relation to the provision of stairlifts, including 'progressive conditions'. Such a guideline adopted by a local authority is legally and administratively possible so long as it does not become a rigid policy.

If it is deemed appropriate to have a stairlift, emergency and future plans should be discussed and recorded. These will be helpful if this form of access is considered to be unsafe at a later date, due to changing needs or circumstances.

- The occupational therapist is responsible for the assessment and must not rely on the recommendation of a stairlift company.
- Every situation must be considered individually.

## Example: Miss Gupta

Miss Gupta, mentioned earlier in this chapter, wanted a stairlift in her new house, as she had in her parental home. Landing space at the top of the stairs was restricted and Miss Gupta's muscular dystrophy was causing increased weakness. Her occupational therapist concluded that a stairlift was inappropriate and her manager supported this.

Miss Gupta was unhappy at her choice being overruled by professionals. Adding to her dissatisfaction, the recommended vertical lift cost more, bringing the total cost of the disabled facilities works over the £20,000 current disabled facilities grant ceiling, with Miss Gupta expected to bear the excess cost. She requested permission to install a stairlift privately with a disabled facilities grant for other necessary adaptations.

Legal advice was sought. This supported the position that where an occupational therapist assessed an individual and recommended what was necessary for that person's safety, then an unsafe provision could not be agreed, either through a statutory grant or private arrangements associated with such a grant. The legal advice was to look at a fair way of helping Miss Gupta. The social services department agreed to purchase, install and maintain a suitable vertical lift as a piece of equipment, (therefore owned by the local authority and not a means tested service) under the Chronically Sick and Disabled Persons Act.

It must be emphasised that this was not the 'correct' solution, but was appropriate in Miss Gupta's situation.

## Example: Mrs Hardy

Mrs Hardy, in her forties, had early stages of multiple sclerosis with no evidence of rapid progression. Her husband was there to help her. She was assessed as needing help with getting up the stairs. Her occupational therapist assessed her ability to use a stairlift safely but queried whether this should be provided. The occupational therapy manager supported the provision because it was a reasonable and appropriate solution in the light of the outcome of an assessment of risk for Mrs Hardy and her carer.

In both cases, the authority applied the policy in a reasonable way, supporting the occupational therapist's ethical need to provide a 'level of satisfactory and safe occupational therapy service' which 'upholds the autonomy of the individual'.

*Resource deficiency*

Occupational therapists have a responsibility to record assessment of need and notify the appropriate manager if they feel that 'a minimum level of satisfactory and safe occupational therapy service to the client and their carers' cannot be achieved because of resource deficiency. 'Occupational therapists should state and substantiate their views to employers about resource and service deficiencies which may have implications for the client'.

Where the 'appropriate manager' is an occupational therapist practising at policy or strategic level the principles of these ethical considerations are applied at this level on behalf of people with disabilities. This gives an opportunity for influencing the way services are provided and resources allocated, based on clearly identified and quantified need and shortfall in provision.

Ultimately, the occupational therapist's code of ethics and professional conduct leads those in the housing field to work with, and advocate for, disabled people at a local and national political level to aim for high quality standards, services and resource levels.

## Through what channels do occupational therapists contribute to improved practice standards in housing?

*Communication* is vital to avoid professional isolation which narrows scope for developing a responsive service for disabled people through mainstream or specialist housing provision. This means interaction with:

1. *Statutory bodies*

   - local authorities, contributing to a co-ordinated approach from relevant departments such as planning, housing and social services through strategies, policies and networks

   - health authorities using resources to enhance housing opportunities for disabled people, for example through initiatives to provide community housing for people with learning disabilities leaving hospital care

   - healthcare providers taking a sensitive and holistic approach to hospital discharge of people who require alternative accommodation or adaptations because of acquired disability.

2. *The private sector.* In particular home designers or builders, who may be offered advice through the local authority planning process (see Chapter 9) and architects and builders completing adaptations.

3. *Publicly supported agencies,* such as Care and Repair (see Chapter 3) and housing associations, of which many are registered with the Housing Corporation.

4. *Voluntary organisations* and user groups which promote partnerships, for example local access groups looking at access to public buildings and new housing scheme proposals, or national organisations such as Scope, which employs occupational therapists who can advise on adaptation specifications.

5. *Professional bodies,* in particular the College of Occupational Therapists who value the client acting on their environment rather than being determined by it and seek constantly to update practice standards.

6. *Other agencies working towards better housing opportunities.* This is important, but difficult to establish where occupational therapists are not represented at senior level.

---

### Example: Doncaster Local Authority Metropolitan Borough Council, Social Services Department

Inadequate communication between occupational therapists and local authority/housing association providers left occupational therapists without influence in decisions about housing opportunities for their disabled clients;

*A new principal occupational therapist* in post has created a focal point for occupational therapy management, with benefits to housing provision expected through:

- regular initial representation on all housing association new build projects

- representation on local authority lettings meetings

- quarterly joint meetings with the disabled facilities grant department.

---

**How do occupational therapists contribute to improved housing policies?**

The situations where occupational therapists make a significant contribution to policy are where the professions role is recognised and promoted at all levels on behalf of people with disabilities. 'Requests for occupational therapy assessments already make up to 20–30% of all social services referrals. Adapting housing is no longer a peripheral matter...' (Heywood 1992).

*Adaptation policies*

These are based on professional guidance such as the *London Boroughs Criteria for Adaptations* modified to meet local need and applied sensitively with each individual.

---

## Example

In one London borough the housing department is committed to giving priority for central heating installations to people with disabilities as part of its policy for spending to improve properties for disabled people because they represent a high percentage of council tenants. The London boroughs' criteria gives guidance only in selecting those disabled people in greatest need because their health would suffer or condition deteriorate without improved heating, based on medical evidence. This does ensure that people at risk have the highest priority.

A housing occupational therapist worked alongside housing officers to research a fair way of meeting the wider demand. The borough now includes in the scheme individual applications from disabled people whose lifestyle, health and comfort would be improved by better home heating. The occupational therapist's confirmation of need helps protect genuine applicants from loss of resources to those claiming this valuable service, but whose disability is not substantial. All others who request improved heating are considered in date order of application, within available resources, whether they be disabled, elderly or parents of young children.

---

*Planning and Allocation Policies*

These are based on the local picture of need for general or specialist housing for people of all abilities.

The National Population Census counts people whose lifestyle is limited by 'long-term illness', but this bears no significant relationship to housing problems. The RADAR publication *Housing, A Question of Influence* (RADAR 1992) had national political support and representation from a range of organisations of people with disabilities, and professionals including occupational therapists. Their recommendations included:

All local authorities should be required to collect information on the number of

- disabled people living in their area
- accessible dwellings in their area, their particular characteristics and locations, in their own stock and others.

The Housing Act 1996 included the requirement for local authorities to set up a housing register on which people with unsatisfactory housing conditions or a need for settled accommodation on medical or welfare grounds are included as a priority for rehousing. Occupational therapists can contribute to setting up and implementing recording and retrieval systems to help disabled people find the available property which suits their needs, and to the planning of future need for property based on evidence of the shortfall in conveniently designed properties, which makes it so hard for people to find suitably accessible homes (see Chapter 4).

---

### Example: The London Borough of Waltham Forest

In the London Borough of Waltham Forest two occupational therapists with distinct areas of responsibility work alongside two disabled persons' housing officers within the housing department. They help local disabled people to make the most of the council and housing association properties, and helps the local authority to have an appropriate housing stock with a system that also lets it to suitable tenants.

For one occupational therapist the main emphasis is on assessment and categorisation of the needs of people with a disability who are requesting more suitable accommodation:

- providing information on disability and present housing
- recommending suitable category of accommodation
- indicating degree of urgency

Occupational therapy assessments are not requested in the majority of cases following people's own self-assessment, only if a situation is complex or unclear. If an occupational therapy report is requested and the tenant/applicant is known to an occupational therapist in one of the area teams, that occupational therapist is asked to provide the report, otherwise the housing occupational therapist will carry out the assessment. Reports inform the medical adviser responsible for awarding priority points. The panel consists of the medical adviser (housing), one of the housing occupational therapists and a disability officer from the housing department.

For the other occupational therapist the emphasis is on identifying suitable council or housing association properties, and advising on new build design:

- identifying potentially convenient vacated or new build, purpose built or adapted properties from the weekly 'voids' list and checking on database if they are categorised
- visiting to view, sketch and categorise suitable properties

---

### Example: The London Borough of Waltham Forest (continued)

- using a computer list to select people who require that size and category of property in that area
- liaising with housing allocations officer to select tenant and offer property
- once an offer is made, arranging for an occupational therapist to visit as necessary to be sure the property is suitable, arranging any adaptations required to meet individual needs.

---

### How do occupational therapists contribute to long-term strategies in housing?

Information and communication are vital ingredients to ensure the right mix of housing in the community. With increased experience in housing comes increased responsibility, based on professional ethics, both to work and to advocate for people with disabilities to the highest levels of personal competence. All therapists should have an expectation of professional support from those practising at a more advanced level when confronted by new challenges or advocating for change.

*Research*

Research, either at informal, local level or with national or international significance, identifies precisely how the built environment affects people and how those with disabilities are disadvantaged.

---

### Example

Occupational therapists and architects worked together with disabled people to research and produce the Wheelchair Housing Design Guide, working through NATWHAG (National Wheelchair Housing Association Group).

---

*Lecturing*

Lecturing, either at universities in the education of occupational therapists to a good level of competence in environmental issues, or at conferences and seminars, promotes the prospect of high standards of housing provision in the community for future generations.

*Writing*

Writing for journals, newsletters and national organisations.

---

### Example

*Pulling Together: Developing Effective Partnerships* (Care and Repair 1994) was written by representatives of the College of Occupational Therapists and Care and Repair Ltd, sharing good examples and successful outcomes for disabled people when organisations work together.

---

*Representation*

Representing the College of Occupational Therapists in responding to national issues.

---

### Example

Meeting with disabled people and civil servants to discuss and influence proposed changes in legislation such as Building Regulations (Part M) and private sector renewals including provision of disabled facilities grants. Current examples of the way legislation affects disabled people encourages central government officers, and hence politicians, to base legislation on real people's lives, not historic views of how disabled people were expected to live in the community.

---

*Promotion of high standards*

The promotion of high standards of professional practice, so that the work of occupational therapists is built on the real concerns of people with disabilities.

---

### Example

Contributing to the practice standards set by the College of Occupational Therapists as they influence good practise in housing. *Back to the Future* (COT 1996) includes guidance on working in housing for members of the profession returning to practice after a break.

---

*Working at a strategic level within the place of employment*

Occupational therapists who seek to address the problems experienced by disabled people, because of inadequately researched or poorly resourced housing policies, require channels of influence to the highest possible levels. Where occupational therapists are welcomed at levels where strategies are discussed and policies made, their contribution to a team, whether in the public, private or 'not-for-profit' sector, can enhance the work of that team.

> In developing joint strategies, housing, health and social services authorities should work together to review the range of provisions available and examine the use of equipment and adaptations and requirements for general and specialised housing. (Housing and Community Care 1997)

---

### Example

In the London Borough of Redbridge an occupational therapist was employed in disability service management, including line management of the occupational therapy teams. The scope of the post permitted regular meetings with other managers in community care and housing services. Together they identified the types of housing required in the community and participated in selection of preferred partners from housing associations who plan and develop housing schemes and associated community resources.

High standards were promoted and monitored. The John Groomes housing association worked alongside these officers and sought views of prospective tenants for a new development. This early involvement meant that general and individual requirements, as agreed between the tenants and their occupational therapists, were planned into the scheme at the appropriate stage of building design and construction.

---

*Building partnerships with users and carers*

Such partnerships, built on listening, informing and involving people, is essential to future community provision in housing.

---

### Example

The London Borough of Redbridge housing department holds an annual housing conference for the local community. Contributors inform the housing strategy. Individuals or representatives of community groups, including groups for disabled people, attend alongside elected members, council officers and private sector representatives.

## Conclusion

This chapter began by considering the different approaches open to disabled people experiencing difficulties because of their housing environment. Where someone with a disability seeks to live at home in the community, but is blocked by the limitations of the building, he or she may choose how to overcome these limitations, harnessing the services of a range of lay or professional people as he or she considers necessary. Occupational therapists are amongst those professionals available, often as part of a team, to offer advice, assessment and assistance in generating options and progressing solutions.

Housing work is complex and sensitive, and all concerned will face uncertainty, compromise and the need for negotiation. A clear understanding of the assessment process and basic design principles are not complete without awareness of the ethical issues raised by a seemingly practical process. In reality, housing issues are not always clear cut, and there are many avenues that an occupational therapist can explore when seeking to contribute to improved practice standards, policies and long-term strategies which support and enable disabled people to live and participate in the community.

Many people who have a disability, be it a physical, sensory, mental health or learning disability, look for someone impartial with whom to discuss the difficulties they experience when living in conventional housing. The occupational therapy profession can offer information based on knowledge both of the nature of disabilities and of the application of legislation, guidance and local good practice in the public, private and not-for-profit sectors. This will assist people to harness the resources which are available to help them to achieve better housing.

The focus of an occupational therapist's professional responsibility is to enable people to make informed choices about their lifestyle. Working within legal and financial constraints, they can interpret and advocate for individuals and groups of people who wish to benefit from practical support or social improvements. Their practical and analytical skills contribute to a creative approach to building design and construction, allocation or sales to meet the spectrum of needs. Participating in local and national systems and networks, occupational therapists share in the current shift towards ensuring that the best possible public or private sector housing is available to those who require it.

## References

'Ethics in practice' (1996a) *British Journal of Occupational Therapy 59(Y)*, 312.
'Clinical reasoning' (1996b) *British Journal of Occupational Therapy 59(S)*, 196–211.

Care and Repair and College of Occupational Therapists (1994) *Pulling Together: Developing Effective Partnerships*. Nottingham: Care and Repair.

*Children Act 1989* London: HMSO.

*Chronically Sick and Disabled Persons Act 1970* London: HMSO.

College of Occupational Therapists Ethics Committee (1996a) *Code of Ethics and Professional Conduct*. London: COT.

College of Occupational Therapists (1996) *Back to the Future*. London: COT.

College of Occupational Therapists (1995) *Realising the Potential*. London: COT.

College of Occupational Therapists Specialist Section in Housing (1996) *Members' Handbook*. Department of the Environment. London: COT.

Department of the Environment. *Housing Grants, Construction and Regeneration Act Part I*. London: DoE.

Harrowell, C. (1993) *Do Deaf People Need Architects*. Unpublished Presentation, Waltham Forest Access Group.

Heywood, F. (1992) *Managing Adaptations: Positive Ideas for Social Services*. Bristol: The Policy Press.

*Housing Act 1996*. London: HMSO.

Kielhofner, G. (1995) *A Model of Human Occupation, Theory and Application*. London: Williams and Wilkins.

London Boroughs Occupational Therapy Managers Group (1990) *Housing and Occupational Therapists: a report by the London Boroughs*. London: Occupational Therapists Housing Group.

Mandelstam, M. (1997) *Equipment for Older or Disabled People and the Law*. London: Jessica Kingsley Publishers.

RADAR (1992) *Housing, A Question of Influence*. London: RADAR.

RADAR (1994) *Housing Newsletter*. London: RADAR.

Social Services Inspectorate/Department of Health (1994) *Occupational Therapy: The Community Contribution*. London: Department of Health.

Walbrook Housing Association Ltd (1994) *Cracking Housing Problems*. Derby: Walbrook Housing Association.

## Further reading

College of Occupational Therapists (1996) *Fact sheet on Professional Discipline and Ethics*. London: COT.

Community Care Development Programmes (1996) *Building Partnerships for Success*. London: Occupational Therapists Housing Group.

Department of the Environment (1995) *Housing Strategies: The Preparation of Guidance for Local Authorities on Housing Strategies*. London: DoE.

Department of Health/Department of the Environment (1996) *Code of Guidance on Parts VI and VII of the Housing Act 1996: Allocation of Housing Accommodation: Homelessness*. London: DoE.

Disabled Persons Accommodation Agency (DPAA) (1995) *The Way Forward for Ken*. London: DPAA.

Department of Health (1997) *Housing and Community Care: Establishing a Strategic Framework*. London: DoH.

*Housing Grants, Construction and Regeneration Act 1996*. London: HMSO.

London Boroughs Occupational Therapy Managers Group (1989): *London Boroughs Criteria for the Provision of Adaptations in Disabled Person's Property*. London: Occupational Therapists Housing Group.

London Borough of Waltham Forest (1994) *Design Guide for People who Use a Wheelchair Indoors.* Unpublished.

McKevitt, D. and Lawton, A. (1994) *Public Sector Management.* Milton Keynes: Open University.

(1994) *Occupational Therapy: The Community Contribution.* Extract from the Wiltshire Community Care Involvement Network SSI Seminar Report.

# Appendix I: Breakdown by employer of membership of the College of Occupational Therapists Specialist Section in Housing

| Employer | Number |
|---|---|
| Local authority social services | 167 |
| Local authority (occupational therapists in specialist housing posts) | 8 |
| Health services | 15 |
| Housing associations | 9 |
| Care and Repair's home improvements agencies | 2 |
| OT bureau | 8 |
| Charities and independent organisations | 5 |
| Educational establishments | 13 |
| OT student | 1 |
| Freelance/Private | 14 |
| Employer not known | 20 |
| **Total** | **255** |

*Source:* COTSSIH Members' Handbook 1996

CHAPTER 3

# The Adaptation Process
*Ian Bradford*

## Introduction

> At present my mother is having to fight to get the adaptations ... to al-
> low me to remain living at home, with my mother who has been in hos-
> pital with a slipped disc through lifting me. I hope she gets this as I do
> not want to live in residential care. (User in Lamb and Layzell 1994,
> p.38)

Getting the right adaptation can make a difference. It can make the difference
between independence and dependence, dignity and indignity, comfort and
discomfort. The right adaptation can provide the user with a safer environment, an environment which offers the opportunity to exercise personal control. The right adaptation can make a difference as to whether a carer can, or
will, continue with their caring role. Ultimately the right adaptation can
make a difference in terms of whether or not the user is able to live in their
home – and wants to.

I want to record my grateful thanks to the following people. Andy Benson who provided the
'users view' and commented on the chapter's relevance to himself as a disabled person; Tim
Bullock, Buildings Advisor, Care and Repair, who wrote two sections – 'specifying work' and
'the work in progress'; Asari Duke, Training and Information Officer, and Mike Ellison,
Policy and Monitoring Officer, Care and Repair, who wrote the grant factsheets reproduced,
in a modified form, in this chapter; Lisa Sims, Regional/Development Secretary at Care and
Repair who uncomplainingly typed and retyped the text; Glen Buchanan at Scottish Homes
and Chris Smith at Care and Repair Forum who advised on text for the section on the grant
system in Scotland.

---

## Example: Mrs Wright

Dorothy Wright, aged 86, couldn't climb the stairs to use the toilet, nor could she get to the outside toilet. An occupational therapist visited and assessed Mrs Wright as needing a level-access shower room and toilet on the ground floor. She declined because of the worry about the mess and disruption.

Mrs Wright was provided with a commode but was so embarrassed at having to ask her neighbour to empty it that she tried to limit its use by cutting down on her fluid intake. It was only after her third admission to hospital with dehydration that, with the help of a home improvement agency, access was created via the pantry to the outside toilet. The work was funded through minor works assistance (predecessor to home repair assistance).

---

Most disabled people want to live their lives in the community as independently as possible. The extent to which that can be achieved depends to a large extent on the accessibility of the built environment, at home and in public. Few homes are built with any real thought for the more complex individual needs of the people who may live in them or use them. When physical disability prevents convenient independent living the first option usually considered is to try and adapt the home.

Getting the right adaptation requires a certain amount of knowledge and, often, a considerable amount of fortitude. The whole process can be confusing, stressful and frustrating.

This chapter aims to unravel and explain the adaptation process from referral to completion. It will describe the key players, consider the main funding options and identify some of the common problems associated with arranging adaptations. Much of what is written is of relevance to readers throughout the United Kingdom. However, apart from specific references to the grant systems in Scotland and Northern Ireland, the chapter refers primarily to the adaptations process in England. Leaders wanting a detailed understanding of this process outside of England should check for national variations.

### Referral to an occupational therapist

Where an adaptation may be required, referral for assessment by an occupational therapist will usually be made to the local authority social services department. Referral might also be made to the hospital occupational therapist or through a private occupational therapy practice. This may occur when, for example, the client is paying for the adaptations themselves and does not want to go through the local authority occupational therapist or where social services have arrangements with other providers of occupational therapy services.

There is no universal referral procedure – different local authorities have adopted a variety of different systems. Normally the referral procedure will incorporate an initial screening process to help determine the most appropriate form of assessment. Some authorities issue potential clients with self-assessment forms. This method may not provide a useful tool in obtaining an accurate assessment of need. The screening process can be used to deflect demand on limited resources, and where successful referral is prevented disabled people may be denied services they need and to which they may be entitled. Richards (1996, p.57) argues that initial screening must contain at least a simple assessment. Failure to do this could be seen as preventing a client from obtaining their right to an assessment under the NHS and Community Care Act 1990 and may leave the authority concerned open to legal challenge.

It is important to be clear about the referral procedure and what to expect once the referral has been made. Social services departments have a duty to provide clear and accessible information. This should include:

- where, when, how and by whom referrals should be made and what happens next
- speed of response and referral
- what to do in the event of a complaint about the procedure or how it is being carried out.

We might learn from Heywood's suggestion as to users' priorities 'Users would like [referral] reception staff to be polite, patient, kind and correctly informed, and above all not to act as an unofficial gate-keeping service' (Heywood 1994, p.25).


## Occupational therapy assessment

A disabled person has a right to an assessment under the Disabled Persons (Services, Consultation and Representation) Act 1986 for services described under Section 2 of the Chronically Sick and Disabled Persons Act, 1970 (CSDP). The CSDP Act refers to the social services departments duty to make arrangements for 'the provision of assistance for that (disabled) person in arranging for the carrying out of any works or adaptations in the home or the provision of any additional facilities designed to secure his greater safety, comfort or convenience' (CSDP Act 1970, Section 2 (i)(e)). The assessment is carried out within the framework of Section 47 of the NHS and Community

Care Act 1990. (See Chapter 1 for more information about relevant legislation.)

An occupational therapy assessment will usually be provided through social services. An assessment may also be carried out by a hospital occupational therapy service or by a private occupational therapist if delegated by social services to one of these. This might occur where social services does not employ its own occupational therapists, or as a means of managing long waiting lists for an assessment by social services occupational therapists. Some social services departments are making use of occupational therapy assistants or other social work staff to carry out an initial assessment or for full assessments for some less complex needs.

Authorities often undertake a preliminary assessment at the referral stage. For example, a number of social services departments have established criteria in order to manage high demand and in an attempt to meet urgent need. This may preclude or give very low priority to certain types of assistance such as washing or bathing needs. There are obvious disadvantages in this approach: in particular it removes the opportunity for more complex needs to emerge during a comprehensive assessment at home. There is also the problem that potential users may be deterred from making legitimate demands on services; effectively creating a hidden, unexpressed demand. It could be argued that such a policy is unlawful if the local authority has developed a device which is not shown to be reasonable, consistent and objective (Richards 1996, p.71).

The occupational therapy assessment will need to consider a number of issues including:

- clients' own assessment of need
- clients' aspirations
- needs of carers and family
- medical condition and prognosis
- social, employment and education needs
- functional ability
- limitations of building.

Where a disabled facilities grant (DFG) application is made, the housing authority must satisfy itself that adaptation works are necessary and appropriate. In doing this, social services must be consulted and the assessment for this would usually fall to the social services occupational therapist. Guidelines from the Department of the Environment (DoE) (DoE 1996, pp.198–199) show that they need to take account of a number of factors, including the following:

- that the works should enable the person to remain in their own home
- that the adaptation should meet the persons assessed need
- to distinguish between the disabled persons 'possibly legitimate aspirations and what is actually needed and for which grant support is fully justified'.

One of the more difficult aspects to gauge is the extent to which a person's existing disability may change over time. Clearly this will be an important consideration in ensuring that appropriate provision is made. From the client's point of view, however, a realistic assessment of a deteriorating condition may not be very welcome.

It is imperative that the assessment takes account of the needs of everyone in the home. The carer, for example, may have particular needs which could be crucial to their being able to continue to provide care or personal assistance. If the carer is providing assistance for a person being assessed for or receiving services under the CSPD Act 1970, the NHS and Community Care Act 1990 or the Children Act 1989, they have the right to request their own assessment under the Carers (Recognition and Services) Act 1995. In taking account of the family needs as a whole it should be possible to maximise the assistance to the disabled person and avoid making recommendations for adaptations or equipment which run contrary to the best interests of other users of the home. For example, there is not likely to be much praise for the installation of fixed, low-level kitchen worktops that are not useable by the rest of the family.

It can be seen that the assessment is a complex process requiring considerable expertise, insight and sensitivity. A number of devices have been developed to assist with this process. The Walbrook Disabled Persons Housing Service in Derby uses what it calls a 'Users' Functional and Environmental Assessment Form'. This is a room by room checklist which provides information to assist with assessment and adaptation design based on anthropometric data, observations about functional ability and prognosis as well as the users expressed needs. A more detailed description about the occupational therapist's considerations during assessment is shown in Chapter 2.

A significant and enduring problem facing many disabled people has been long delays for occupational therapy assessments. In 1993 average waiting time was 4 months (Heywood 1996, p.5) and although this is unacceptable for people with urgent needs it is a major improvement over the situation in 1990 when the average wait for assessment was 11 months (Social Services Inspectorate 1994, p.10). This is a clear demonstration of the efforts that most social services departments have made to reduce waiting lists often through the appointment of an extra occupational therapist or occupational therapy assistants. During the period 1990–1993 the median increase in expenditure on occupational therapy staff was 74 per cent. To put this into context, in the four years since 1990 the number of requests to social services departments for adaptations has risen by an average of 50 per cent. (Heywood 1996, p.1)

When a DFG is being applied for it will usually be necessary for one of the local housing authority grant officers to be involved. The grant officers administer grants on behalf of the authority and will need to assess the client's home and determine if the proposed adaptation is 'reasonable and practicable' in relation to the property. Delays in the adaptation process have not been restricted to the occupational therapy assessment stage. Many local housing authorities have had considerable difficulties meeting their obligations to provide grant aid. This has often led to very lengthy delays. Ironically then, social services departments' efforts to clear their waiting lists have all too often just shifted the list elsewhere in the process. Waiting lists can be thoroughly frustrating, inconvenient and even dangerous for clients (Age Concern England 1996, p.19). Furthermore, clients are often not given any realistic assessment of how much longer they will have to wait (Social Services Inspectorate 1994, p.26).

## Specifying work

Building work is no different to many other kinds of activity in that the preparatory stages are all-important if a quality result is to be achieved first time. The transition from the assessment of a client's needs to the specifications for the work which the builder receives offers ample opportunity for errors, misunderstandings and problems to be created which can be difficult, costly and upsetting to resolve once the builders are on site and the job is underway.

### Detail

In adapting a client's home, it is their individual needs which must be translated into the scheme proposal and whilst their general needs may be easily communicated, it is often small details which make the difference between a successful scheme and one which could have been a lot better. It can be argued that particularly with adaptation work, the achilles heel principle applies – the scheme is only as good as its weakest link and one apparently small detail overlooked can undermine the success of the whole project.

### Terminology

Terminology is important and is a frequent source of confusion. In many cases of smaller-scale adaptation work, the final description of the building work will be confirmed to the client, the builder, grants officers, occupational therapists and so on in the form of a schedule of works. This essentially is a list of descriptive clauses identifying the work, item by item, in sufficient detail to be sure that what is required is understood by all parties. This document may well be supported by a detailed specification document. Traditionally used by quantity surveyors to accurately forecast the cost of larger jobs, the specification tends to be a lengthy document and covers quality requirements relevant to all jobs rather than any one particular job. To save on repetition, the specification document may well refer to industry standards such as British Standards and codes of practice and is used as a reference document. It is quite possible and perhaps desirable to reference it in the schedule of works or even to extract some key elements of it for inclusion within the schedule. It is the schedule of works that forms the principle working document to be used on site as a checklist for the work in progress. The other key controlling documents are drawings (plans, elevations and sections) and the building contract which identifies the responsibilities of the parties.

### The role of the occupational therapist

The occupational therapist's role is crucially important in starting this process. The assessment of the client's needs inevitably leads to a specification recommending how those needs are to be met. A range of feasible options for clients to consider is vital. The level of detail of this occupational therapist specification must be such that it accurately describes what is required. This may be relatively straightforward when considering equipment, but occupational therapists are not trained as building surveyors and ideally these roles should be clearly separated. The information produced by the occupational therapist will specify many of the factors relating to the existing building in terms of its structure, the form of the construction, electricity, water supply or any associated repairs which may be needed. He/she will not be expected to instruct a builder and will rely on technical advice from a qualified person in drawing up the final specification.

There may also be significant constraints on what can be achieved regardless of cost due to the site, or as a result of the need for planning permission and building control approval. Clients who live in conservation areas may find particular restrictions on what can be achieved and, at times, it may require a significant level of liaison and negotiation to arrive at a solution.

Whilst it is generally good practice to refer to a quality or performance standard rather than individual products or services, there may be factors which uniquely require particular manufacturers or suppliers to be nominated.

Many experienced occupational therapists will be able to offer this wide range of specialist design skills and construction knowledge, using this expertise when assessing needs and specifying how those needs are to be met. A good understanding by all those involved, of the subtle factors affecting any proposed scheme will help towards better communication and ensure clients are well informed and supported in the choices they make.

*Client choice*

Numerous factors need to be taken into account in deciding precisely what the final scheme proposal will be and how the recommendations of the occupational therapist are to be addressed. There will inevitably be options open to the client and choices will have to be made taking cost, practicality and aesthetics into account. It may help to identify between options if a client can visit another home in which the proposed adaptation has been previously provided or installed. This gives the client the opportunity to try the facility, see what it looks like and discuss any 'pros and cons' with its owner/user. It can also allow the occupational therapist to assess the appropriateness of proposed provision. The use of computer aided design software (CAD) can be helpful in providing effective diagrammatic impressions of options under consideration.

Much adaptation work is driven by practical consideration and clients may well be so delighted at the prospect of their needs being addressed that other considerations get overlooked. Aesthetics play an important part in all our lives and people with disabilities similarly will have preferences for design, style, colour, quality of finish and so on for the equipment they need. These choices must be incorporated into the schedule of works/specification documents to ensure they are allowed for in the builder's quotation for the work. Where cost constraints tend to limit the choice to the lowest price item, the market is sufficiently competitive for choices still to be made and new products are coming onto the market all the time. Keeping abreast of these developments is itself a substantial task and subscription to relevant journals and information systems, together with occasional visits to trade shows, are essential.

Similarly, the design choices to be made in altering the house should not ignore aesthetic consideration. Factors which need to be considered here include choices of materials, scale and proportion. A poorly designed ramp or extension may provide the solution to mobility difficulties but may also result in a lowering of value of the house, just as poor detailing may create future maintenance problems such as damp occurring in the home due to a ramp bridging the damp proof course. It may also unnecessarily draw attention to the fact that an occupier has a disability which may cause clients anxiety.

### The role of consultants

There is clearly a role in such adaptations work for occupational therapists to work closely with architects, surveyors or other technical staff with particular experience in this field both at the design and specification stage, as well as administering the contract once work is progressed on site. Similarly, other consultants may be particularly useful whether independent specialists or those linked to particular manufacturers or suppliers. As with any team it is essential to identify a team leader who at the very least is responsible for co-ordinating input.

---

### Skills mix

In the London Borough of Lewisham the community occupational therapy service has a building surveyor and a lift engineer based within the team. This provides the team with the expert advisers required and facilitates efficiency, consultation, communication and good practice.

---

Cost will inevitably dominate the proposals and may prove to be a negative influence on the final scheme. In considering options for both adapting the fabric of the building as well as for the provision of new equipment, the cost implications need to be identified and articulated throughout the design and specifying process. Architects, surveyors, builders and grants officers familiar with this type of work will be in a position to offer good advice and indicate likely costs in open discussion with occupational therapists and clients.

When providing new facilities, clearly, a long narrow extension to a property will cost more than a compact one of equal floor area and will certainly cost more to heat in winter. On the other hand, converting an existing room to provide the new facilities may well cost less than either of the other options. It may be possible to reduce costs by considering second-hand and reconditioned equipment (e.g. stairlifts) or by equipment being loaned by social services. Reclaimed building materials can be used which may represent a cost saving but which can also help a new extension blend with the existing home. Such materials should be approved by the architect or surveyor in charge of the job and must be obtained only from reputable sources so as to be sure of their quality and durability. Warranties and insurances may also be affected by the use of reclaimed materials and clients must be appropriately advised.

When grants are being used to provide the finance, it may be that only with additional resources can the client's wishes be fully realised. Clearly the grants section of the housing authority is central to the funding of much adaptations work and will be closely involved throughout.

### Finalising the specification

Once all the factors affecting the scheme have been balanced and negotiated, they must be accurately reflected in the final schedule of works and specification (if used) in order for competitive quotes to be sought from builders and for the control of the works, once the job starts. If done properly, the builders should be clear about what they are being asked to provide and their prices should come in reasonably close to the estimated cost. If this approach is not taken there will be numerous queries from builders in advance of their quotation or else assumptions will be made which then cause problems once the work is underway. The quotes received will vary significantly, making it very difficult to be sure that like is being compared with like, and confusion may be built in as a result of builders asking for clarification when visiting to price up the job and various 'extras' being offered or discussed. Any additional items must be costed and approved by the client and checked by the occupational therapist to ensure they do not undermine the ability of the scheme to meet the needs of the client.

Furthermore, if a local authority grant is covering the cost of the works which must be judged to be necessary and appropriate, reasonable and practical, any additional works will similarly need to be approved by the housing authority.

It is essential that all the work proposed is adequately identified in the schedule of works, supported as appropriate by drawings and a specification document and that these form the controlling documents together with the building contract.

## Paying for adaptations

> I am very dissatisfied ... I have to use a chemical toilet as I cannot yet get
> upstairs. My wife who is 70 has to empty it upstairs. I applied for a grant
> for the toilet which we have room for ... but was told that we would
> have to find the first £3000 of a grant – so no toilet. (User in Lamb and
> Layzell 1994, p.37)

Finding the money for adaptation works can, on the face of it, appear a
daunting task. There are, in fact, a number of sources of money which can be
accessed, the following are the most commonly used.

### Local authority grants, England and Wales

Chapter 1 describes the background to and details of the implementation of
housing renewal grants. The information here summarises the key elements
of the grant system.

A new grant system for England and Wales was introduced in December
1996. In relation to adaptations the following three types of grant are most
relevant.

#### I. RENOVATION GRANT

A renovation grant is a discretionary grant for larger scale repair and
improvement works. It is administered by the local housing authority.
Different local authorities will have different priorities for who can get a
grant, but these should be published by the authority.

To be eligible for a renovation grant, the person must:

- be an owner or private tenant with an obligation to carry out the
  works
- have occupied the property for at least three years prior to applying
  for a grant, unless:
  - the property is in a renewal area
  - the council allow an application to be made earlier
  - the building works are for fire precautions
  - the work is to convert a property.

The property must also be at least ten years old prior to the application.

A renovation grant can be awarded for the following items:

- to bring a property up to a legal standard for human habitation
- to bring a property up to a standard of reasonable repair
- to provide thermal insulation

- to provide facilities for space heating
- to improve internal arrangements within a property
- to provide a fire escape or other fire precautions
- to improve construction or physical condition of a property
- to improve services or amenities within a property
- to convert an existing property.

All renovation grants are means tested through what is called a 'test of resources'. The test of resources is used to calculate how much a person may have to contribute to the cost of carrying out the work. Anyone on income support or income based job seekers' allowance will receive a 100 per cent grant for approved works.

(This information is adapted from Care and Repair *Grant Factsheet No 1*. December 1996.)

## 2. DISABLED FACILITIES GRANT

A disabled facilities grant (DFG) is a cash grant to help disabled people with the cost of adaptations and is administered by the local housing authority.

To be eligible for a DFG, the person must be either:

- an owner-occupier
- a private tenant
- a private landlord of disabled tenant(s)
- a council tenant
- a housing association tenant.

Before awarding a DFG, the authority must be satisfied that the proposed work is reasonable and practicable, taking into account the age and condition of the home. It must also be satisfied that proposed works are necessary and appropriate for the disabled person for whose benefit they are to be carried out. It must consult with the social services department about this. This usually involves social services sending a social service authority occupational therapist to carry out an assessment of need.

There are two types of DFG: mandatory and discretionary. (See Chapter 1 for a definition of mandatory works.)

The maximum value of a mandatory DFG is £20,000 in England and £24,000 in Wales. If the work costs more than the maximum, the authority has a discretion to pay extra grant.

DFGs are subject to the 'test of resources'. People claiming income support or income based job seekers' allowance will receive 100 per cent grant for approved works. The only income and capital taken into account in the test of resources for a DFG is that of the disabled person and their partner. If the disabled person is a child or young person, the test of resources is applied to the person who is responsible for him or her.

The authority may delay payment of a mandatory DFG (or part of it) for up to 12 months from the date of application. (Adapted from Care and Repair *Grant Factsheet No 2*. December 1996.)

### 3. HOME REPAIR ASSISTANCE

Home repair assistance (HRA) is available to help pay for small-scale repairs, improvement or adaptations to the home and is administered by the local housing authority. Different authorities will have different priorities for who can get assistance, but the authority should publish these priorities.

To be eligible for HRA a person must:

- be aged 18 or over
- live in the dwelling as their only or main residence, or be applying for assistance for the benefit of a person who is 60 years old or more, or disabled or infirm
- be an owner-occupier or private tenant or have a right of exclusive occupation of the property for at least five years
- have a power or duty to carry out the building works
- be aged 60 or more, or disabled, or infirm, (or a carer of someone in one of these three categories) or in receipt of one of the following benefits: income support, income based job seekers' allowance, housing benefit, family credit, council tax benefit or disability working allowance.

HRA is also available to some occupiers of mobile homes and house-boats.

There is no restriction on the type of repairs, improvements or adaptations which can be funded by HRA. Assistance can be in the form of a cash grant or materials or both. The maximum amount of assistance that can be paid is £2000 per application and £4000 in any three year period. (Adapted from Care and Repair *Grant Factsheet No 3*.[1] December 1996.)

---

1    The Department of Transport, Environment and the Regions and the Welsh Office produces a series of three booklets giving more detailed information of the above grants. The address to apply for these free publications is given at the end of this chapter.

*Home improvement and repairs grants (Scotland)*

The grant system in Scotland was reformed in 1997. There are two main categories of grant aid available: Improvement Grants and Repairs Grants. In addition, help may be available to provide standard amenties.
Eligibility

- Owner or tenant of the property (tenants must obtain written consent from the owner)
- Usually, the property must be more than ten years old
- the property must be in council tax band A, B, C, D, E
- grant allocation targeted to worst housing and to occupants in financial need
- on completion of the work the property must meet agreed standards

1. IMPROVEMENT GRANT

For improvements to the property and to make property suitable for occupants with disabilties.

- Discretionary (mandatory if the house is below the 'tolerable standard' or is in a Housing Action Area).
- (Usually) up to 75 per cent of the approved expense limit of £12,600 for improvement/conversion, up to 75 per cent for other eligible works.
- Councils can make a case to the Scottish Office for an increase above £12,600 and provide grant up to 75 per cent where an improvement has been made or up to 90 per cent (in cases of financial hardship).
- Standard amenity grant, up to 50 per cent of approved expense limit of £3010 for standard amenities and £3450 for repairs

2. REPAIRS GRANT

For work to the internal and external fabric of the house in order to maintain the useful life of the property.

- Discretionary (mandatory if the house is served with a Repairs notice by the council).
- (Usually) up to 50 per cent of the approved expense limit of £5500.
- Up to 90 per cent of the approved expense limit of £5500 for lead plumbing and radon gas works.

Enquiries about the detailed operation of the current system in each of Scotland's 32 local authorities should be routed through the private sector grants section which is usually located within the council's housing department.[2]

### Housing grants, Northern Ireland

A system of grant aid is available to home owners, tenants and landlords (not tenants of the Housing Executive or housing associations) through the Northern Ireland Housing Executive. Its key elements are as follows:

1. RENOVATION GRANT

- mandatory
- to make homes fit for human habitation
- maximum grant £20,000
- means tested.

2. DISABLED FACILITIES GRANT

- mandatory
- facilitating access to and from the home (similar to criteria used in for the DFG in England)
- the Housing Executive will consult with the Health and Social Services Board to obtain a recommendation
- maximum grant £20,000
- means tested.

3. MINOR WORKS ASSISTANCE

- discretionary
- for small, essential works to the home
- available to people on income related benefits
- types of assistance:
    - staying put, small repairs or adaptations

---

2   For further information, refer to the free booklet 'House Improvement and Repairs Grant' (Spring 1997), issued by The Scottish Office Development Department (available from SODD, Victoria Quay, Edinburgh, EH6 6QQ).

- for people over 60
- elderly resident – to enable an older person to stay on a permanent basis with someone else.
- patch and mend – assistance for property in clearance or redevelopment areas
- lead pipes
- disabled adaptations – small-scale adaptations.

Applications must be supported by an occupational therapist recommendation.

Minor works assistance takes the form of a cash grant or materials up to a maximum of £1080 per annum or £3240 in any three-year period.

### Funding adaptations in different tenures

Different housing tenures create some differences in terms of the funding options available.

- Council tenants are entitled to apply for a DFG, but many local authorities have developed their own policies on adapting their properties.

- Tenants of social landlords (Housing Associations) are eligible to apply for a DFG. Alternatively their landlord may decide to fund the adaptation themselves. Where the landlord is registered with the Housing Corporation it can apply for funding for adaptations costing in excess of £500, providing it does not have more than £500,000 in the rent surplus fund. Although the housing corporation has no statutory duty to fund such works it has in practice been a major source of financial assistance. However the amount granted by the holding corporation has declined during the last year 1996/7, and seems set to fall further.

- Private tenants may apply for a grant providing the landlord agrees and is prepared to comply with the relevant conditions and undertakings. The local authority may choose to waive these conditions in certain cases. The landlord can apply him/herself if the tenant doesn't have a contractual power or duty to undertake works to the home.

- Tenants of houses in multiple occupation may face further complications.

Tenants are advised to seek guidance both from the landlord and the local housing authority grant department.

### Social services department

Social services departments have a duty under Section 2 of the CSDP Act 1970 to make arrangements for adaptations. This means that social services may need to help their client find the money to pay for the work or to consider funding the works when for example, a DFG is not available, when the cost of the work exceeds the mandatory limit or to assist with the householder's assessed contribution. Many social services departments routinely pay for items of equipment, leaving local (housing) authorities to fund work involving adaptations to the home. This discussion has been expanded elsewhere, and at the time of writing, the debate concerning the responsibilities of social services departments looks set to continue and to be influenced by legal precedents.

The Community Care (Direct Payments) Act 1996 came into force on 1 April 1997. This gave social services departments the power to make direct payments to people with disabilities in order that they can purchase their own care services. Direct payments are possible towards the cost of aids and adaptations providing they are items for which social services themselves have a responsibility to provide (i.e. they should not be used as a substitute for a disabled facilities grant).

Social services departments have the power to recover the cost, or part of it, from the client. Decisions about the amount payable will be based on a test of financial resources. Any such 'means test' should take account of all of the households essential outgoings – something the DFG test of resources is often criticised for not doing.

### Family Fund

The Family Fund is a government financed scheme administered by the Joseph Rowntree Foundation.

It is intended to help relieve the stress caused by the care of a disabled child. The fund is concerned to avoid paying for items for which the local authority has a duty to provide but will sometimes agree to pay towards the cost of aids and adaptations providing the social services department is also contributing.

*Community care grants*

Community care grants are one of three types of discretionary payment under the Department of Social Security's Social Fund administered by the Benefits Agency. It is intended to help priority groups such as older people and people with disabilities to remain living in the community, to return from institutional care or to ease exceptional pressure on families.

Community care grants are discretionary to people who are on income support or income based job seekers' allowance. The grant will be reduced on a pound-for-pound basis for any savings over £500 (£1000 if the person is aged 60 or over).

Grants will not be given where a local authority has a statutory duty to meet the need.

*National health service*

A number of items of equipment are available through the NHS. These include low vision aids, hearing aids, communication aids, wheelchairs, environmental control equipment (i.e. a central control operating alarms, doors, telephone, heating etc.) and walking aids. The social services occupational therapist should be aware of what is available and may be required to support the application following an assessment. Items provided through the NHS are on a loan basis.

*Employment service*

A disabled person working, or intending to work from home may be entitled to some assistance towards equipment or adaptations through the 'Access to Work' scheme. However, a good 'business' case would have to be made in order to qualify and it would be necessary to show that the assistance requested would be towards a provision that would not be required by a non-disabled person. For example, a computer probably wouldn't be funded but special software might be.

Some items of equipment are available on loan to enable disabled people to pursue employment or education.

*Personal resources*

The person requiring an adaptation to their home may be in a position to fund the works through their own resources – income, savings or a loan.

Home owners may want to consider using an equity release scheme. These are available through some banks and building societies and overcome the problem of finding large repayments. There are several types of scheme and anyone contemplating this route should seek independent financial advice.

Income support and income based job seekers' allowance are means-tested benefits paid to top up other benefits or earnings or to provide a basic income if no other money is coming in. People eligible to claim may be able to receive extra payment to cover the interest on a loan for adaptation work. Waiting periods apply in the case of claimants under 60 years of age and the rate of interest payable is stipulated by law. Income support/income based job seekers' allowance claimants should contact the Benefits Agency for more information.

*Charitable sources*

There are numerous local, regional and national charitable sources which may be willing to assist financially. These include ex-service charities, trade unions, ex-employees associations, churches, self-help or special interest groups, Rotary Clubs and so on. Citizens Advice Bureaux (CAB), libraries or councils for voluntary service are useful places to seek advice on charitable sources.

*Home improvement agencies (HIAS) / The Disabled Persons Housing Service (DPHS)*

These organisations, details of which are shown at the end of this chapter, are able to advise on funding works and in some cases may have a limited hardship fund available. They are also able to provide considerable practical and personal support to people needing repairs or adaptations to their homes.

> The main strengths of the service they [home improvement agencies] offered were in their effectiveness at supplying financial advice and help … (Mackintosh, Leather and McCafferty 1993, p.xi)

Details can be obtained from the local housing authority, social services department, Citizens Advice Bureau or from the relevant national body listed at the end of this chapter.

---

### Example: Mrs Amis

Eileen Amis is 79 years old and has arthritis which causes very limited mobility. She lives alone in an inter-war bungalow, receives state pension and has little or no savings.

The steps to Mrs Amis's property were in a very poor state, as was the handrail. This caused her considerable difficulty leaving her home and

---

### Example: Mrs Amis (continued)

---

throughout the winter she became a virtual prisoner in her home, too afraid to venture out and too afraid of being 'ripped off' to arrange the necessary repairs to her steps and handrail.

A neighbour of Mrs Amis contacted the local home improvement agency. The agency employed a handyperson who visited and carried out the necessary repairs at a cost of only £4.00 to Mrs Amis.

---

*VAT*

Certain adaptation works are zero rated for VAT. The local customs and excise office will be able to advise and can provide an explanatory leaflet (701/7/94 – *VAT Reliefs For People With Disabilities*).

## Progressing the work

### Quotations and tenders

Once the scheme proposals have been finalised and the necessary documents produced, builders can be approached. Providing the documentation is adequate, builders should be asked to provide a quotation for the work rather than an estimate. A quotation represents a firm offer to carry out the work described for the sum of money stated. An estimate is no more than a best guess and almost invariably leads to lengthy negotiations over the price.

Quotations may be sought from a number of builders on a competitive basis. Best practice is to formalise this into a tendering process whereby all the builders are approached at the same time, provided strictly with the same information and required to return their tenders (i.e. quotations) by a specified deadline in a sealed envelope. The tenders are logged, opened and witnessed all at the same time before being evaluated. The purpose of this is to ensure builders are competing on fair and equal terms which is in the interests of all the parties concerned.

A key principal of contract law hinges on the terms 'offer' and 'acceptance'. The letter of invitation to tender should state clearly that it does not constitute an offer. It should also state that there is no undertaking to accept the lowest or any of the tenders received. This ensures full control of the point at which an offer is accepted and thus a contract is entered into.

*Competent builders*

Finding a competent builder is a crucial part of the adaptations process. No matter how much control is exercised over the documentation or how much time may be devoted to monitoring the progress of the work, great reliance is put on the builders to carry out the work satisfactorily. Much of what goes on during building work is covered up on completion and problems may not surface for quite some time. Clients should be advised to take great care in selecting builders. They must not only be skilled technically, they must have excellent health and safety and customer care practices, and be fully aware of current policy and practices, together with the legislation which governs all their activities.

There is no magic formula to identify such builders. There is understandably a high level of anxiety over the 'cowboy' element. However, it should be remembered that builders are often criticised for doing an unsatisfactory job when the real explanation is either that far too little money was available to pay for the work required, or that the contract documentation/specification was inadequate and the builder was not properly instructed.

Nevertheless, factors to consider in identifying builders include:

- local reputation
- experience of similar types of work
- length of time in business
- trades employed directly and the arrangements for subcontracting
- validity of insurances and membership of trade bodies
- references from bank, trade suppliers, former customers
- evidence of accident record and health and safety competence
- equal opportunities awareness and customer care policy
- information on county court judgements
- management and administrative competence
- tax and VAT status.

It should also be remembered that circumstances can change very quickly and builders known from past experience to be capable of delivering a good service may change their practice if their financial survival is at stake. It can be very difficult to identify when a builder is financially at risk but one sign can be to offer an unrealistically low quote for a job with the builder hoping to negotiate increases in the price once the contract has been won. Good documentation and contract administration will prevent this.

*Customer care*

Customer care practices are all-important with adaptation work and clients who are unhappy with their builder will often rapidly lose patience. Having alterations to the house is stressful enough for everyone and coping with the inevitable mess and disruption from a firm of builders can be a powerful disincentive to having the work done at all. Good communication and progressing the work to an agreed timetable will help ease the process.

Whilst many clients will wish to remain at home during the building work, it may be desirable for some to stay elsewhere temporarily. When essential services are disrupted and when potentially hazardous operations are underway, builders will generally expect to have sole possession of the site. Alternative accommodation may be available from friends, relatives, local authorities and housing associations. If the client does move out, it is important to state clearly in writing who has the responsibility for the security of the house, who takes charge of the keys and what if any insurance obligations result.

*The building contract*

Once a builder has been selected and the necessary practical arrangements sorted out, the contract can be let. The importance of a written building contract cannot be overstated. The purpose of the contract is to formalise the arrangements between the two parties to the contract – the employer (disabled person) and the builder. It identifies the duties and responsibilities of the parties and covers the following:

- parties to the contract
- location of the site
- arrangements for contract administration
- nature of work and the price agreed
- arrangements for payments
- arrangements for varying the work and cost as necessary
- arrangements for resolving disputes
- arrangements for insurance
- arrangements for terminating the contract other than on completion of the building work
- arrangements for dealing with defects.

Whilst it is possible to draft a letter to cover all these various matters, it is much better to use a standard form of contract in which the wording has been carefully considered in the light of construction disputes. Many building contracts are lengthy documents full of legal jargon, but others exist which are written in plain English which can be used even for very small-scale works. Many problems which arise between employer and builder once work has started, can be traced to inadequate information or confusion over what is expected, problems that can be addressed systematically with a suitable building contract to use in conjunction with the schedule of works/ specification.

*Contract administration*

Perhaps one of the most important elements is the role of a contract administrator. Ideally an architect, surveyor or other technical officer will be appointed to act on behalf of the employer in administering the contract and carrying out various duties according to the conditions of the contract. The contract administrator will keep the employer advised of the progress of the work and seek instructions from the employer from time to time. The contract administrator will be involved in inspecting the progress of the work, authorising payments and in issuing instructions to the builder, perhaps to vary the work from what was originally planned. Builders often carry out apparently minor adjustments to the work to compensate for inadequate information or perhaps simply because it may be easier for them to carry out the work. Given the tight tolerances in adaptation work, this can result in the scheme failing to meet expectations and any variations should be formally approved and may well require the input of an occupational therapist in exercising judgement. Additionally, if the works are being funded by a local authority grant, the grants officer must be consulted and approval sought for a grant to cover the cost of the variations.

The contract administrator cannot carry out all the duties for the employers, for example only the employer, as one of the parties to the contract, can terminate the contract. Occupational therapists may find themselves assisting clients in carrying out some of these duties in the absence of a contract administrator being appointed. Their expertise in assessing need and specifying equipment and adaptations does not necessarily equip them to deal with issues of contract law or matters relating to the building structure, safe working practices or unforeseen works, such as timber rot and faulty wiring. Some assistance can be given by grants officers when the works relate to grant funding, but the contract administrators role is best provided by an independent, experienced construction professional.

On completion of an adaptation, a visit by the occupational therapist involved is required to ensure that all facilities are functioning as they should and that the work has been completed to his or her satisfaction. The client's contract administrator, the occupational therapist and, when grant funded, the grants officer should make a joint visit to ensure all are in agreement.

Once the work has been completed, the contract may stipulate that a defects liability period will come into force and a percentage of the funds may be held back by way of a retention to encourage a builder to return and put right any problems which arise in that period.

It is important that the client is fully briefed on how to use new equipment or facilities with which they have been provided and that they are issued with copies of warranties, instruction books and any arrangements for the return of loaned equipment in the future. Information should also be provided for routine maintenance, and emergency call out and insurers should be notified of the final details of the adaptation works.

A follow-up visit by the occupational therapist will ensure clients are able to use their new facilities safely and effectively and also identify any further support needs.

### Sources of support and advice

> Particular care is needed in making a success of home adaptations. There is an increasing trend to leave the actual management of building work and other contractors with the clients themselves. In the inspection, some users complained to SSI of distressing experiences which this had caused, and more generally of the delays and breakdown in communications often experienced. A major home adaptation is a very stressful episode for anyone, but the more so for disabled people and their carers. (Social Services Inspectorate 1994, p.34)

Anyone who has had any significant work carried out in the home will understand what an unpleasant experience it can be. Quite apart from the disruption and mess there are the problems of what needs to be done, how it can be paid for, who will do it and whether it has been done properly. Add to this the likelihood of delays in getting assessments or in processing the grant application and the bureaucratic procedures and it is hardly surprising that many people needing adaptations simply fail to proceed with the necessary works. The Pieda Report (referred to in Heywood and Smart 1996, p.126) shows a national dropout rate of 30 per cent after initial enquiry and before applying for a DFG.

Local authorities are encouraged to carry out a preliminary enquiry system (Department of the Environment 1996). This should provide potential grant applicants with information about their grant entitlements and the authorities' published policies on allocation of discretionary grants. This is a positive step but may deter clients if they learn that they will be required to contribute to the cost of the works or that a grant will not be made. When this happens the person can fail to seek an occupational therapist assessment (to which they are entitled) and may not be aware of alternative sources of funding. Authorities using preliminary enquiry systems, therefore, need to be aware of, and to inform clients about, resource availability outside of the grant system.

Help may be available to disabled people seeking to achieve an adaptation to their home from the following.

*Home improvement agencies*

Home improvement agencies (HIAs) are non-profit making organisations helping older people and people with disabilities to repair and adapt their homes. Staff visit people in the own homes and help them through the whole process of deciding what needs to be done, arranging the finance and organising the building work.

A key element of the service is bringing together the relevant experts – client, occupational therapist, grant officer and others – and assembling and dovetailing all the component parts of the service such as grants, loans and building contracts.

There are around 200 HIAs in England (at April 1998). Of these, 162 are part-funded by the Department of the Environment, Transport and the Region (DETR) and are managed by a number of different bodies; mainly housing associations (70%) and local authorities (16%). The agency network in England is co-ordinated by Care and Repair England receiving financial support from DETR. Other networks exist in Scotland, Wales and Northern Ireland. Details of how to contact the national bodies, who can advise on the whereabouts of local HIAs, are given at the end of this chapter.

---

## Example: Mr and Mrs Tyler

Mr and Mrs Tyler live in a 1970s semi-detached house. They are living on a low income but have a large mortgage. Their four-year-old son is severely disabled with cerebral palsy. They needed ground-floor bedroom and bathroom facilities for him. The HIA assisted Mr and Mrs Tyler to apply for a disabled facilities grant.

The occupational therapist agreed that ground-floor facilities were necessary. The housing authority decided that it would be reasonable to convert the existing semi-integral garage into a bedroom and shower room and

---

### Example: Mr and Mrs Tyler (continued)

---

toilet. With close co-operation with the occupational therapist the work was carried out to provide level access facilities and a ramp to the front door. In addition a ceiling mounted hoist was installed between the bedroom and the shower room.

The work was financed through a mixture of sources which the agency helped Mr and Mrs Tyler to obtain.

The total cost of work was £13,249.42; the DFG contributed £12,261.22. The social services department provided £488.20 and Mr and Mrs Tyler contributed £500 themselves.

(Care and Repair 1994)

---

HIAs have received increasing recognition as significant providers of community care services. Working with and for their clients they are able to take away much of the 'sting' of arranging adaptation works and help save occupational therapists time which might otherwise have been diverted to supporting the client through the process.

*The Disabled Persons Housing Service*

Disabled persons housing services (DPHS) have been established in a number of areas. These offer a one-stop shop for disabled people of all ages where they can receive expert and practical information, advice, support and guidance on all aspects of their housing need. This includes assistance with grants and funding as well as technical aspects of housing, 'move on' advice and support and help in arranging adaptations to the home. (Further details of the work of DPHS can be found in Chapter 4.)

*Local authority agency service*

Local housing authorities have a responsibility for administering disabled facility and other housing renovation grant applications. Most offer advice and guidance to applicants for a grant but some, including the 26 DETR funded agencies, provide a comprehensive HIA service.

## Assessment of agency services

A study commissioned by the DoE (MacKintosh, Leather and McCafferty 1993, p.xi) found that all three types of agencies (HIA, DPHS and local authority agency services) provided 'an extremely valuable and distinct service to their clients which if properly co-ordinated at a local level could meet all the needs of disabled people for housing advice and help...'. The study went on to demonstrate very high levels of client satisfaction (87% overall) but did indicate that people with a need for more intensive help would be better served by agencies offering a comprehensive range of support through the whole process.

*Private agency services*

A number of private home adaptation agency services have been set up by, amongst others, private occupational therapy practices or building surveyors practices. Some local authorities have chosen to contract with them to provide a support service to grant applicants – paying their fee out of the grant. It would be feasible to contract an occupational therapist based with one of these agencies to undertake the 'necessary and appropriate' assessment for a DFG, although the cost of that assessment may not be recoverable from the grant. Clients may choose to use one of these agencies to assist them to have privately funded adaptation works carried out. It would be in their interest to check first that they can offer the appropriate level of service and expertise and to establish the fee payable.

## Example

Camden London Borough Council funded St Pancras Care and Repair to employ an agency occupational therapist to assess and advise clients applying for a DFG. The occupational therapist was given delegated authority to assess if the adaptations were necessary and appropriate. Supervision was provided by the senior occupational therapist at social services.

## Joint working – The collective response to problem solving

> the procedure for assessing and agreeing funding for adaptations to property was lengthy and complex, with delays and duplication. (Arblaster *et al.* 1996, p.12)

Arranging adaptations can be difficult enough without having also to negotiate unnecessary barriers between and sometimes within organisations. Research has identified a number of common issues creating barriers and preventing effective joint working (Department of Health 1996, p.5). They include:

- different levels of authority and decision making process
- different agendas, priorities and stakeholders
- different legal frameworks
- different systems
- different cultures and languages
- lack of knowledge about other agencies working in the field.

It is probably reasonable to add to this list the problem associated with increasing demands on restricted departmental budgets. As Arblaster (1996, p.12) observed, 'identifying which agency was responsible for adaptations was also a problem. "What adaptations we (housing) should fund and what (adaptations) social services should fund – it's a grey area and an acute problem as we've over committed our money."' Fortunately there were rays of hope. 'In some areas problems such as these had been addressed and there were examples of successful inter-agency collaboration to provide home adaptations' (p.12).

When budgets are tight and staff are under considerable pressure the synergy created by effective joint working may help resolve the problems. Joint working can, and should, take place at a number of different levels, strategic and operational. At a strategic level this may take the form of joint commissioning, ideally involving health, social services and housing.

---

### Example

In parts of Derbyshire joint panels of officers from districts and county authorities meet to consider adaptation issues and to review needs and priorities. These panels, which have been complemented by local members committees, have helped develop trust, raised the adaptation profile and won political support. (From Heywood 1996)

---

*Figure 3.1: Model for Joint Working*

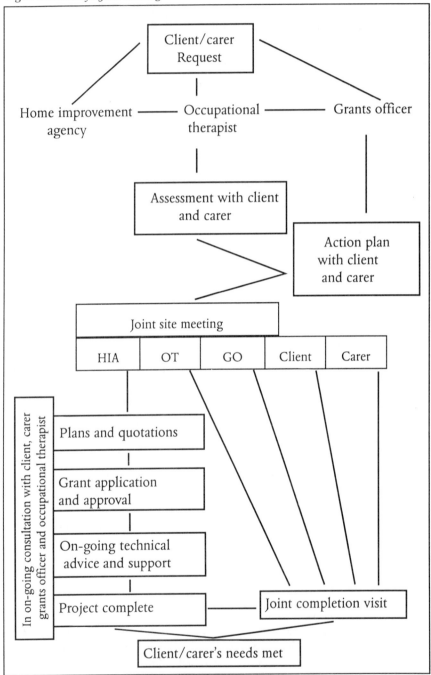

*Source:* Pulling Together: developing effective partnerships (Care and Repair/College of
    Occupational Therapists 1994).

Excellent examples of joint working between occupational therapists, grant departments, and home improvement agencies have emerged in the field of adaptations. In this the occupational therapist carries out the initial assessment and provides any necessary on-going professional advice. A plan of action is agreed between the grant officer, occupational therapist and home improvement agency. The home improvement agency, in conjunction with the client, grant officer and occupational therapist, will use its experienced staff to make sure that the work is carried out properly and to the client's satisfaction.

Care and Repair and the College of Occupational Therapists produced a joint publication to promote collaborative working. This sets out five factors for effective joint working.

### 1. Communication

Clear channels of communication need to be established as a prerequisite to any joint working arrangements and must be maintained throughout the process, for example:

- organise regular meetings
- know who the contact people are
- remember to communicate with all the relevant parties, especially the client
- the involvement of the representative from the occupational therapy team on the home improvement agency management or advisory committee is beneficial. Similarly, home improvement agencies' representation in occupational therapists decision making processes can be an aid to communication.

### 2. Agreeing procedures

Working arrangements must be agreed and written down, and include referral procedures, joint visits, response times, criteria and how to deal with difficult or contentious issues. Procedures need to be in place to ensure efficient referral back to the occupational therapist. All procedures should reflect realistic expectations and explicitly identify the limits of each party's responsibilities and policy constraints. Clarifying roles will be essential in order to encourage respect for each other's professionalism, avoid potential conflict and ensure that clients have access to the best possible service.

### 3. Policy

Successful partnerships depend upon commitment at all levels. Managers need to agree policy and practices that promote and support joint working and that address any local sensitive issues.

### 4. Training

Training needs must be considered as a priority at the beginning of the working partnership. These should involve appropriate induction training and a sharing in each others' training courses. Issues to address may include:

- development of team working skills
- awareness of the respective roles and expertise
- effects of disability
- different needs arising from cultural and religious beliefs
- the nature and effects of poor housing and disrepair.

### 5. Adequacy of resources

Working partnerships bring many rewards but it is necessary to recognise that there are resource implications such as staff time to attend meetings or to engage in joint assessment. An increase in demand on services may require a corresponding increase in resources. Some home improvement agencies, for example, negotiated funding from health and social services authorities in order to meet the workload.

(Care and Repair/College of Occupational Therapists 1994, p.8–10)

Joint working may not hold all of the answers but where there is a commitment to collectively strive for solutions to meet the need there is a much better chance of success through the creative use of shared resources.

### The user's view

Research carried out by and with disabled people (Heywood 1996, p.4) identifies the seven key components of a good adaptation service:

- one person co-ordinating the process from start to finish
- minimal wait for assessment
- the priorities and values of the disabled person respected
- swift implementation after assessment

- well-organised, well-supervised implementation, causing minimum disruption

- high quality end product, not ugly or embarrassing and enhancing the quality of life

- service available to all who need it. People should not be excluded by poor quality information, by the existence of or inadequacies of the means test or by prioritisation.

---

### Example: Andy

Andy lives alone in a late-Edwardian semi in a small, former mining community in North Warwickshire. He has cerebral palsy and in recent years has experienced a deterioration in his mobility.

Getting to the upstairs toilet and bathroom were becoming a real trial and using the bath was both difficult and painful. The heating and hot water system operated on a solid fuel boiler and this required a considerable effort to maintain.

There was a clear need for some adaptations to Andy's home. The occupational therapist visited promptly to discuss Andy's needs fully. He arranged a joint visit with the borough council's grant officer. It was agreed that a level-access shower and toilet should be installed in what was at that time a pantry and outhouse. Access to the new facility would be via a lobby off the kitchen. A new gas fired boiler was to be fitted too.

Quotations had to be obtained; two for the alterations and two for the heating work. The occupational therapist had given advice on the most suitable type of shower unit.

The whole process took about five months from start to finish. Andy was delighted with the end result – he didn't need to climb the stairs to use the toilet, could wash quickly, easily and safely and didn't need to go outside for coal.

---

This then is a success story in terms of outcome. The process itself was also largely successful because both the occupational therapist and the grant officer ensured that Andy's wishes were heard and, in his own words 'I was made to feel part of the team'. However, even when things go well, there is room for improvement.

The first criticism is that Andy was left very much to fend for himself in arranging for the plans to be drawn up to the occupational therapist's specification, and in getting building quotes. At one point the plans needed to be re-drawn because the toilet had to be re-sited. This was actually quite stressful and time consuming. Fortunately, Andy is a capable person who communicates well and has many friends and associates. Someone else may not have been able to negotiate this first hurdle.

A second problem related to a seriously long delay in getting the boiler connected to the gas supply. Andy had to wait over a week for this during some bitterly cold weather. This created considerable discomfort and pushed up the electricity bill through intensive use of electric heaters.

The third area of concern for Andy was the mess and upheaval experienced while his home was adapted. The builder did his best but it was, in Andy's words, 'harassing – I felt very anxious, but I put up with it because of the overall improvement it would make to my life'.

So what would have improved matters? Major adaptations are always likely to disturb daily routine and to produce a degree of anxiety. Additional personal and practical support can make a considerable difference to a statisfactory outcome.


## Conclusion

Getting the right adaptation to the home is often the crucial factor determining independence. This chapter plots a course through the process, identifying potential problems and some solutions.

On the face of it the journey to a successful adaptation takes the traveller through a somewhat hostile environment. For some, and especially those with limited resources, just accessing the system may seem to present more than a few hazards which are likely to end the journey before it has even begun, for example, lack of clear referral procedures, filtering out, eligibility criteria designed to target need (but which may appear to ration services) and long delays. There are clear messages here about the need for all parties concerned, from service users down, to understand policy, procedures and the rights conveyed by legislation. It is also clear that all parties need to develop joint strategies to ensure clear, consistent and appropriate processes to ease access to services and to avoid deterring appropriate demand.

Having been assessed as needing adaptation work someone has to translate need into a specification for the work. This requires attention to detail, clarity of communication, use of commonly understood terminology and preparation of appropriate schedules and drawings. There are choices to make and practical solutions to be found which demand the full involvement of the user. Tensions may arise here in as much as decisions may be driven by financial constraints rather more than user or professional adviser preference.

Finding the money to pay for the work can seem problematic yet there are a number of sources of help available, the most significant of these being the housing renewal grant system. Other options might be available when a grant is either not payable or does not cover the full cost.

For many people the prospect of engaging builders or contractors to do work on their home can be a fearsome experience. Spectres of cowboy builders emerge, fuelled by press reports. Then there is the worry about the disruption and ensuring satisfactory completion. Fortunately unscrupulous builders are very much in the minority and with the right approach and care it is possible to progress work satisfactorily.

This journey to a much needed adaptation seems by now to have taken a turn through a minefield zone. It is not surprising that, all too often, disabled people are deterred and fail to complete the journey. The right sort of assistance can help here. The occupational therapist may be able to provide this but it can be time consuming and not necessarily the best use of their time. It is not surprising then that in many areas there is considerable statutory support for home improvement agencies. Other sources of help include disabled persons housing services, local authority grant departments and private agency services.

Further barriers are created by the very organisations vested with the responsibility of facilitating the adaptation. These are generally the barriers created within and between those organisations which can so easily inhibit successful outcomes. Whilst we might understand why the barriers have been created, every effort must be made to breach them. Organisations working together to find solutions can so often create a synergy that will result in a successful outcome.

Ultimately, the journey will be judged by the users themselves. The final part of the chapter has set out some guidance on what users want from an adaptation service. This section shows that even largely successful services can be improved at little cost if proper consideration is given to customer care. It is that very objective of providing customer care that may be the key to the creation of an efficient, effective and appropriate adaptation service.

## References

Age Concern England (1996) *Stuck on the Waiting List: Older People and Equipment for Independent Living.* London: Age Concern England.

Arblaster, L., Conway, J., Foreman, A. and Hawtin, M. (1996) *Asking the Impossible? Inter-agency Working to Address the Housing and Social Care Needs of People in Ordinary Housing.* Bristol: The Policy Press.

Care and Repair (1994) *Poor Housing – Who Cares? The Housing Circumstances of Home Improvement Agency Clients.* Nottingham: Care and Repair.

Care and Repair (1996) *Grant Factsheets 1, 2 and 3.* Nottingham: Care and Repair.

Care and Repair/College of Occupational Therapists (1994) *Pulling Together: Developing Effective Partnerships.* Nottingham: Care and Repair.

*Carers (Recognition and Services) Act 1995.* London: HMSO.

*Children Act 1989.* London: HMSO.

*Chronically Sick and Disabled Persons Act 1970.* London: HMSO.

*Community Care (Direct Payments) Act 1996.* London: HMSO.

Department of the Environment (1996) *Private Sector Renewal: A Strategic Approach.* Circular 17/96. London: HMSO.

Department of Health (1996) *A Development Pack for Joint Commissioning.* London: Department of Health.

*Disabled Persons (Services, Consultation and Representations) Act 1986.* London: HMSO.

Heywood, F. (1994) *Adaptations: Finding Ways to Say Yes.* Bristol: SAUS Publications.

Heywood, F. (1996) *Managing Adaptations: Positive Ideas for Social Services.* Bristol: The Policy Press.

Heywood, F. and Smart, G. (1996) *Funding Adaptations: The Need to Co-operate.* Bristol: The Policy Press.

Lamb, B. and Layzell, S. (1994) *Disabled in Britain: A World Apart.* London: SCOPE.

Mackintosh, S., Leather, P. and McCafferty P. (1993) *The Role of Housing Agency Services in Helping Disabled People.* London: HMSO.

*NHS and Community Care Act 1990.* London: HMSO.

Richards, M. (1996) *Community Care and Older People: Rights, Remedies and Finances.* Bristol: Jordan Publishing Ltd.

Social Services Inspectorate (1994) *Occupational Therapy: The Community Contribution. Report on Local Authority Occupational Therapy Services.* London: Department of Health.

## Useful addresses

*Home improvement agencies – national co-ordinating bodies/contacts:*

### *England:* Care and Repair England
Castle House, Kirtley Drive, Nottingham, NG7 1LD.
Tel: 0115 979 9091.

### *Wales:* Care and Repair Cymru
Norbury House, Norbury Road, Cardiff, CF5 3AS.
Tel: 01222 576286.

### *Scotland:* Care and Repair Forum Scotland
c/o Glasgow Care and Repair, 553 Shields Road, Glasgow, G41 2RW.
Tel: 0141 221 9879.

### *Northern Ireland:* Fold Housing Association
Fold House, 3–6 Redburn Street, Holywood, Co. Down, BT18 9HZ.
Tel: 01232 428314.

*Disabled Persons Housing Service*

### National Disabled Persons Housing Service
Brunswick House, Deighton Close, Wetherby,
West Yorkshire, LS22 7GZ.
Tel: 01937 588580.

Department of the Environment, Transport and the Regions,
Eland House, Bressenden Place, London SW1E 5DU.
Tel: 0171 890 3496

For publications contact: Department of the Environment, Transport and
the Regions, Blackhorse Road, London SE99 6TT.
Tel: 0181 691 9191, Fax: 0181 694 0099.

CHAPTER 4

# Ways of Obtaining Appropriate or Adapted Housing

*Jackie Parsons*

## Introduction

This chapter considers the issues concerning ways of obtaining access to appropriate or adapted suitable housing for people with disabilities. It will lead those involved through the maze of information essential in order to assist in the decision making processes involved in moving to a new home. It looks at accessing information on housing need and what the user, or those assisting the user, needs to know. This includes waiting lists and housing policies within the social housing sector, and associated issues of overcrowding, harassment, domestic violence and homelessness, some of which may also be relevant. It assists in identifying how priority status is achieved and the policies with regard to accommodation offers are explained.

Meeting the need of people with disabilities requiring alternative accommodation is investigated and both social rented housing and owner occupation options are illustrated. Several examples of good practice in different

Grateful thanks are given to all those individuals who contributed towards this chapter by providing examples of good practice. Particular thanks go to: Debbie Stevenson, Service Manager, Milton Keynes Community NHS Trust; Richard Parrott of the Sheffield Learning Disabilities Information Project; Chris Read from the City of Nottingham Housing Department; Leon Jenkins of the Disabled Persons Accommodation Agency; Heather Rees and Cheryl Hague, Sheffield Disability Housing Service; Geoffrey Sproson and Angela Needham from HOMES; Rosalind Gill, Housing Disability Team Leader, Greenwich; Jill Pritchard and Jan Drummond, Fife Council; Marie Stobie, Aberdeen City Council; Janet McArthy, London Borough of Waltham Forest; and Rosemary Kemp, West Cumbria Health Care NHS Trust. Thank you also to others who made valuable observations with regard to the content of this chapter, including members of the Sheffield Forum of People with Disabilities; Ginny Shaw, Director of the National Disabled Persons Housing Service; and all the other chapter contributors to this book.

areas of the country are examined. Moving across areas, including information about the Housing Organisations Mobility and Exchange Services (HOMES) is also included.

When a decision has been made to move to alternative accommodation, people have options to consider with regard to their future housing. This includes, on the simplest level, where they want to live, what kind of home they want to live in, who they intend to live with, when they would like to move and how they are going to achieve it. This can be a traumatic time and, along with others, the occupational therapist has a role to play in enabling a person with a disability to make decisions about his or her future housing need.

## Access to information

Information is the key requirement of any house hunter. Information will be required for the person or persons needing rehousing and will be controlled by their individual needs, the needs of their carer and the nature of their disability. Factors to consider will include information about different property types and sizes including existing and new build plans, property location including local facilities and terrain, how to access suitable properties including renting and purchasing options, financial advice, local authority and housing association eligibility and application procedures and so on. Geographical location is often the most important issue of concern and is determined by a number of factors, including the availability of family and other support, schools, job location of self and other family members and existing familiarity with an area.

As a result of the 1996 Housing Act, local authorities have to be able to provide information about eligibility to apply for a place on their housing register. Anyone on the register is then entitled to sufficient general information to allow him or her to assess how long it is likely to be before housing is allocated, either by a local authority letting or by nomination to a registered social landlord (mostly housing associations including some almshouses/trusts who are registered with the Housing Corporation). A copy of their allocation scheme must be available for inspection in their office and they must send a copy, at a reasonable charge, to anyone requesting it. They must also produce a summary to be given out free on request.

One way of obtaining appropriate information is through a disabled persons housing service (DPHS). The role of a DPHS is to provide a professional and comprehensive service to people, regardless of tenure, age or income, who are experiencing housing problems as a result of their disability. In several areas a DPHS has been established or is in the process of being set up. The first DPHS was founded by Walbrook Housing Association in Derby in 1985 and the second one was established in Sheffield in 1993. Hammersmith and Fulham, Papworth and Lothian followed suit and there is an active national organisation (National Disabled Persons Housing Service) with several more DPHSs coming on line. Accreditation standards to be reached to be eligible to become a DPHS are currently being developed. Occupational therapists are ideally suited for employment within a disabled persons housing service as they are able to assess both properties and people and attempt to match the two together, as well as being able to carry out managerial and developmental roles within the organisation.

Sheffield Disability Housing Service is an example of a DPHS. It employs an occupational therapy manager and occupational therapy housing advisers. It is registered as an Industrial and Provident Society with charitable status. Over 50 per cent of the management committee must be representative of people with a disability. Its range of services includes information provision; a rehousing register that enables suitable client nominations to be put forward to housing providers; an adaptations recommendation service; and advice to housing developers on future housing need. It has a vital information gathering and dissemination role and people requiring alternative accommodation within the Sheffield area can contact the staff for advice and information with regard to their housing need. Practical help and advice is offered on either moving to a new home or adapting an existing one.

### Housing registers (waiting lists)

Access to social housing involves making a housing application to the housing organisation concerned, be it either a local authority or housing association. Each local authority and housing association usually has its own application form to fill in, which can take a considerable amount of time, effort and duplication for the applicant.

It is worth finding out beforehand whether a person requiring rehousing is eligible to be on the waiting list concerned. In the case of the local authority this is determined by Section 161 of the 1996 Housing Act, which states that:

> A local authority may allocate housing only to a 'qualifying person'. It is for the local authority to define who is a qualifying person, subject to a power of the Secretary of State to lay down that particular categories of person must or must not be included in the definition.

For example, Mansfield District Council's Housing Allocations scheme from April 1997 states, under the heading of 'qualifying persons', that they will normally only allow any person aged 18 years and over with a local connection to join their housing register, subject to those classes of persons who are specifically excluded from registration under regulations issued by the Secretary of State. These regulations refer to the rights of refugees, immigrants and non-intentionally or threatened homeless persons. Mansfield District Council also state that current or former tenants who have an outstanding debt to the revenue account will be able to register as a qualifying person but would not normally be made an offer of accommodation whilst this debt remains outstanding.

In the case of local authority housing lists, the applicant can also state if they wish to be considered for nomination to a housing association property as well as a local authority owned property. Most local authorities have nomination rights to a given percentage of properties owned by housing associations and this can vary. Fifty per cent is usual but in some cases up to 100 per cent nomination rights can be held for certain housing schemes.

Some areas are investigating the idea of a common waiting register, covering all local authority and housing association properties within a given area. This has its advantages to the client in that only one application form needs to be filled in to access all possible tenancies. This is only operating in a few areas in view of the logistics involved. It is difficult to satisfy all the criteria and need variations and information technology standardisation requirements for different housing bodies. Section 162 of the 1996 Housing Act allows common waiting lists to continue and new ones to be set up.

Sheffield Disability Housing Service, along with the other DPHSs, holds its own database of people with disabilities who require alternative accommodation. An open referral system is in operation and people requiring rehousing can go onto the database register, initially by filling in a self-assessment application form. The majority of people will then receive a visit in their own homes by a housing adviser (who is an occupational therapist) who will assess their particular housing need and provide information on the properties available within their chosen geographical area. Assistance to fill in other relevant housing application forms can be given and letters of support are usually supplied alongside to increase the applicants chances of being accepted or given higher priority points by a housing organisation.

Information on housing need applies to all user groups, including people with learning disabilities. Here, a project is described that illustrates the importance of information from both the users viewpoint and for a future planning and strategic development function. In 1994 in Sheffield the Learning Disability Accommodation Project began on a three-year joint-funded basis. Planning and strategic development is its primary function but the research and information collected for that purpose has proved useful as a specialist resource of information that is very much in demand from users, carers, purchasers and providers of accommodation and related care packages.

The project has collected information on to a database of all the accommodation options open to people with a learning disability in Sheffield. This ranges from the larger, specialist type of accommodation provided by hostels through to nursing and residential care provision, homes run by housing associations and on to adult and family placement schemes and supported living schemes where people have their own tenancies and require varying levels of support ranging from 24-hour care to on-call. Information is also held about local independent charities offering accommodation services who have no formal contract with the authorities. The project is concerned that people with learning disabilities are not precluded from other kinds of accommodation options open to them, depending on individual need, for example, specialist elderly and sheltered housing, accommodation for people with mental health or physical disability problems. The Young Men's and Women's Christian Associations have both shown an interest in providing places for people with learning disabilities.

Accommodation providers will contact the project staff and inform them of vacancies. The information is recorded and passed on to social service team managers and fieldwork social workers. They in turn identify possible suitable applicants and the decisions regarding suitability rests with the service provider and the service purchaser.

The project staff keep their own list of people requiring housing and will advise them of the accommodation on offer where appropriate. Staff will advise the person or their representative to apply directly to the providers of relevant accommodation, bearing in mind the appropriateness of the care levels required by each individual to ensure the best match possible.

The project is analysing present and future housing need for the 2400 Sheffield residents with a learning disability, using the Sheffield Case Register database, set up in 1974 and renowned to be one of the best in the country, as its main source of information. The project has determined that there will be an increase in the amount of accommodation and care required over the next 10 to 15 years as a result of:

- more people in the 25–40 year old age group who are living with carers who are ageing or elderly
- more severely disabled people in younger age groups who tend to come into care younger than less severely disabled people
- increasing life expectancies of people with a learning disability which reduces turnover of places within existing accommodation.

A parallel analysis of carer need in the city confirms these facts. Related to these issues there will be an expected increase in the number of emergency admissions because of the increasing number of people now living with elderly carers. The need for good quality emergency accommodation and good quality care levels has been recognised as the current deficit has been identified as a problem within the present system, sometimes resulting in expensive, out of city placements.

A 'quality of life' evaluation for people already living in the existing identified accommodation has also been carried out by the project staff and has identified those who are inappropriately placed who may need move-on accommodation. It has also highlighted a shortage of suitable places for people with autism, behaviour problems and mental health problems.

Amongst its findings, the Learning Disability Accommodation Project has highlighted the need for an active and interactive information and advisory service on accommodation need, open to all who require the information.

### Rehousing policies

There are numerous policies and procedures that have to be adhered to or overcome in order to be successful in being offered a suitable choice of alternative accommodation within the social housing sector. It is therefore vital that the person requiring rehousing is aware of these policies before deciding whether to proceed with an application or not. This includes information relating to: allocation and special eligibility rules; age restrictions to certain properties; the implications of existing rent arrears or unsatisfactory existing property conditions if the client is already living in the social rented sector; the rules regarding pets; relocation through employment; definitions of harassment; statutory overcrowding rules; domestic violence issues and homeless definitions (Sheffield City Council 1996). People with disabilities may have obvious housing needs on account of their disability, but these needs should not be looked at in isolation as they may have other social needs that are equally important.

#### ALLOCATION LISTS

A housing list is made up of a number of housing allocation lists, which are based upon estates or distinct housing areas. Within each estate there can be separate lists for the different property types, usually determined by the number of bedrooms. Applicants can choose which allocation lists to be put on to, but there are rules about the size and type of property an applicant may be offered. There are usually general rules applying to pregnant women, lone-parent families and child access in the event of divorce and separation. A person may have only one application on the housing list and this is cancelled when they become a tenant or joint tenant. Applicants are placed on an allocation list in order, depending on the number of points or level of priority they have been awarded.

### SPECIAL ELIGIBILITY RULES

There are usually special eligibility rules in addition to the general ones, including, for example, councils who will not offer families with more than one child a tenancy in a multi-storey flat. Special eligibility rules apply to properties set aside or designated for elderly people, or ground-floor accommodation or purpose built or adapted properties for disabled people. A tenant deemed as suitable for an elderly person's property usually has to be aged 60 or over (or 55 in some authorities), or have been awarded medical priority, or be eligible if the property is age banded.

### AGE BANDING

Age banding is where a property has been set aside for elderly people but if there is no one over 60 on the allocation list, then the property will be offered on an age banding basis instead, that is 50 to 59, 40 to 49, 30 to 39 and under 30. In the case of joint applications the age of the eldest person applies.

### DEBT TO HOUSING REVENUE ACCOUNT (RENT ARREARS)

Any tenant who is in arrears with their rent will jeopardise their chances of rehousing.

### SATISFACTORY PROPERTY CONDITION

An applicant already housed in local authority property must ensure their current property is in a satisfactory condition before an offer of alternative property will be made.

### PETS

The local policy regarding the keeping of pets is usually that pets 'free to roam' such as dogs and cats cannot be kept in properties with a shared entrance, unless the other existing tenants give consent. The rules concerning the keeping of pets in rented social housing is particularly important to many older and disabled people. Many elderly people with an old and trusted pet/best friend, will not consider being parted from him or her. This can result in the turning down of appropriate level access accommodation that would otherwise improve their independence.

NEW EMPLOYMENT

People who are moving into an area to work may be awarded priority points by the local authority if they need to be rehoused in order to take up their job. They may also be considered for an offer of housing, sometimes temporary, if it is too far for that person to travel to work each day, subject to the new employer's confirmation.

HARASSMENT

Harassment may be defined as sustained and deliberate interference with the peace and comfort of any person in relation to the enjoyment of their property. Moving away from this is not necessarily the only option and where possible, action should be taken against the person doing the harassing. Most local authorities will award higher priority to victims of harassment, be it in relation to race, sex, sexuality, disability or religion.

OVERCROWDING

There are statutory overcrowding rules laid down in Sections 325 and 326 of the 1985 Housing Act, giving room and space standards. Statutory overcrowding is when the number of people sleeping in a property is more than the permitted number, or two people of the opposite sex who are over ten years old and who do not normally live together as man and wife are forced to sleep in the same room. Children under one year may not count and children under ten may count as half a person for calculation purposes. Local authorities and housing associations will use their own formulas to work out the permitted number of persons per number of rooms and these may be lower than the standards set out in the 1985 Act, although they cannot be higher. Overcrowding can occur when two separate council tenants want to live together but this would lead to overcrowding in the larger of the two properties and housing points may be awarded for this. Overcrowding may be eased by a household within a household being rehoused.

DOMESTIC VIOLENCE

In cases of domestic violence, priority for housing the victim is usually given by a local authority or a housing association. A tenant, joint tenant or someone who would have been eligible to be a joint tenant, who has been treated violently or been threatened with violence by the partner, will usually be eligible for priority housing to a property similar to their own. A tenant who has been treated violently or threatened with violence at or near the property by a former partner who does not live at the property may also be eligible for housing but at less priority than the first situation.

HOMELESSNESS

To be considered as homeless by a housing authority, an applicant has to fulfil certain criteria relating to their eligibility for assistance and their priority need (Department of the Environment/Department of Health 1996, p.73–74). During this consideration period, the authority is under a duty to secure accommodation pending a decision as to what duty under Part VII of the Housing Act 1996 the applicant is owed. For example, if the applicant is eligible for assistance, homeless, in priority need and not homeless intentionally then the authority is under a duty to provide advice and assistance to enable the applicant to secure other suitable accommodation available in the area. If the applicant meets all the criteria mentioned above, a local connection with the area in which they are applying has to be established:

- they are or were in the past normally living in that area
- they are employed in that area
- they have family associations in that area
- there are other special circumstances.

If no local connection is established and the applicant has a connection with another area, the local authority has a duty to provide secure accommodation until the referral is agreed by the other authority.

MEDICAL PRIORITY

Medical priority can be given when someone's medical condition indicates they should move to more suitable property. An assessment to determine the level of priority is carried out by housing department personnel who can include occupational therapists, or independent advisers such as general practitioners. A recommendation for a medical priority assessment is often made by an occupational therapist, and a letter of support is often the first step on the ladder to housing. Priority status can sometimes be determined without seeing the client, hence the importance of a comprehensive support letter or report.

A medical priority assessor is usually a person with an appropriate qualification to be so (such as an occupational therapist or a nurse), and they may visit the applicant in their own home, or in hospital if this is appropriate, to determine their eligibility for medical priority status on grounds of disability. They will take into consideration present accommodation, if there is one, how the applicant's health is affected by it and how the applicant's health could be improved by rehousing. They will discuss with the applicant the type of property and area required. The more areas the applicant is prepared to accept, the quicker and easier it will be for them to be rehoused.

Sometimes the assessor will request the applicant to sign a form giving permission for their doctor to give information to the housing department if it is decided that this is required.

If medical priority is refused, the applicant will still have their application on the normal housing list, but they have the right to ask for the decision to be reviewed. If this is the case a review will be carried out by an independent medical adviser, who is usually a doctor. If medical priority is accepted then the applicant will be informed of this and will be told the area, type and size of accommodation that will be offered.

Housing registers are formulated on the basis of area, property type and size of accommodation required. Points are allocated to applicants on the basis of need and this applies equally to new applicants and existing tenants who wish to transfer to a different local authority property. Other factors will also need taking into consideration such as social grounds, over or under occupation of existing home and time spent on the waiting list.

There can be different levels of need for medical priority housing status. For example, one local authority defines need thus:

First priority need:

- a person being discharged from hospital where their home is totally unsuitable for their needs

- a person who is completely unable to cope in their present home

- a person who has spent a long time in institutional care and is ready to leave this care to live independently or with an identified and confirmed support package.

Second priority need:

- a person who cannot get in or out of their home, cannot reach essential facilities within their home, or who has a medical or disability problem that is affected by their home in some way;

- a person leaving residential care or a hostel if that person is ready to live independently or has an identified and confirmed support package.

Third priority need:

- a person who can use their existing facilities at home and in their local area such as shops and buses, but with whom there is clear evidence that being rehoused would improve their quality of life or their health or disability.

OFFERS OF ACCOMMODATION

Between two and three offers are usually made and if they are all refused then the priority may be cancelled or suspended. Some occupational therapists are concerned that applicants are made offers which are not suitable for their needs, so the applicant has to turn them down and therefore forfeits an offer. In Aberdeen, the housing department is advised if the occupational therapist is involved and he or she will be asked to view a property first before any offer is made to the client. If the occupational therapist refuses the offer on the grounds of its unsuitability then it will not count as an offer to the client.

The problem of inappropriate offers is a recognised difficulty which is potentially improved with the introduction of property registers providing more accurate information concerning individual properties. It has been known for a housing department to categorise a property as 'adapted' even if it only has a hand rail fitted to some part of the building. The property has then been unsuitably reoffered when vacant to someone awaiting medical priority housing. An increasing number of housing departments are employing occupational therapists to be responsible for the allocation of their adapted or purpose built properties, as they have the special skills and training necessary to assess both the people and the properties and to 'match' or allocate most appropriately.

BEDROOM NUMBERS AND OCCUPANCY LEVELS

Housing organisations vary in their flexibility with regard to the provision of a two-bedroom property for a couple. A proven medical need for separate bedrooms is often required and the occupational therapist can expect conflict with housing providers over this issue. Many single people require a second bedroom for relatives to stay and this issue is of particular concern to elderly people who are rightly worried about being ill at home and not having enough available space for a relative/carer to stay when necessary. Many elderly and disabled people prefer to stay put in large, unsuitable houses than be forced to cope with a one-bedroom property with insufficient space for their assessed needs and preferences. A policy on the provision of an extra room may assist in some cases, hopefully with some input at the policy design stage from an occupational therapist.

In Aberdeen, the occupational therapist is a member of the 'disabled special needs group' and if he or she presents a case for the need for two bedrooms for a client at this meeting, the community medical officer has the discretionary powers to authorise the allocation of the required size of property.

## Meeting the need

Having made a decision to move to different accommodation and having considered the information on housing options available, the next stage in accessing suitable accommodation is meeting that need. There are various options available and choice will depend on a combination of several factors relating to individual and family need as previously mentioned, including property size, type and geographical location, proximity to schools, employment and shops. Financial decisions have to be made and financial position is usually the main deciding factor in whether to rent or buy a new home. This part of the chapter looks at the different housing options and how different housing providers have analysed and taken action to improve the service they provide for people with disabilities.

### Rented social housing

Social housing is defined as housing available through local authorities and housing associations for rent. Once eligibility to be on their housing register or waiting list has been established and an application made, it is then a matter of waiting for an offer of accommodation from the relevant housing organisation.

In order to improve on the service provided for people with disabilities, many organisations have used the services of occupational therapists to assist with:

- the identification of properties suitable or adaptable for people with disabilities
- the redesign of housing application forms to assist in identifying the needs of people with disabilities
- the matching and selection process of identifying the most suitable applicant for a vacant property
- involvement in the design of computerised information storage, retrieval and selection systems integral to the matching processes
- staff training on disability awareness issues
- accessing appropriate information on housing stock and availability (for example through leaflet design) for potential users
- advising on adaptations for existing and prospective tenants
- waiting list management
- involvement and influence at the property design and development stage.

The following examples of good practice illustrate the role the occupational therapist has to play in ensuring that, as far as is practically possible successful matching of people with disabilities to accommodation suited to their needs, is achieved.

KINGDOM HOUSING ASSOCIATION

One example of how the occupational therapist works to achieve these principles is at Kingdom Housing Association in Fife, Scotland, where in the early 1990s a secondment arrangement between the housing association and Fife Council was set up, enabling two occupational therapists to work part time within the association. They were initially involved with the design of the application form, assessment of applications, review of the Kingdom Design Guide and advice on adaptations and were seen as a general resource in terms of specialist knowledge on disability. Figure 4.1 describes the role of the occupational therapist within Kingdom Housing Association.

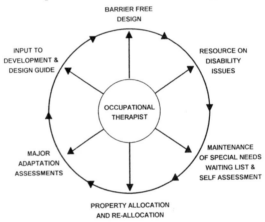

*Figure 4.1: The role of the occupational therapist in a housing association*
Source: Adapted from Kingdom Housing Association.

The occupational therapist assesses every self-assessment application form made on the grounds of special needs. Points can be awarded where someone's medical condition affects their housing need and where there is a problem with their accommodation not matching their needs. The occupational therapist will make recommendations on the type of housing required, such as ground floor, ground floor with level access, mobility or wheelchair standard housing. Recommendations are also made with regard to other specific needs such as access to carers or specific adaptation requirements. This assessment can be made with supporting information from, for example, the disabled applicant themself, their general practitioner, social worker, or other involved occupational therapist.

The applicant's information is stored on computer and used to assist in the suitable allocation of a property. This will include the area in which they wish to live, the size and type of the property wanted and any specific requirements. A visit is not usually made to the applicant until a particular property, identified as suitable for their needs, becomes available. Several applicants can be visited at once to establish who is in most need and the applicant with the most priority points is not necessarily the one who will be offered the property first.

A full survey of all Kingdom Housing Association's properties was carried out in the early 1990s and the information stored on to their computerised system. This identifies each property, lists their attributes and adaptations and classifies them in terms of accessibility. All new properties built or all properties having adaptation work are similarly classified in an ongoing manner. This property information is essential for the occupational therapists and housing officers who carry out the matching process for new and reallocated properties. The more straightforward matching can be done by the housing officers in relation to ground-floor properties and those with minor adaptations, but the mobility and wheelchair standard housing allocations require input from the occupational therapist. In the case of new developments, applicants requiring mobility and wheelchair standard housing will be identified in the early stages, although this is sometimes difficult due to the timescales involved as peoples' needs change and they may move elsewhere in the meantime.

With regard to waiting list management, the occupational therapist regularly provides feedback and information to the development section with regard to the nature of the needs of applicants still on the waiting list.

WALTHAM FOREST

An example of how a local authority has set up a successful system of property allocation to those best suited to the property is in the London Borough of Waltham Forest, which has set up and has been using property registers for some time. Occupational therapists are working from within the housing department, categorising properties as they become void, or training housing voids surveyors to categorise properties to the same standards whilst carrying out their routine inspection. The information collected and stored onto a database is shown in Figure 4.2.

Standard data entry codes to describe each part are used, for example yes/no answers, numbers of bedrooms or steps and type descriptions.

An occupational therapist working to carry out Waltham Forest's property assessments finds that most properties in their area fit into the categories reasonably well. A sketch plan of the property showing its layout is often

## Figure 4.2: Notice of vacation – survey details

| | | |
|---|---|---|
| Property type | Floor | Number of bedrooms |
| Number of living rooms | Garden | Downstairs WC |
| Downstairs bathroom | Inside steps | Floor of access |
| Access steps (front) | Access steps (back) | Lift to property |
| Balcony | Pram shed present | Cooking type |
| Water heating type | Space heating type | Elderly dwelling |
| Suitable for disabled | Chairlift present | Suitable for chairlift |
| Hilly location | Entrycom system | Type of security device |
| Garage/car port | | |

drawn on site by the occupational therapist, for additional information. The property information gathered is essential when the later task of matching a person to a property is carried out. From the work initiated by Waltham Forest, similar models have developed in Milton Keynes and Kent, as described later in this chapter.

MILTON KEYNES

A further example of local authority initiative is in Milton Keynes where, in 1996, Milton Keynes Borough Council carried out a research project to establish a classification system for properties with an adaptation. The background to this was a combination of an increasing demand on housing stock by tenants with special needs, including mobility and increasing dependency, and the lack of information available to identify their adapted housing stock. Their housing computer system was only able to identify an adapted property by an 'indicator' on the screen, with no accompanying description of the level of adaptation that had been carried out.

The project proposal was to produce a list of adapted council properties, classified according to agreed definitions. The purpose of this classification was to enable a better matching of tenants to properties during the allocation process. This made the health employed occupational therapists' role within the system easier, as they act as agents for the local authority and survey properties for particular people to decide if they would meet recognised needs.

The project involved:

- researching other similar projects conducted by other housing providers
- examining their existing internal procedures and data capture systems

- developing property classifications and facility codes
- surveying and classifying all the properties indicated as adapted on the present system
- determining new computer data requirements.

Questionnaires were sent direct to the tenants of the identified properties, with an 80 per cent response rate. The remaining 20 per cent of the properties were later assessed by the housing staff to complete the picture of their adapted housing stock. All the questionnaires were returned to the project worker and community occupational therapy service manager, who classified every property. The housing type classification system is as follows:

*Category A*

Specially built or adapted to wheelchair standard (wide doorways, suitable turning circles etc.) with parking facilities and scooter/wheelchair storage. Full wheelchair mobility to *all* facilities within property. Wheelchair access to first floor via vertical lift or stairlift.

*Category B*

Specially built or adapted to wheelchair standards to accommodate access to basic facilities, i.e. ramp/level access. Wheelchair access to main facilities, i.e. bathroom, bedroom and living area. May include access to first floor via a stairlift.

*Category C*

Mobility standard housing or ordinary accommodation adapted with ramped/level access or house with stairlift.

*Category D*

Ordinary accommodation with no more than two steps internally or externally, house with stairlift or maisonette/flat with lift access.

*Category E*

Ordinary accommodation with no more than one flight of stairs to facilities, internally or externally.

*Category F*

Ordinary housing with single minor adaptations.

Property facility codes were introduced to describe the adaptations present within a property and an example is shown here:

|  | **Description** | **Code** |
| --- | --- | --- |
| **Showers** | Shower over bath | SO1 |
|  | Shower tray | SO2 |
|  | Flat floor shower | SO3 |
|  | Prefabricated shower unit | SO4 |
|  | Additional shower facilities | SO5 |

| | Description | Code |
|---|---|---|
| **Kitchens** | Kitchen wall unit/s lowered | KO1 |
| | Kitchen work top/s lowered | KO2 |
| | Wheelchair designed kitchen | KO3 |

Other descriptions and codes are used for adaptations for baths, basins, toilets, windows, ceiling track hoists, home extensions, heating, doors, walls, stairs, electrical and access (Corbett 1996; London Boroughs Occupational Therapy Managers Group 1996).

NOTTINGHAM

In 1995 a one-year, joint funded project was arranged between Nottingham City Council Housing Department and Nottingham County Council Social Services Department. The project was called the 'Disabled Persons and Adapted Properties Register' and it employed a full-time information technology development and research officer and a part-time occupational therapist. The aims of the project were as follows:

- identification and categorisation of the needs of customers with disabilities who are seeking to move into more suitably adapted accommodation

- research of adaptations in both the public and private sector and the introduction of standard categories to enable practical matching with customer need

- research into the access needs of users of such information

- selection, design, development and implementation of a suitable computer system to maintain the register and allow access by identified user groups

- identification and implementation of methods and sources of updating the information contained within the register.

The expected benefits of the project were to keep disabled people informed of all suitable accommodation and to help them to rent, sell or buy adapted properties in order to move to a more suitable home. It would also enable housing providers to make more efficient use of their present resources and identify demand to inform their future strategic planning.

The project received a six-month extension and ran for a total of eighteen months. This period has now ended and Nottingham City Council Housing Department continues to maintain and improve register software.

Properties are categorised into a number of levels which enable them to be matched to applicants from the details provided by the applicants on their completed self-assessment forms. The software assigns the category to the property as it is input into the system; it then matches a property to a suitable applicant. The decision was made to categorise properties rather than applicants due to negative feedback received from potential user groups.

The success of the self-assessment of applicants has been assessed by occupational therapists 'loaned' from social services and has been found to have a high degree of accuracy.

A visit by an occupational therapist or by the housing department's medical referrals officer is made with the applicant to a property to ensure the property would meet the needs of the applicant, *before* a final allocation of the property is made.

GREENWICH

The London Borough of Greenwich has deliberately taken a step back to examine the whole issue of adapted and accessible housing from a strategic point of view. Their first step was to set up a housing based disability team comprising senior occupational therapists and building surveyors experienced in the design of major adaptations and accessible housing. They found great benefits in putting the two professions together and many seemingly intractable problems have been solved by sharing ideas, learning to see things from each other's viewpoint and working towards the same goals. As it is a housing department based team, there is commitment from senior managers to ensure the maximum number of accessible homes, with subsequent budgetary increase to support this. The team deal with individual requests for adaptations and they manage the list of wheelchair users seeking housing. The team has built up a relationship with the estate management personnel and has trained estate officers to look out for properties that have become vacant and which might be suitable for adaptation. The occupational therapists' knowledge of the council housing stock has meant that they can match clients to the right property and then follow through any adaptations that might be necessary. The team are in the process of setting up a computerised database of adapted and adaptable housing that can be accessed from any computer outlet in the department's many satellite offices.

Greenwich's housing disability team also play a role in influencing the design of new build social housing. An agreement has been negotiated with the main local housing associations that in every new development 15 per cent of dwellings should be fully accessible to wheelchair users. They have produced a design guide for wheelchair accessible housing and plan to hold seminars for local architects and house developers as part of a strategy to encourage private sector developers to consider the needs of people with disabilities. By taking a long-term approach the team is developing a strategy that raises the profile of disability issues in housing and is helping to set the agenda on how to meet the increasing demand for this type of housing in the future (Gill 1996).

NORTH CUMBRIA

In an effort to obtain information from people with disabilities on their view of housing issues, a review of the housing needs of people with a physical disability was carried out in 1996 in North Cumbria. One of the main outcomes of the research is that people prefer to remain in their existing home with suitable equipment and adaptations wherever possible. This is being reflected in the increasing occupational therapy workloads and it is a trend that is expected to continue. It found that equipment and adaptation budgets are not keeping pace with demand, whilst at the same time the government is cutting back on renovation grants and reducing its own contribution through subsidy. Where housing was considered to be the only practical option, concern was expressed about current limited service user consultation. In a rural, hilly area such as North Cumbria, there is also a limited choice of suitable accommodation (North Cumbria Housing Forum 1996).

*Disabled persons housing services (DPHS)*

In past and present times, much thought has gone into the complicated issue of matching the right person to the right property. The logistics of this exercise have thankfully been simplified in recent years with the increasing use of computers to carry out data analysis and processing – many different computerised programmes will have been tried, tested and hopefully implemented in various parts of the country with regard to property registers. The function of a DPHS is to assist a person seeking a property suitable for their needs and a large part of their role is in setting up and managing systems that enable them to identify the right property for the right person, based on the information they receive. They can have a wide remit and can be involved in advising on all types of house tenure or purchase options. Two separate examples of different methods used to achieve this process in Kent and Sheffield are described here.

KENT

In Kent, the Disabled Persons' Accommodation Agency (DPAA), in consultation with a user group, set out to match people to property through its classification system of matching a person who fitted a description of type A, to a property that matched a description of type A, and so on down to type G.

Other areas which have adopted and amended the Kent system have found resistance to the people classification system by user groups and have therefore tended to concentrate mainly on the property categorisation system, as in the Milton Keynes example. Kent however, has not encountered such resistance and are still using their people classification system, as described here.

### Type A

People whose legs are not able to support their weight and who need to use a wheel-chair when indoors and outdoors.

### Type B

People who use wheelchairs but are able to walk to a limited extent. They cannot climb steps and stairs.

### Type C

People who do not use wheelchairs but walk with difficulty. They cannot climb steps and stairs.

### Type D

People who do not use wheelchairs, walk with difficulty, but can manage one or two steps.

### Type E

People who do not use wheelchairs but cannot manage more than one flight of stairs.

### Type F

People who need a downstairs toilet. People requiring additional room for treatment.

### Type G

People with a disability or medical problem requiring more suitable accommodation which does not fall into the above categories. (DPAA 1995).

The DPAA staff are then able to match people to properties, although in practice the system has not yet been given a fair trial as the project is still being developed and very few properties have been offered to date. Experience so far has shown that it is easy to classify people in the A–E range as mobility levels are the predominating factor, but the F–G classification is more difficult as they are not so well defined.

The head of the Kent Occupational Therapy Bureau represents the occupational therapy service on the management committee of the DPAA. The DPAA has a close relationship with the bureau and will usually refer a housing applicant on to the service for an assessment if they have not been visited in the recent past. The DPAA is very satisfied with the service it receives and with the short response times involved.

SHEFFIELD

At Sheffield Disability Housing Service, the initial matching process of an individual or household to a property is carried out by the computer and selects people based on their requirements for:

- the number of bedrooms in the property
- the property type
- the postal district of the property.

Further optional fields select on:

- minimum age
- maximum age
- wheelchair users (yes or no)
- disability group.

Although applicants are selected in date order from the database, it is not necessarily the one who has waited longest who has first priority. The occupational therapist carefully reviews each person on the shortlist, takes all factors into consideration, and discusses cases with other colleagues before making a decision as to who to offer a property to first. There is no limit on the number of property offers the service can make.

### Housing Organisations Mobility and Exchange Services (HOMES)

HOMES' role is to make it easier for people to move home in the local authority and housing association sectors through two schemes: the HOMES Mobility scheme and the Homeswap scheme. Both of these free schemes can be used for short and long distance moves.

HOMES MOBILITY SCHEME

The HOMES Mobility Scheme is a nationwide network of housing organis-ations who work together to help people move from one area to another, to fill vacant properties in other areas. Most councils and housing associations throughout England, Northern Ireland, Scotland and Wales participate in this scheme. Anyone considering a move through this scheme has to approach their landlord in the first instance to see if they fit the criteria to be eligible to apply. Anyone needing to move for at least one of the following reasons will usually be eligible:

- to be closer to relatives or friends so that they can give or receive support

- taking up a job that is too far away to travel to every day

- other particular reasons, such as domestic violence or harassment.

The person completes a HOMES Mobility Scheme nomination form and returns the form to their landlord. The landlord then consults the HOMES directory to try and find a landlord who can help in the appropriate area. The directory contains information about the type of property each landlord has and it will include information about mobility or wheelchair standard accommodation if these are available.

The landlord then contacts the appropriate landlord and, if they are able to help, sends them the completed application form. A copy of the form is also sent to HOMES. When the receiving landlord has suitable accommodation to offer it will notify the applicant's landlord and the applicant decides whether he or she wishes to pursue the offer made.

In addition to the directory, an 'offers and appeals' bulletin is published monthly and distributed to all participating landlords. Any landlord offering or requesting a certain type of accommodation can go into the bulletin, so for example a landlord having difficulty letting adapted or purpose built disabled person's accommodation could put an appeal for applicants in the bulletin.

HOMESWAP SCHEME

The Homeswap scheme is another option. Swapping homes with a tenant in the area requested can be a good way of moving. Once registered on the Homeswap scheme, the applicant's details and what they are looking for is displayed on a list in the areas chosen. Both partners in any exchange need the permission of both landlords to swap homes. The onus is on the applicant to check the displayed lists regularly. If an adapted or purpose built accommodation for a disabled person is part of the swapping arrangements, then the landlords will satisfy themselves that the accommodation will continue to house a person who requires that level of adaptation. If this is not to be the case, then the landlord has grounds for withholding consent under the 1985 Housing Act. If both applicants require similar levels of accommodation then the exchange will usually be allowed to proceed. This is a similar scheme run on the same principles as the mutual exchange schemes operated by local authorities within their own areas (HOMES 1993).

HOMES STATISTICS

HOMES is currently not able to access information from its register regarding the percentage of scheme users who have a disability, although it has a current project group looking at this in relation to changing the database details to allow this to happen.

HOMES statistics for house transfers made during 1995/96 looks at the reasons why people want to move:

- 44 per cent to receive support from family or friends
- 16 per cent for health reasons
- 9 per cent to give support to family or friends
- 6 per cent to escape domestic violence or harassment
- 4 per cent to be nearer present job
- 3 per cent to change to a new job
- 2 per cent need larger or smaller accommodation
- 2 per cent to take up a new job following unemployment
- 14 per cent for other social reasons.

### NATIONAL REGISTER OF ACCESSIBLE HOUSING

In 1992 HOMES, in conjunction with the Housing Associations' Charitable Trust (HACT), appointed a development worker to investigate the need for a national register of accessible housing for wheelchair users, based in Liverpool and to run for one year. During the year a register was built up of 167 people wanting accommodation in the area where the scheme operated and the project was offered 37 properties for nomination, mainly from housing associations. Sixteen households accepted the property offered. The project highlighted the mismatch of accommodation to need. The property most clearly in demand was for two bedrooms and yet the majority of property offered only had one bedroom. There was a shortage of three-bedroom properties offered and no four-bedroom properties were offered at all, in spite of there being a demand.

Issues raised by the project were:

- units with one bedroom are still being built, whereas two-bedroom accommodation is far more commonly required
- families requiring three or more bedrooms have a very poor chance of being rehoused
- there is an emphasis on building sheltered accommodation for wheelchair users over retirement age and a lack of attention to the needs of younger people. Housing for young adults who want to leave home or residential care or move to be nearer a job is very scarce.

This mismatch is believed to be caused by a lack of information about need, which makes it possible for planners to ignore the housing needs of wheelchair users.

In HOMES' (1995) view, it is not practical to set up a separate scheme for wheelchair users on a national basis. The client group is too small and the existing accommodation too scarce. It believes that initiatives are required at local levels to build up information about supply and demand.

### Mutual exchange scheme

Mutual exchanges within an area between local authority tenants and other secure or assured tenants may usually be made as long as both landlords agree in writing. Tenants with low priority status on the housing register may find this method quicker than waiting for their turn to come. Tenants of a local authority who wish to consider a mutual exchange will have their names and addresses put on public display within their housing division and it may be circulated to other tenants who are interested in an exchange. Certain criteria apply with regard to the size of the property and the number of household members, the state of the property, tenants having a clear rent account and so on before permission will be granted. Permission will be refused if an adapted property for a disabled person was involved in an exchange that resulted in a non-disabled person occupying the property. Consultation with an occupational therapist is preferred when people with disabilities are involved in a mutual exchange.

### Owner occupation

Occupational therapists might come across situations where owner-occupiers are living in their own property which they find totally unsuitable because of their physical disability. If it is not practical to adapt the property then they can either choose to stay put or to move to alternative accommodation. It is here where many people may experience financial difficulties in not being able to afford to purchase a property suitable for their needs as the property required may need to be bigger, probably a bungalow.

If a person can afford to purchase a property, finding one can be a daunting task as there is usually very little choice of wheelchair accessible accommodation available. Estate agency personnel are generally not equipped to cope with identifying suitable, wheelchair accessible housing and there is a general dearth of information around. If requested, an occupational therapist may be able to assist a person with a disability to access suitable housing in the owner-occupier market.

Care managers for complex cases, often appointed via the courts in litigation cases and often occupational therapists themselves, may see the task of finding suitable housing for their client as a necessary part of their role if this is what is required for the client. In the absence of appropriate housing, and client finances permitting, occupational therapists may be involved in the identification of land and the individual design requirements for a disabled person as the only way to ensure access to a suitable property to live in.

The Kent Disabled Persons' Accommodation Agency (DPAA) has found that it receives information about adapted properties for sale, especially in the flatter coastal areas where people have retired. They have then searched their register and found a lack of suitable people requiring housing who can afford the purchase price of most of the properties on offer. One of the original aims of the DPAA was to become self-financing by asking for subscriptions from various agencies, including estate agents, to pay for the service they received from the DPAA in assisting in the process of finding buyers for adapted properties. This objective has not yet been achieved.

OWNER-OCCUPIERS MOVING TO RENTED ACCOMMODATION

If an owner-occupier decides to apply for housing in rented property owned by the local authority or a housing association, then they must comply with strict conditions, such as:

- not having enough equity to buy another suitable property
- having an urgent medical/social need.

Applicants who now own their ex-local authority property may also be treated in the same manner. There are no guidelines available from the Housing Corporation with regard to owner-occupier eligibility for re-housing into housing association properties, which leaves individual associations to decide their own policies and procedures regarding this issue. Housing associations have an obligation to consider owner-occupiers for housing into their properties. They should be more flexible towards clients who cannot afford to upgrade their owner-occupier status by purchasing a property better suited to their needs as a disabled person.

Low priority is often awarded to an owner-occupier on a waiting list for local authority or housing association accommodation, which can mean a waiting time of several years depending on the popularity of the area and property type chosen by the applicant. For example, in Aberdeen owner-occupiers have the same rights as existing tenants, although they are kept on a separate group classification within the overall waiting list, which is unique to the city.

If a joint owner moves out of the property but still remains a joint owner then the same eligibility rules can apply. The rules will not apply once a property has been sold, or contracts have been exchanged or the title passed to someone else. Once an owner-occupier is rehoused into rented social housing, then they may have to agree to take all reasonable steps to sell or dispose of their property within six months. This might include renting it out to a tenant. An applicant who also owns other residential accommodation anywhere in the United Kingdom will usually be treated in the same manner.

In Milton Keynes, an occupational therapist is asked to assess an application from an owner-occupier if housing on disability need is requested. They are asked to establish whether the present house will meet their needs or not and what needs they will have if they move into local authority owned accommodation. In practice, occupational therapists have found that many owner-occupiers do not really wish to move and that the provision of an adaptation may enable them to continue living in their own homes. Many would-be housing applicants are simply not aware of the availability of the disabled facilities grant system to assist them with the provision of an adaptation or major piece of equipment such as a stairlift to enable them to stay put.

When an owner-occupier considers a move to rented accommodation, there are initial financial implications. Once the tenancy agreement is signed, the tenant has to start paying rent on their new home, regardless of the fact that they may still have a house to sell and a mortgage to pay. There are general principles that apply within the housing benefits system that apply to this situation but each case is assessed individually, making it difficult to predict the outcome of possible interim financial assistance or to offer advice appropriately. Factors that are taken into consideration include individual savings and the person's housing equity status. The housing organisation offering the property is unable to wait for the prospective tenant to sort themselves out financially as it will incur a void (loss of rent) on the property that would be unacceptable. These combining factors can result in suitable housing being turned down by disabled people as they are not able to cope with the financial complications and risks involved, thereby denying them access to suitable housing.

LOW COST HOME OWNERSHIP SCHEMES
The Housing Corporation funds a number of 'low cost home ownership' schemes designed to make it possible for people on lower incomes to buy a home of their own.

SHARED OWNERSHIP

Shared ownership is described as a property which the occupant part rents, usually from a housing association, and part owns, usually in multiples of 25 per cent. This allows low income households to get a foot on the ladder of home ownership and is particularly suited to people with disabilities who are reliant on state benefits. In a recent case study, an occupational therapist from a Disabled Persons Housing Service took a lead role in deciding who was to be offered three two-bedroom bungalows built to wheelchair housing standards by a housing association and offered for sale on a shared owner-ship basis. The occupational therapist was involved in shortlisting potential applicants, visiting each one to assess their current situation and interest in the scheme and assisting the housing association personnel to decide who to offer the properties to. Once this had been achieved, the occupational therapist and the prospective purchasers discussed and agreed individual requirements and these were passed on to the contractor who incorporated them into the properties. In one case a care package was to be required and this was initiated by the occupational therapist and referred to the social services department. This scheme enabled three severely disabled people to access appropriate housing to suit their own individual circumstances.

DO-IT-YOURSELF SHARED OWNERSHIP (DIYSO)

DIYSO is a form of low cost home ownership introduced to help people who cannot afford to buy a home outright. Through DIYSO a property is selected on the open market, the client buys a share of the property and pays rent on the remainder to the housing association or local authority administering the scheme. Gradually further shares may be bought until eventually the home is owned outright. This only applies to properties bought in England.

The property purchased can be either new or existing, it must be of a size appropriate to the housing need and the value and price of the property must be within a certain limit set down for the area of purchase. Individual housing associations may impose additional restrictions as to the age, type and condition of the property selected.

The scheme is intended for people who cannot afford to buy a suitable home any other way. They are usually first time buyers and priority is given to local authority or housing association tenants who are releasing accom-modation suitable for housing homeless households. Other people in hous-ing need may also be considered for the scheme. Buyers must be able to obtain their own mortgage to meet their purchase costs and have sufficient savings to cover associated costs such as legal fees, house survey and valuation report, stamp duty and in many cases a deposit. Bear in mind that DIYSO schemes may not operate in all areas, funds may be limited and demand may be high.

### TENANTS INCENTIVE SCHEME

Through this scheme tenants of participating housing associations or local authorities, who have been tenants for at least two years, are assisted with a cash payment to purchase and move to a home of their own, which they have selected on the open market, thus releasing their rented home to help house a homeless household in the area.

### LEASEHOLD FOR ELDERLY PEOPLE

This scheme enables people over 55 years to buy a sheltered housing association home on a shared ownership basis and is normally newly built one- or two-bedroom flats or bungalows. Depending on the money they have available, they can buy either a 25 per cent, 50 per cent or 75 per cent share, either by raising a mortgage or cash (more often cash from the sale of the present home). Rent is paid on the part not owned, but as the maximum share that can be bought is 75 per cent, no rent is paid when 75 per cent is owned. As the scheme is intended to help elderly people, resales are limited to people who are also 55 years or over. The housing association arranges a range of services, such as external maintenance and repair, landscaping, window cleaning and a warden call system. All buyers will have to pay the service charge regardless of what percentage of the property they own.

### SELF-BUILD SCHEME

A group of people living in the same area may form a 'self build housing association' to build their own homes. The Housing Corporation can help these groups to raise money if they are in real need.

## Conclusion

In conclusion, suitable housing for people with disabilities continues to be a scarce resource. Until this fundamental problem is resolved, housing organisations will continue to act as gatekeepers for their high demand properties and will continue to need special waiting lists and to make allocations based on priority need. There is a long way to go yet before appropriate housing for people with disabilities, regardless of tenure, will become accessible as and when it is required. The examples illustrated within this chapter show innovation and determination to succeed and are to be commended. They should be used as examples of good practice for other housing organisations.

Access to appropriate or adaptable housing for people with disabilities varies considerably, depending on the area lived in and how much priority the subject is given. New housing legislation must continue to push the problems of access forwards to stop housing organisations from continuing to give the whole subject low priority. In the absence of legislation which includes and guarantees equal opportunities for disabled people in choosing their preferred housing, the procedures and examples described within this chapter will be needed to alleviate the discrimination and inequality for people living in the community.

## Glossary

| | |
|---|---|
| *Age banding* | Where a property is set aside for elderly people, but there is no one over 60 on the allocation list. The property will be offered on an age banding basis instead, that is 50 to 60, 40 to 50, 30 to 40, under 30. |
| *Allocation* | Where an applicant's details are matched to a property which may lead to an offer. |
| *Applicant* | A person aged 16 or over who has filled in and signed a re-housing application form and is eligible to be registered on the housing list. |
| *Household* | This can be a single person or it can mean a group of people who live or want to live together. This does not include people who just want to share a property and then live separately within it. |
| *Household within a household* | Where two or more households share the same property. |
| *Housing association* | A non-profit making organisation which provides homes for rent. |
| *Intentionally homeless* | Where someone has deliberately done, or not done, something which means they cannot continue to live in their property, they may be intentionally homeless. |
| *Joint tenant* | Where two or more people are tenants of the same property. |
| *Like for like* | Where two properties are the same size and type as each other. |
| *Lone parent* | Where a person has not got a partner living with them, and has a child or children under the age of 18 living permanently with them. |
| *Money owed to the Housing Revenue Account* | This is usually any money owed to the housing department, and includes rent arrears, former tenant arrears, re-chargeable repairs and housing benefit overpayments on council rents. |
| *Offer* | Where an applicant is given the chance to look at an empty property and decide if they want to become the tenant. |

| | |
|---|---|
| *Permitted number* | The legal maximum number of persons who can live in a property before it is overcrowded by law. |
| *Roofless* | An applicant who has literally nowhere to live or stay. |
| *Secure tenancy* | A tenancy granted to a council tenant. The council can only regain possession of the property in certain situations and if the court agrees. |
| *Similar demand property* | A property for which an applicant needs a similar number of points to the home they live in now. |

## References

Corbett, S. (1996) *Project to Establish a Classification System for Properties with an Adaptation.* Milton Keynes: Milton Keynes Community NHS Trust/Milton Keynes Borough Council.

Department of the Environment/Department of Health (1996) *Code of Guidance on Parts VI and VII of the Housing Act 1996: Allocation of Housing Accommodation – Homelessness.* London: DoE.

DPAA supported by Joseph Rowntree Foundation (1994) *Disabled Persons Accommodation Agency. The Way Forward for Kent.*

Gill, R. (1996) 'Providing accessible homes – taking up the challenge of the new millennium.' *Occupational Therapy News,* July, p.17.

*Housing Act 1985.* London: HMSO.

*Housing Act 1996.* London: HMSO.

HOMES (1993) *Makes it Happen.: Homes.* London: HOMES.

HOMES (1990) *There's No Place Like HOMES.* London: HOMES.

HOMES (1993) HOMES – Opening a door to accessible housing.

Joseph Rowntree Foundation (1995) *Housing Needs of People with Physical Disability.* York: Joseph Rowntree Foundation.

London Boroughs Occupational Therapy Managers Group (1990) *Housing and Occupational Therapists.* London: London Boroughs Occupational Therapy Managers Group.

North Cumbria Housing Forum (1996) *The Housing Needs of People with a Disability.* Keswick: NCHF.

Sheffield City Council (1996) *Sheffield City Council Rehousing Policy,* issue 2, August.

# CHAPTER 5

# Regulations, Standards, Design Guides and Plans

*Trevor Dodd*

## Introduction

This chapter aims to give a broad outline of:

1. regulations which impact on building design
2. national standards which relate to special needs building design
3. the guidance available to assist in the design process
4. how to make sense of plans and drawings.

The roles of the groups involved and the influences which may impact on the design process will also be considered.

### Background

Over the years building regulations and standards applicable to housing have been developed, but it is only relatively recently that the housing needs of disabled people have been considered. In 1976 Selwyn Goldsmith brought out the third edition of his book *Designing for the Disabled* which discussed the psychological, economic and practical issues involved in greater depth than the earlier editions of 1963 and 1967. This third edition is still regarded by many as the definitive reference book for anyone involved in building homes for disabled people. He researched the space requirements and suitable layouts for homes which would enable disabled people to move around and access the facilities within them. This valuable work helped bring to the fore

My love and thanks go to my partner Ruth for her patience and help. Thanks also go to Sid Huseyin for all her hard work in deciphering and typing several drafts of my chapter and Chapter 2.

the need to consider all people when planning housing developments (Goldsmith 1976). The London Borough of Islington was one of the forerunners in developing a policy guide to assist in the building and adaptation of houses for people using wheelchairs (Islington Council 1986). Since then, many other local authorities and organisations have followed suit using previous texts as a basis and altering them to suit local opinion and circumstances. In the early 1980s the London Borough of Lambeth Occupational Therapy Department set up 'obstacle courses' and measured the spaces required to manoeuvre wheelchairs around, and the heights at which to place fixtures and fittings.

The contribution disabled people can make to the development of not just local access guides but national policy on designing homes, is considerable. The Chronically Sick and Disabled Persons Act (CSDP Act) 1970 recommends that local authorities consult with local disability groups and the guidelines issued to accompany the National Health and Community Care Act 1991 place an obligation on local authorities to liaise with local disability groups (Department of Health 1991). National disability groups are being consulted on issues such as the proposed alterations to the building regulations which is covered later in this chapter. The more progressive authorities have always made a point of consulting with disabled people to achieve designs which are likely to meet the general requirements of disabled people (providing wheelchair circulation space and suitable positioning of fixtures and fittings), leaving only minor adjustments (kitchen work-surface height or the position of grab rails) to meet the special needs of individuals.

Since it began in 1969 The Centre for Accessible Environments (CAE) has taken a leading role in raising the awareness of those involved in access issues, particularly architects. Initially an information and advisory service, it developed into one of the leading organisations on disability issues relating to the built environment. CAE acts as consultancy, information service and training body and is committed to the provision of buildings that are accessible to everyone. CAE is an incorporated charitable company which has received support and grant monies from the Department of Health since 1977, grants from the Department of the Environment and financial assistance from donations and joint ventures with other organisations, such as the Joseph Rowntree Foundation.

Since 1973 Habinteg Housing Association have been striving to ensure that the housing needs of disabled people are addressed in all their new build schemes. All their homes were built to mobility standard, and the bathrooms and kitchens had the flexibility to allow for future adaptations. In 1994 they made a commitment to build all their houses to Lifetime Homes standards.

They also build 25 per cent of properties to full wheelchair standard as laid down in their own access guide (Habinteg Housing Association 1992).

In 1984 the Access Committee for England (ACE) was established to provide a focus for national issues related to the accessibility of the built environment. It is currently funded by grants from a number of government departments as well as trusts and foundations. It has close links with the Royal Association for Disability and Rehabilitation (RADAR). The committee consists of one-third building users, one-third building regulators and one-third building providers. Through this collaborative approach the committee will promote guidance on access policy issues which meets the needs of users that is enforceable by regulators and achievable by providers.

ACE are active in promoting access issues addressed by the Disability Discrimination Act (1995), promoting the appointment of designated access officers in local authorities, providing information and training to access groups and providing training to service providers and employers on access issues. ACE have also played a part in promoting the extension of the building regulations to cover access into and around private dwellings (Access Committee for England 1992).

National groups such as the National Wheelchair Housing Association Group (NATWHAG) have, in conjunction with Home Housing Trust, been instrumental in commissioning a new design guide. The Housing Corporation is backing the project and proposes to adopt it as the standard for homes to be built to accommodate permanent wheelchair users. Local disability groups are having greater input into what happens environmentally to ensure access in their area is more suited to the needs of everyone. Together, voluntary and professional organisations are pressing those responsible to place more emphasis on what is now being termed 'barrier free environments'. Organisations like the Joseph Rowntree Foundation (JRF) are pioneering new designs for homes with the potential to accommodate people, whatever their age or needs, for as long as they wish to live there. They have called them Lifetime Homes. This is an ongoing process which will inevitably change with the development of new materials, technology and equipment (details are given later in this chapter).

Educational courses are now being run which have moved away from the medical model of care and are focusing on a social model. The Architectural Association (AA) in London has run a course entitled 'Environmental Access' since 1993. It takes a proactive stance towards promoting awareness on access issues among professionals involved with design and the environment. The philosophy behind the course is that access issues are environmental not health related.

Support for accessible homes comes from many quarters. Sally Greengross, director general of Age Concern England, is quoted as saying 'The government and designers must urgently address the severe shortage of new homes built to meet the needs of an ageing population. Accessible housing is not a luxury but a basic human necessity' (*Therapy Weekly* 1996).

## Legislation

The background to the relevant legislation, both existing and proposed, is dealt with in Chapter 1. Suffice to say that any new legislation or subsequent amendments would be slow to come into force. This highlights the need for full consultation between relevant bodies prior to the formation of any proposal.

### Building regulations

These legally enforceable regulations cover how any building should be constructed with respect to aspects such as ventilation, natural light levels, drainage, wall construction, fire safety, energy conservation and so on. They were introduced nationally in 1965 as recommendations, and became compulsory in 1985 (Department of the Environment 1991). Although prescriptive, they allow a certain amount of interpretation in how the design meets the regulations, giving architects and surveyors the freedom to express their own creative ideas. The building regulations are enforced by building control officers appointed by local authorities. These officers must be consulted when adaptations are proposed to private dwellings where the basic fabric of the property is affected, for example, where an extension is being built to provide a ground-floor shower room and bedroom. Here consideration needs to be given to the drainage, provision and maintenance of natural light and ventilation to new and existing rooms affected by the extension. The depth of the foundations and structure of the walls and roof also need to comply with regulations.

### Regulations relating to access in public buildings

Regulations relating to access to public buildings and facilities within them for wheelchair users, were introduced on 1 August 1985 by the Department of the Environment (DoE). These regulations were revised in 1991 and came into force in 1992. They are known as Part M of the Building Regulations 1991 Access and Facilities for Disabled People (DoE 1992). These regulations set out to ensure a suitable means of access for people with a disability is provided to all new buildings, and stipulate that they must be able to move freely around the building once inside, with access to all facilities. Dimensions required for suitable access are given in guidance notes which accompany Part M.

### Regulations relating to access in private dwellings

Other than the general building regulations there are no specific ones addressing access issues and disabilities.

A draft proposal to extend the building regulations to cover new homes (DoE 1995) was produced by the DoE in January 1995, sent out for consultation, and as yet has not been redrafted. They announced late in 1996 that further discussions with the House Builders Federation will take place on extending Part M. The proposal is to ask a small number of local authorities to identify sites on which studies can be carried out. The objectives are to quantify the cost and the design impact of applying Part M to dwellings. The DoE will compare the impact of their own proposals with those made by respondents to the 1995 consultation. This is likely to be a lengthy process but it is hoped that it will result in a positive outcome and the implementation of Part M to new dwellings. At the time of going to press, an announcement has been made by the Construction Minister, who stated in March 1998 that Part M would be extended to cover new dwellings. It is proposed that it will go before Parliament in 1998 and come into force in 1999.

The draft proposals look to ensure that private dwellings are built to give ground-floor accessibility, or what has been termed 'visitability'. This means that a disabled person will be able to enter the property and have access to a toilet and living room. In essence it should enable disabled people to visit other homes but will give only partial access for someone with a disability who lives in the property. Major adaptations are likely to be necessary to achieve this. It is not the government's intention at this stage to ensure homes are built which allow access into, and around the whole property by those people who use wheelchairs. This may of course change before the proposals become law.

If these proposals are adopted, it will be a small step towards creating homes accessible to all. Standards set out by ACE have been used as the main source of reference for the proposals (ACE 1992). The design issues addressed in the draft are:

1. level or ramped access from the pavement to the front door
2. front doors designed to allow wheelchairs to pass through
3. corridors, passages and internal doors which allow circulation by wheelchair users

4. toilets on the ground floor which are accessible and provided in properties over a specified floor area (equivalent to a three-bedroom house)

5. switches and sockets which are at a height reachable from a seated position.

6. passenger lifts, when provided, which are of a suitable size to accommodate an unaccompanied wheelchair user, thus allowing disabled people to visit people who live in a flat above ground floor. Only buildings containing 12 or more flats above ground level will have to provide an accessible lift.

Although welcome if introduced in the proposed form, the new proposals would set space standards which are minimal compared to the recommendations set down in many design guides for accessible housing. This is likely to lead to new homes being built to the minimum standard, which would not address the difficulties many disabled people have as regards accessible housing; for example, the DoE wheelchair housing standard (Housing Development Directorate 1975) specifies dimensions that are often taken to be ideal but were intended to be minimum standards.

### Health and safety regulations

In 1995 new regulations came into force which relate to the health and safety of anyone involved in the construction of a building. The Construction (Design and Management) Regulations 1994 (CDM) place a responsibility on anyone involved in the design of a building, including adaptations, to ensure that those carrying out the work, visiting the site or living there are safe (Health and Safety Executive 1994).

### The potential benefits of enforceable standards

Legislation which makes dwellings accessible for disabled people would have concomitant benefits for all people as their circumstances change. For example:

- everyone would have an equal opportunity to move home to wherever they wished, in the knowledge that it would be accessible

- only minor adaptations to suit individual needs would be required, thus saving money for individual home owners, governments and local authorities

- the need to move home because it was no longer accessible would be removed; most people would be able to remain in their homes for as long as they wished
- family life would be disrupted less by the need for major adaptations
- parents with young children in prams would be able to get in and out of their homes more easily
- individuals with temporary disabilities would have fewer difficulties moving around at home
- elderly people who experience difficulties brought on by the ageing process would be able to adapt their own homes at greatly reduced cost; this would be of great benefit as reduced resources in local authorities are often targeted at the most severely disabled people, which in turn can result in long waiting times for assessment and particularly provision of a service
- disabled people would have more freedom to visit relatives and friends in the knowledge that they can enter the property and access necessary facilities.

Arguments against the introduction of regulations have been raised by the construction industry and others. They have included the following.

- *Technical difficulties in providing level thresholds which do not allow water egress.* Much research has been done; many architects and surveyors believe it is no longer a problem if the correct design is used. Also, provision of a porch or canopy protects the door and threshold.

- *Increased costs in providing what are currently non-standard features, such as lower switches, would have to be passed on to the consumer.* If carried out while building work is going on, these costs are minimal and unnoticeable in the overall cost of the property.

- *Non-standard materials, such as wider door frames, would be more difficult to obtain and more costly.* Current non-standard materials would become standard and the costs would reduce.

- *Fewer dwellings could be built on any piece of land if larger space standards were required.* Certainly more creative designs and use of the land would be required, but noticeable cost increases for purchasers may only occur on very small sites. The increasing number of registered social landlords who build to these standards already would seem to refute this argument.

- *Individual choice about how a home should be designed would be seriously reduced, i.e. all properties would look the same.* This is not supportable as the design of any property is only limited by the creative talents of the architect and the nature of the landscape.

- *Rents or mortgages would be higher to compensate for increased costs and place the homes beyond the financial means of many people.* This would not appear to be supported by the increasing number of properties already built to lifetime standards and occupied by families.

The Government has to decide whether the objections are valid and whether they outweigh the benefits.


## Design standards

A number of differing standards have been proposed since the early 1970s, and a variety of terms have been used to describe homes built to accommodate disabled people with differing levels of need. Some terms refer to similar, if not identical, standards, some reflect changes in thinking about what are the housing needs of the whole of society. Some of these standards and terms will be considered in this section. They are only recommendations and not compulsory. Some examples of standards are given at the end of this chapter in Appendices I, II and III.


### Space standards in housing

The basis for the currently accepted standards is that specific sizes of households require certain sizes of living space. In 1961, the Parker Morris Committee attempted to relate the amount of floor space required to the activities necessary for normal family life (DoE 1961). It produced recommended standards which have been applied to all local authority housing since 1967, and some private developers have adhered to them. For general needs housing, Parker Morris standards have been widely accepted as desirable and put forward as suitable for housing which would meet the needs of people with some degree of disability (see 'mobility housing' below).

In 1968 the DOE published a bulletin entitled *Space in the Home* (DoE 1968). This was a follow-up to the Parker Morris recommendations. It illustrates some of the activities the house design has to cater for, sets out suggested space and furniture requirements, and provides an analysis of a house plan to illustrate the recommendations of the Parker Morris Committee, relating to space requirements. The bulletin gives the space required to carry out a whole range of activities such as circulation around a double bed, drying a child after a bath and using the dustbin.

Selwyn Goldsmith wrote two articles for *The Architect's Journal* (1974, 1975) in which he proposed suitable design elements for what was termed mobility housing and wheelchair housing respectively. These recommendations were adopted by the Housing Development Directorate (HDD) and printed as the occasional papers 2/74 and 2/75 (HDD 1974, 1975; further information on these follows). He suggested that Parker Morris space standards were suitable for mobility housing, but more space was required for wheelchair users. He reiterated this in *Designing for the Disabled* (1976).

Research by Karn and Sheridan (1994) reported a gradual deterioration since 1974 in the space standards of new build homes built by registered social landlords. By that they meant space standards had fallen significantly below Parker Morris. They also found the dwellings were designed in such a way that adaptations were difficult to achieve at a later date. Some local authorities, such as Greenwich Council in London, still actively encourage their local registered social landlords to build new homes to Parker Morris space standards and Lifetime Homes design standards.

*Mobility housing*

In 1974 a DoE circular was issued by the HDD to local authorities, recommending that, where practicable, ordinary housing should be designed which is suitable for disabled people to live in. This HDD Occasional Paper *Mobility Housing* (HDD 1974 was reprinted from Selwyn Goldsmith's article in *The Architect's Journal* (Goldsmith 1974) and a third impression was published in 1987. It is a widely accepted standard but often not fully implemented.

The paper proposed that this type of property would not be a substitute for wheelchair accessible housing, but that it would widen the choice of accommodation for people with some degree of disability. It would also increase the number of properties available for those with disabilities, while reducing the need for adaptations. Parker Morris space standards were deemed suitable for this type of property, these being applied to public sector housing at that time. As a general rule, mobility housing should be suitable for all ambulant people and people who use wheelchairs but are able to stand to transfer and move a few steps.

Three principle requirements set down in the paper are:

1.  Entrances to homes need to be accessible to people who use wheelchairs.

2. Internal planning must allow for ease of movement by ambulant disabled people, including those who have wheelchairs but do not use them all the time.

3. A bathroom, toilet and at least one bedroom are at entrance level.

The design guidelines given to achieve mobility standards are:

1. The entrance must be ramped or have a level approach and a flush threshold.

2. Entrances and principal rooms (living room, dining room, kitchen and at least one bedroom) must have 900mm doorsets, and circulation spaces serving these rooms must be at least 900mm wide.

3. Bathroom and toilet must be at the same level as the entrance.

A list of other desirable design features is also included, and covers:

- doors and windows
- walls and floors
- electrical and heating services
- kitchen fittings
- bathroom and toilet fittings
- vehicle storage
- garden paths.

A range of examples of suitable plans for the ground floor are given.

### Wheelchair housing

In 1975 a second HDD Occasional Paper *Wheelchair Housing* (HDD 1975) was circulated to local authorities. This, like *Mobility Housing*, was reprinted from Goldsmith's article in *The Architect's Journal* (Goldsmith 1975) and a second impression was published in April 1980. These recommendations relate to housing for:

- people who are permanent wheelchair users
- people with large wheelchairs
- people who use wheelchairs while working in the kitchen
- people who use a wheelchair for bathroom use, for example, they undress in the bedroom and use a wheelchair to reach the bathroom.

Space standards more generous than Parker Morris are recommended for this type of housing. The principle requirements are:

1. Entrances to homes need to be accessible to people who use wheelchairs.
2. Internal planning must allow for ease of movement by ambulant disabled people, including those who have wheelchairs but do not use them all the time.
3. A bathroom, toilet and at least one bedroom are at entrance level.
4. Allowance must be made for a person using a wheelchair to move around the property.

The design guidelines given to achieve wheelchair standards are:

1. The entrance must be ramped or have a level approach and a flush threshold.
2. Entrances and principal rooms (living room, dining room, kitchen and at least one bedroom) must have 900mm doorsets, and circulation spaces serving these rooms must allow for a wheelchair to turn, i.e. a 1500mm diameter space.
3. Bathroom and toilet should be at entrance level but, if not, a straight flight staircase is recommended and upper-floor doorsets and circulation spaces should be the same as on the ground floor. Alternatively space for a wheelchair accessible through a floor lift could be provided.

A list of design features is given which is more detailed than for mobility housing and covers:

- the site to be built on
- door and windows
- taps
- floor finishes
- heating
- electrical services
- provision for hoists
- alarm systems
- kitchen fixtures and fittings
- living room features
- bedroom features
- bathroom and toilet features
- wheelchair storage

- garaging
- fire protection.

The detail given is commensurate with that found in the majority of books and access guides on designing for disabled people. Examples are given of layouts suitable to meet wheelchair housing standards.

*British Standards*

The British Standards Institute (BSI) has produced two codes of good practice directly relating to housing and disabled people.

1. BS5619: 1978 *Code of Practice for Design of Housing for the Convenience of Disabled People* (British Standards Institute 1978).

This states that ordinary housing should be designed so that it is convenient for disabled people to visit but, more important, enables disabled people to live in the property. The recommendations given are a list of desirable features which should be included wherever practicable. The benefits of designing in such a way are believed to affect not only disabled people, but elderly people, parents with young children and able-bodied people. The code details all the features of design found in most design guides currently available. It covers recommendations for:

- the approaches to a dwelling
- the interior design
- the building services.

The paper emphasises that the guidelines relate to general needs housing and not specifically to special housing for people with a disability. It is intended that the design recommendations will have the benefit of enabling a person to carry on living in a property if they become disabled. In essence this code of practice is supporting the values of lifetime homes.

2. BS5810: 1979 *Code of Practice for Access for the Disabled to Buildings* (formerly CP96: Part 1) (British Standards Institute 1979).

This code covers recommendations of good practice in relation to new buildings used by the general public, both as visitors and as employees. It is also suggested that the recommendations should be applied to the adaptation of existing buildings. The code is set for revision under major ergonomic research to be commissioned by the DoE.

These recommended standards cover the same design features as are found in Part M of the building regulations relating to public buildings: the approach to the building, the internal planning, toilet design and some general recommendations on features such as wall and floor surfaces, switch heights and signage.

### Accessible general housing

In 1992 the Access Committee for England (ACE) published a document called *Building Homes for Successive Generations*. It was produced to argue for extending Part M of the building regulations to cover new dwellings. ACE came up with design guidance proposals which would compliment the recommendations set down for mobility housing and enable new build properties to be accessible to disabled people. The principles behind the design guidance are that:

- approaches and entrances should be accessible to all people, including wheelchair users
- areas used by visitors should be accessible to wheelchair users
- dwellings on more than one level should be designed to allow easy movement internally and be amenable to modification for people with limited mobility.

Design features deemed essential were:

1. wherever feasible entrances should be level or gently ramped
2. access to parking spaces should be easy to reach in a wheelchair
3. lifts to flats above ground floor should be wheelchair accessible
4. all thresholds should be level
5. door widths and circulation space in halls should allow disabled people to move around unobstructed
6. homes on more than one storey should have a toilet at entrance level, and the staircase should allow for the future installation of a stairlift or space identified that could accommodate a through floor lift.

These items relate to the structure of the building and are expensive to alter or provide at a later date. ACE expressed a belief that the benefits of the recommendations clearly outweighed any resulting additional costs. ACE believes that there are no significant extra costs in achieving an accessible standard, except at the lower end of the housing market where a ground floor toilet is not normally included and space allowances are reduced. Designing properties to an accessible standard at the lower price end of the market is still desirable as many disabled people are among the poorest sectors of society, and therefore only able to afford cheaper houses. Also, elderly people often move to smaller, more easily managed homes and would benefit from the design features recommended.

All the essential recommendations were taken on board by the government when it drew up its draft proposals for extending Part M of the building regulations to cover new dwellings, except for the very last point. No mention was made of staircase design, probably because these proposals set out to provide visitability standards only (see the earlier section 'Regulations relating to access in private dwellings').

## Lifetime Homes

Lifetime Homes (LTH) are properties built to a design which will meet the needs of an occupier throughout his or her lifetime. The design allows for the needs of all age groups and life events such as temporary disabilities. Lifetime homes incorporate features which allow access into and around the property for everyone. They are easily adaptable at minimum cost so that they can accommodate a range of disabilities (Lifetime Homes Group 1993).

Unlike many properties where the adaptation has been provided years after it was built and is not in keeping with the rest of the property, Lifetime Homes need look no different from the other neighbouring properties. No stigma need by felt by disabled householders because their home stands out. The commonly stated objection to having ramps and handrails outside the property because of the fear of highlighting the homes of perceived vulnerable residents, would no longer apply.

The 1991 National Census (Office of Population Censuses and Surveys 1992) indicated that one in four households included one or more persons with a limiting long-term illness. Half of these households were owner-occupied or privately rented. When left to the discretion of the private developer very little progress has been made on the supply of accessible homes for sale. The government's consultation document *Measures to Tackle Discrimination Against Disabled People* (DoE 1994) quotes a cost to the government of £245 million, via the disabled facilities grant, in three years, to adapt the homes of disabled people. On top of this is the cost to local authorities for adaptations. Building homes which last a lifetime would be more economical in the long term. Frances Heywood recommends both local authorities and the Housing Corporation adopt Lifetime Homes standards in all new build schemes (Heywood and Smart 1996). Her research into a number of studies looking at the costs of adaptations and building to LTH standards shows that adaptation costs could be significantly reduced by building to LTH standard. Costs of building in LTH features appeared to be minimal and this was especially true for larger properties of three bedrooms and above.

Scottish Homes, a national housing agency, is carrying out research into the cost of initially providing properties built to a barrier free standard compared to the cost of adaptation work. Adaptations use significant amounts of their funds which is not surprising given the increasing number of elderly people in the population and the disability which all too often accompanies old age (Scottish Homes 1996).

The Joseph Rowntree Foundation (JRF) was at the forefront of discussions to develop housing which is not built exclusively for disabled people, but is still able to meet their needs. Discussions between ACE, housing associations, architects, disability groups and the JRF resulted in the concept of Lifetime Homes being developed and in 1994 put into practice with the building of 126 homes near York. The criteria are as follows.

1.  *Outside*

    - convenient car parking close by
    - approach paths which are suitably wide and level or gently sloping
    - covered and illuminated entrance without steps
    - a handrail where steps are unavoidable.

2.  *Inside*

    - wide front door and ample hall space to turn around
    - ground-floor toilet with a basin
    - ground-floor living room with a possible bed space
    - doors that are convenient to use
    - windows that are easy to open/operate.

3.  *Services*

    - safe and convenient bathroom
    - kitchen with units planned for safety
    - switches and controls that are easy to reach and use.

4.  *Structure*

    - walls in bathrooms and toilets able to take handrails
    - ceilings in bathrooms and bedrooms strong enough for a hoist
    - stairs with suitable handrails, to bath sides if necessary.

If adopted nationally then all people, whether disabled or not, would have a real choice about where they live and when they choose to move, not having this imposed on them because their current home is no longer suitable for their changing needs. All too often, rehousing is the only viable option for a disabled person because adaptations are not feasible or too costly. Having accepted this rehousing option the number of alternative properties available which would meet their needs is very limited.

In 1996 at the annual general meeting of the College of Occupational Therapists Specialist Section in Housing (COTSSIH), a representative of the Derbyshire Coalition of Disabled People expressed his belief that this standard was preferred by many disabled people who consider it to be an integral part of their equal opportunities campaign.

Support for this concept is growing despite arguments from some sections of the building trade that there are significant increased cost implications, and that design constraints will result in all properties looking identical. These arguments have been countered by some architects, registered social landlords and a number of professionals and disability groups and appear not to have any substance. This is substantiated by studies cited by Frances Heywood in her book *Funding Adaptations* (Heywood and Smart 1996). Research and debate continues into how the recommended housing features can best be achieved.

## Guidance available to assist with the design process

### Design guides

The role of design guides is to educate all those involved in building projects, in what is acceptable good practice. They address the general needs of disabled people in relation to the built environment, and can be applied to most housing projects. Proper use of a design guide should result in properties being built which require only minor adaptations for a succession of owners/residents, rather than costly and disruptive major adaptations.

Design guides have been produced by disability groups, occupational therapists, architects, access officers and housing associations in this country and abroad. One of the first was Selwyn Goldsmith's *Designing for the Disabled*, (Goldsmith 1976) the third edition of which is still being used. Since then the production of design guides has continued.

In 1987 the European Committee held a conference on accessibility for disabled people and recommended that European standards for accessibility be developed. In 1990 the *European Manual for an Accessible Built Environment* was produced by the Central Coordinating Committee for the Promotion of Accessibility, based in the Netherlands. It was an attempt to set up a European standard, but as yet has not been adopted by all member states.

Occupational therapists working in partnership with local disabled people resulted in Waltham Forest's policy design guide (London Borough of Waltham Forest 1992). This sets out what features are deemed essential and which are desirable. It does not set out to be prescriptive about how to design accessible homes but gives the necessary information to achieve them.

Without reinventing the wheel, the need for ongoing work in research into accessible homes remains. New technologies, methods and equipment constitute an ongoing process to ensure the best possible homes are built in the future. As professionals knowledegable in a range of disabling conditions and focused on assisting disabled people to maximise their independence, more occupational therapists could take a lead in this through research and collaborative work with disabled people and architects.

The widely acknowledged objectives of any design guide for the home should be to ensure that:

- individuals have access into their home
- facilities within the home are accessible and usable
- the safety of the home users is addressed
- day-to-day maintenance of the home is considered
- the domestic service controls are easily accessible, e.g. for water, gas, electricity.

Specified space standards which allow safe, obstruction free movement should be set down, based on the abilities of a wide variety of individuals with differing disabling conditions. The layout of internal fixtures should also be stated to ensure safety and ease of use. Built in flexibility is required to allow the property to be used by people with differing abilities.

Design guides tend to fall into several types concerning:

- general environmental issues looking at public areas, street furniture, shop interiors, access into public buildings
- adapting existing private dwellings, covering entrance into and movement around the property, and access to the facilities within the home
- the design of newly built properties to standards suitable for both people with mobility problems and wheelchair users
- the design of buildings for those with sensory loss
- special needs groups such as those with learning difficulties
- those requiring sheltered accommodation
- various combinations of all the above.

They all vary in style from being very prescriptive to just listing features categorised as essential or desirable (see the further reading section at the end of the chapter for more details).

What would appear to be slight variations in recommended space requirements can be found in the various regulations, design standards and guides. The opening width of the front door given in BS5619 (British Standards Institute 1978) and Lifetime Homes, differs by only 50mm and may seem very little, but it could make the difference between a disabled person being able to enter a property or not. A range of sizes from 750 to 1500mm are quoted for corridor widths, but it is not just the width of the corridor which must be considered. Radiators on the wall could reduce the width to an impassable size; the turn into a doorway may be too acute to get through. The turning circle for a wheelchair user is quoted as 1200mm in the draft Part M Building Regulations covering new dwellings, however in the vast majority of other standards and guides it is 1500mm – 1700mm, with 2000mm offering space for someone using a large semi-reclining wheelchair. If insufficient space is given, the property may become inaccessible to wheelchair users. In the majority of cases a minimum size is quoted with the expectation that it will be exceeded wherever practicable. Unfortunately, minimum sizes are all too often those built to, and this is surely a good reason for setting a minimum which is large enough to accommodate if not all, then the majority of disabled people.

The fact that there are so many different design guides, written by various professional groups up and down the country, means that there is a range of specifications for door widths, ramp gradients and so on. This is because different types of wheelchair may be used for gauging these requirements, and opinions vary as to how much extra space is needed. Hence, problems arise in homes which have been built supposedly to wheelchair standard, but which prove not to be suitable once the tenant moves in. Ignorance, other priorities or ineffective use of design guides is usually the reason.

In the last 25 years many organisations, institutions and providers of housing have strived to produce their own standards of good practice in designing for disability. Each guide has contributed to the debate although the large number of guides has led to confusion for potential users and professionals alike. Few have been based on recent in-depth research which fully involves disabled people. To achieve the best possible range of options in any new build development or rehabilitation of an existing building, a multi-disciplinary approach is most likely to succeed (see Chapter 2).

*Design brief for an individual or specific development*

Design briefs relate to one particular adaptation or development catering for individual needs. This is usually achieved by the occupational therapists working with clients to generate possible solutions, surveyors confirming what is technically possible and the client choosing which option they prefer. Design guides give information on those options and offer technical solutions and advice on what is good practice. However, each individual or development will require a specific solution to his or her housing problem. Where disabled people require support from public funds to adapt their home, there may be conflict between what they would ideally prefer and what can be justified and offered by their local authority. It often falls to the occupational therapist to help negotiate a compromise which is acceptable to all concerned, based on government guidelines and locally agreed criteria. Once an adaptation has been agreed by all parties, the occupational therapist should ensure that the client is kept fully informed at every stage, consult with the client regularly and act as advocate as and when necessary.

*Designing for new properties*

Local authorities are discouraged by central government from entering into joint ventures with other organisations in order to build new homes, and often have insufficient funds of their own. It therefore falls largely on registered social landlords who have access to private funds and opportunities to bid for public resources (see Chapter 6) and private developers to meet the wide range of housing needs of the nation. As long ago as 1975 the government was encouraging the private sector to take into account the needs of disabled people. This is clearly stated in HDD OP 2/75 *Wheelchair Housing* (HDD 1975). The government, disability groups and occupational therapists have all spent a great deal of energy in persuading all developers of the benefits of building to accessible standards. The Disability Discrimination Act 1995 now adds its weight to these efforts.

The Housing Corporation has set its own standards which it expects registered social landlords to follow on all new build developments. *Scheme Development Standards* lists essential and desirable features for general housing as well as special properties for wheelchair users (Housing Corporation 1995). The general housing standards are in effect mobility standards.

Some authorities, such as Greenwich Council in London, have begun to use their influence to persuade registered social landlords to build houses to Lifetime Homes standards as a general principle. It will take some time for these initiatives to have any real impact on the availability of accessibe properties, but it is a move in the right direction. In addition, any properties being built to wheelchair standard by the registered social landlords in Greenwich are expected to take into account the recommendations made in the access guide adopted by the council (Greenwich Housing Services 1996). This example of good practice offers a model which may be adopted by other local authorities.

A different situation arises with new build compared to adaptation, in that specific individual housing needs only become influential once someone has agreed to accept the tenancy. The important issue is ensuring that the properties can accommodate the widest possible range of individuals, and would require only minor adaptations to meet individual needs. Referral to design guides in the early stages can give the architects a clearer picture of what is required. This in turn emphasises the importance of ensuring that the content of the guides is reliable. Design guides should complement face-to-face meetings between all those concerned in the project. The latter should take place so that issues can be resolved at the earliest possible opportunity.

(The roles of individual professionals and service users are covered fully in Chapter 3.)

### Designing for minority ethnic groups

It is important to consider the needs of ethnic minority disabled people, taking into account their cultural and religious needs while focusing on the needs of the individual. Once again, a prescriptive approach should be avoided as needs and aspirations are not static regardless of which group is considered. Second and third generations may have very different needs and aspirations from the first generation migrants. Also social, cultural and religious variations exist within ethnic minority groups. The design needs of disabled ethnic minority people can be met by using general access design principles while considering their ethnic needs. A clear understanding of the culture and its religion is essential if a building development is to be successful for the intended occupants. Examples of issues which may need to be considered are:

- whether large extended families share accommodation or whether they prefer to live in close proximity

- security of the proposed site in its widest sense, as minority ethnic groups continue to experience crime above the national norm

- whether the orientation of dwellings and relationships of one room to another is important

- whether additional space needs to be provided to allow traditional work activities to take place in the home

- whether an area is required for religious purposes

- whether, as cooking practices vary significantly and greater volumes may be cooked at any one time, separate areas are required for different types of food and extra ventilation is necessary

- whether bathing needs include the need for running water for religious reasons.

All these issues and more are covered in the guide *Accommodating Diversity* (National Federation of Housing Associations 1993).

### Designing for visually impaired people

The Royal National Institution for the Blind (RNIB) believes as many as 1.7 million people in the United Kingdom have some form of visual impairment. With an increasing elderly population this figure is likely to rise, highlighting the need to incorporate design features suitable for those people with visual impairment.

The following are main areas of concern relating to designing for people with visual impairments.

1. *Layout.* It is important that a clear mental picture of the building can be formed. This will be assisted if the layout is logical and straightforward.

2. *Visibility.* Colour and tone contrasts are effective in helping to identify the building's features and to avoid hazards. For example, contrast between the door and its frame, light switches and the wall, grab rails and wall.

3. *Lighting.* It is very important to get the lighting correct for all building users, not just visually impaired people. Adjustable lighting levels and proper positioning of light sources will help avoid glare, dazzle and optical illusions. For example, lights positioned so as not to create pools of light, paint or wall finishes which do not create glare, and windows positioned carefully so as not to dazzle the occupier in areas of risk such as at the top of the stairs.

4. *Texture.* Changes in texture in floor covering and on rails can give cues as to the position of doorways or top/bottom of staircases.

The above issues are fully explored in the book *Building Sight* (Barker, Barrick and Wilson 1995).

*Designing for sheltered accommodation*

Sheltered accommodation aims to enable elderly people to remain in the community while taking into account a range of abilities and care needs. A mixture of unit types will allow independent living by people who use wheelchairs as well as those who may only have minor difficulties at home, caused by the ageing process. It is desirable for the majority of flats to have one bedroom able to accommodate two people and in addition some two-bedroom flats which would allow for the needs of carers. All the flats need to be self-contained with an alarm link for summoning assistance. It is desirable that communal facilities are accessible to all the tenants, and all floors above ground level ought to be accessible via a lift large enough to accommodate a wheelchair user and at least one other person. Consideration of designing for visual impairment is essential (see previous section). Flats designated for wheelchair users should have all the design features necessary to allow independent access to all the rooms, facilities and service controls.

The majority of flats, if designed to mobility standard, will allow wheelchair users access into the flat and to the lounge and toilet.

*Fire regulations and means of escape*

In some instances there is clear regulatory guidance, for example: means of escape in case of fire from communal areas. Mechanisms for access and egress may be compromised due to fire regulations. Fire regulations, as specified in the Building Regulations, do not apply to private dwellings. However some households may choose to plan for two alternative exits from a bungalow for instance, but fire protection measures, such as half hour fire resistance doors, may be installed.

## Plans

Plans are line drawings produced by architects and surveyors, usually to a client's specification or brief. There will be views from above, known as plan views, or from the side, i.e. elevations. The plan view shows the line of the walls both internal and external, position of doors, windows and staircase if more than one floor. Each level of the building will have a plan to give a picture of the whole building. The elevations will show the property from all four (or more) sides as it will be from outside, and there may be views of the bathroom and kitchen to show the layout of the fixtures and fittings. The plans may have very little detail or a lot of detail, and often several plans will be drawn for each particular property design. Some will show wall construction, or routes for drainage, positions of electrical fittings, or details of kitchen layout. The individual designer will decide what is on each drawing based on maintaining clarity (so that it is easy for construction workers to see what is required), minimising the number of pieces of paper and the time needed to produce the drawings. Each plan is given a reference number, letter and date. When alterations to the original drawings are made the resultant drawing is known as a revision, and the reference letter and date are changed. The alterations are usually listed at the side of the drawing.

All the drawings are to scale, an appropriate scale being chosen depending on how much detail is required. A site plan may be 1:100 while a kitchen layout may be 1:20. Special scales are commercially available for translation of the scales into metric dimensions. Measurements made with these scales are less accurate with the smaller scales, for example 1:250, as the thickness of the drawn lines can greatly distort the translated dimensions.

Alongside the plans, written instructions will be produced by the architect. These are called specifications and give details of how the property is to be built. The specification will give step-by-step instructions about the whole construction, including the type of bricks used, the type of foundations, how any timber should be prepared and finished and how many coats of paint on the walls. These are important documents and community occupational therapists and all those involved need to become familiar with the terminology used in the building trade. In this way they are able to understand what is included in the specification relating to the areas of most concern to them, such as ceiling construction able to accommodate hoist tracks; the clear opening width of all doorways and wall construction in areas likely to require grab rails.

Reading plans is a skill which occupational therapists can learn with professional instruction and practice. Courses on reading plans are organised by professional bodies such as the College of Occupational Therapists in conjunction with The Centre for Accessible Environments in London, and by some local authorities. Courses should include:

- what plans are for
- legislation relating to building
- what plans look like and how different elements are represented
- scales and how to interpret them
- interpretation of plans
- how to draw to scale
- relating plans to actual buildings
- common terminology

- creative adaptation of buildings
- checking for access.

Up until about ten years ago plans were always hand drawn, which allowed for a certain amount of individualism in the presentation. Now computer aided design (CAD) programmes are available which assist the architect/ surveyor in drawing up plans. The scale can be preset, as can the line thickness and paper size. Different elements in the drawing can be given different colours, for example windows could be red, doors blue, walls yellow. This would enable non-professionals and professionals to see the layout more clearly. For competent CAD users:

- the drawing process becomes faster than with hand drawing
- the style of the drawings becomes more standardised
- greater accuracy is possible
- clearer presentation can be achieved
- storage requirements are reduced as several plans stored on single discs will take up less space.

In the future it is likely that people will design buildings with increasing use of computer systems capable of giving three dimensional views, allowing the user to move through the building on the computer screen. Such technology would enhance the prospects of eliminating avoidable mistakes and, more important, enable all those who have difficulty in conceptualising space from a flat sheet, professionals and disabled people alike, to understand more fully and appreciate the consequences of their endeavours. With the advances in virtual reality that have already taken place, there is a high probability that designing in this way will become the norm in the foreseeable future.

## Conclusion

Legislation to ensure the provision of accessible homes for disabled people is slowly being implemented. For some years standards have been recommended which would have improved accessibility to homes had they been law. Ensuring that the best possible standards, not the minimum requirements, are employed is essential.

Recognition of the value of a barrier free environment is taking place and improvements have been made in securing equal housing opportunities for disabled people. The promotion of the issues by disabled people is making a considerable impact on broadening the housing options for all sectors of the community.

The regulations and standards implemented eventually by law will set the broad design requirements, while the design guides will assist with the details and possible solutions to ensure that regulations are met. Using design guides to encourage flexible and lateral thinking is the best way to attain suitable solutions to designing for both general and individual needs of disabled people.

The importance of understanding plans cannot be under-estimated. Spotting the problems and pitfalls as early as possible and suggesting solutions, is of immense value to ensure a smooth transition from conception to completion.

Occupational therapists should be to the fore in promoting good design and encouraging full consultation at every stage between all the relevant parties. Not only would the important issue of promoting equality in housing for elderly and disabled people be addressed, but economic problems would be eased by good housing design. Huge amounts of money are spent nationally in adapting homes and providing statutory services for people who require assistance in inaccessible homes.

Designing homes which are accessible to all, do not stand out as different, and which can be adapted if necessary at minimal cost and disruption, promises to be the way forward for the whole of society.

## Appendix I: A local authority's defined standards

*Visitability and mobility standards as defined by a local authority*

VISITABILITY

Visitability housing is designed for the convenience of households covering all age groups, from people who are elderly, or infirm. It allows for visits by disabled people, and could possibly be adapted for a disabled resident.

MOBILITY

Mobility housing has features with general appeal, but is designed specific-ally for disabled residents. It is based on research showing that most disabled people who are not permanent wheelchair users can live comfortably with small modifications to ordinary housing.

## Appendix II: A housing association's standards

*A Scottish housing associations standard*

NEGOTIABLE

The most basic permissible and lowest standard, this allows a wheelchair user access to the lowest level of a house or a flat even if they have to be assisted up steps. Once in the house or flat, they should be able to move freely around on that level. There may not, however, be an accessible toilet available at entrance level.

### LIVABLE

This allows an independent wheelchair user unassisted access to the lowest level of a house or flat. Once in the house or flat, they should be able to move freely around on that level. A usable bathroom or shower-room and toilet, and a room suitable for use as a bedroom should be available at entrance level.

### VISITABLE

The preferred minimum standard, this allows an independent wheelchair user unassisted access to the lowest level of a house or flat. Once inside they should be able to move freely around on that level. An accessible toilet should be available, but a usable toilet is preferred as this would give a wheelchair user unaided access to, and use of, the toilet.

### UNIVERSAL

This is a house or flat designed to an appropriate wheelchair standard such as set out by the Habinteg Housing Association design guide. This, by implication, is the optimum standard in barrier free housing.

## Appendix III: Proposed European standards

*European standards proposed in 1987 at European Committee Conference*

### INTEGRAL ACCESSIBILITY

The built environment is arranged so that it allows everyone to function in the most independent and natural way possible.

### VISITABILITY

A dwelling or public building is visitable if any visitor can reach the entrance and all the facilities that a visitor is normally allowed to use.

### ADAPTABILITY

The physical and spacial capacity of houses or other individually used areas can be rearranged easily whenever the need to do so occurs.

# References

Access Committee for England (1992) *Criteria for Accessible General Housing: Building Homes for Successive Generations.* London: ACE.

British Standards Institute (1978) *Code of Practice for Design of Housing for the Convenience of Disabled People B55619.* London: BSI.

British Standards Institute (1979) *Code of Practice for Access for the Disabled into Buildings B55810.* London: BSI.

Barker, P., Barrick. J. and Wilson, R. (1995) *Building Sight.* London: HMSO.

Central Coordinating Committee for the Promotion of Accessibility (1990) *European Manual for an Accessible Built Environment.* Rijewijk, the Netherlands: Central Coordinating Committee for the Promotion of Accessibility.

*Chronically Sick and Disabled Persons Act 1970.* London: HMSO.

Department of the Environment (1961) *Homes for Today and Tomorrow.* London: HMSO.

Department of the Environment (1968) *Space in the Home.* London: HMSO.

Department of the Environment (1991) *Building Regulations 1991.* London: HMSO.

Department of the Environment (1992) *Building Regulations 1991 Access and Facilities for Disabled People Part M.* London: HMSO.

Department of the Environment (1995) *Building Regulations 1991 New Dwellings Access and Facilities for Disabled People Part M.* London: HMSO.

Department of the Environment (1994) *Measures to Tackle Discrimination Against Disabled People* London: HMSO.

*Disability Discrimination Act 1995.* London: HMSO.

Greenwich Housing Services (1996) *Accessible Homes: Mobility for Wheelchair Users within Private Dwellings.* London: Greenwich Council.

Goldsmith, S. (1974) 'Mobility housing'. *The Architect's Journal,* 3.7.74, 43–50.

Goldsmith, S. (1975) 'Wheelchair housing'. *The Architect's Journal,* 25.6.75, 1319–1344.

Goldsmith, S. (1963/1976) *Designing for the Disabled.* London: RIBA Publications Ltd.

Habinteg Housing Association (1992) *A Design Guide and Technical Manual for Accessible New Build Housing* Habinteg Housing Association Ltd. London: Habinteg Housing Association.

Health and Safety Executive (1994) *Construction (Design and Management) Regulations (1994)* Construction sheets Nos. 39, 40, 41. Suffolk: HSE Publications.

Heywood, F. and Smart, G. (1996) *Funding Adaptations: The Need to Cooperate.* Bristol: The Policy Press.

Housing Corporation (1995) *Scheme Development Standards.* London: The Housing Corporation.

Housing Development Directorate (1974) *Mobility Housing.* Development Directorate Occasional Paper (HDD OP) 2/74. London: HMSO.

Housing Development Directorate (1975) *Wheelchair Housing.* Development Directorate Occasional Paper (HDD OP) 2/75. London: HMSO.

Islington Council (1989) *Housing for People with Disabilities: A Design Guide.* London: Islington Council Architectural Department.

Karn, V. and Sheridan, L. (1994) *New Homes in the 1990s: A Study of Design, Space Amenities in Housing Association and Private Sector Housing.* London: Housing Centre Trust.

Lifetime Homes Group (1993) *Lifetime Homes.* York: Joseph Rowntree Foundation.

London Borough of Waltham Forest (1992) *Design Guide for Disabled Person Accommodation: Indoor Wheelchair Users.* London: London Borough of Waltham Forest.

National Federation of Housing Associations (1993) *Accommodating Diversity: The Design of Housing for Minority Ethnic, Religious and Cultural Groups.* London: National Federation of Housing Associations.

*National Health Service and Community Care Act 1991.* London: HMSO.

Office of Population Censuses and Surveys (1992) *1991 Census County Monitors.* London: OPCS.

Scottish Homes (1996) *The Physical Quality of Housing: Housing for Older People and Disabled People a Consultation on Design Guidance.* Edinburgh: Scottish Homes.

*Therapy Weekly* (1996) 23, 20, 2, November 14.

## Further reading

Bone, S. (1996) *Buildings for All to Use – Good Practice Guidance for Improving Existing Public Buildings for People with Disabilities.* London: Construction Industry Research and Information Association.

Canadian Standards Association (1990) *Barrier-Free Design: A National Standard for Canada.* Ontario: Candian Standards Association.

Habinteg Housing Association (1995) *Homes for All.* London: Habinteg Housing Association.

Hackney Council (1990) *Design for Better Living.* London: Hackney Council.

Holmes-Siedle, J. (1996) *Barrier-Free Design: A Manual for Building Designers and Managers.* Oxford: Butterworth Architecture.

Lewisham and Southwark Learning Disabilities Service (1995) *Moving On: Housing Design for People with Special Needs.* London: Lewisham and Southwark Learning Disability Service.

London Borough of Waltham Forest (1993) *Warden-Supervised Sheltered Housing for Elderly People.* London: London Borough of Waltham Forest.

Powell-Smith, V. and Billington, M.J. (1992) *The Building Regulations,* Ninth Edition. Oxford: Blackwell Scientific Publications.

Thorpe, S. (1986) *Reading Plans.* London: Access Committee for England.

Thorpe, S. (1997) Wheelchair Housing Design Guide. Hertfordshire: Construction Research Communications Ltd.

Tutt, P. and Adler, D. (1985) *New Metric Handbook.* London: The Architectural Press.

Walbrook Housing Association (1992) *Cracking Housing Problems.* Derby: Walbrook Housing Association Ltd.

Wylde, M., Baron-Robbins, A. and Clark, S. (1994) *Building for a Lifetime: The Design and Construction of Fully Accessible Homes.* USA: Taunton Press Inc.

# CHAPTER 6

# New Build Developments

## Madeleine Middle

### Introduction

This chapter is based on the author's practical knowledge of new build housing.

All the examples used are from the author's own experience working with housing providers and local authorities. Names have been changed or omitted to maintain confidentiality for disabled people and housing providers.

The different sectors of new build housing are defined as follows:

1. *Public sector*

   - social housing (for rent or shared ownership) formerly known as public sector housing.

2. *Private sector*

   - private housing developments for sale or rent
   - one-off private developments.

The author will

- look at the needs of disabled people and how these needs can be met
- consider the role of the local authority as the enabler in achieving new build property

The author wishes to acknowledge the valuable support and input of Walbrook Housing Association, particularly colleagues in the Disabled Persons Housing Service, Architects and Development departments. Also the contribution made by Paul Matthews from the viewpoint of a disabled person and Michael Watts, Access Officer for Derby City Council, for their valuable comments during the preparation of the chapter.

- discuss the roles to be played by all involved in the new build process
- explain all the essential stages which have to be achieved in providing new build housing
- look at the detailed process of providing new housing in each of the identified housing sectors. The detailed process refers to the system operated in England, but similar systems do operate in the rest of the United Kingdom.

**What are the sectors of New Build Development?**

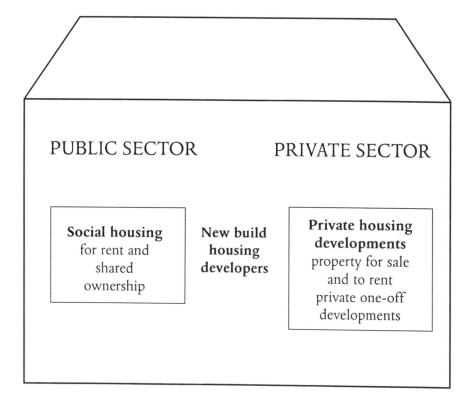

PUBLIC SECTOR          PRIVATE SECTOR

**Social housing** for rent and shared ownership

**New build housing developers**

**Private housing developments** property for sale and to rent private one-off developments

*Figure 6.1: The sectors of new build development*

*Public sector*

SOCIAL HOUSING FOR RENT OR SHARED OWNERSHIP

This is defined as all property developed by registered social landlords (RSL). This term includes housing associations and private landlords who are registered with the Housing Corporation, which is the central body in England for funding and controlling the standards of housing associations. RSLs work in conjunction with the local authority to meet identified housing need and, in return for grants, keep rents affordable. The RSL has a charitable or not-for-profit status.

RSLs now have a vast assortment of property which they manage and rent to people who are unable to afford to purchase or privately rent. The type of property could be family houses or flats, sheltered housing schemes or accommodation such as hostels for homeless people or those with drugs or alcohol related problems. The RSL also works closely with social services and health authorities to provide accommodation for supported housing schemes, to facilitate discharge from residential care and to house people with special needs. Many disabled people have to rely on social housing because of their low income: in the author's experience they are often living on state benefits.

Shared ownership housing is included in the social housing sector and is defined as property which the occupant part rents and part owns. The minimum share to purchase is usually 25 per cent but may be 50 per cent of the total value of the property. This enables first time buyers on low incomes to enter property ownership. The remaining share of 75 per cent is rented from the developer, usually a housing association, and additional 25 per cent shares may be bought when the occupant can afford to do so.

*Private sector*

PRIVATE HOUSING DEVELOPMENTS FOR SALE OR RENT

Private sector developments are undertaken by house builders for profit. The price of property varies vastly to cater for and attract a very wide market of potential buyers.

Housing developers build property in the private sector to provide specialist types of accommodation for sale. An example of this is the growing number of private developers who build a scheme of self-contained flats or bungalows for elderly people to purchase. This is usually a small complex with a resident caretaker or a warden providing a service. An annual service charge is then paid. This gives elderly people the choice of owning their property whilst living in a sheltered, supported environment.

Private developers are also building property specifically for private renting on a commercial basis. This is an area which is increasing to meet the needs of those who do not wish to or are unable to purchase property or rent property in the public sector.

ONE-OFF DEVELOPMENTS

This type of development accounts for a very small proportion of the total new build property, but it is worthy of note because it can achieve results for a disabled person which are not possible on large private sector schemes.

Purchasers or tenants would be able to live in a property which would have been designed to meet their individual needs and in a location which is right for them.

A one-off property usually results from a landowner wishing to develop part of his land. It could be a large garden with planning permission for a single new build dwelling.

The landowner might act as the developer and build for their own use to rent or, alternatively, sell the land to a small local builder.

This type of development has a great deal of potential for disabled people who can afford to purchase land and build or who have the opportunity to rent such a property. It has been used by disabled people who have been awarded large compensation claims to enable them to achieve purpose built accommodation in their chosen area. (To find out about opportunities for such developments read the list of outline planning applications in local newspapers and go to the planning departments for information.)

---

### Example: Derek Ford

Derek Ford, aged 25, received a large compensation claim for the spinal injuries he received in a road traffic accident which resulted in him being a wheelchair user needing 24-hour care. Before the accident he lived with his parents, but their property was no longer suitable for his needs. He wished to remain in the area and maintain contact with his family whilst living independently. A plot of land was available locally which he purchased with his trust fund. The occupational therapist, specialising in housing, worked with him to establish a design brief. An architect was employed to produce working drawings. The young man, his family, the occupational therapist and architect all worked together to achieve the end result with the building contractors. The property was funded from the trust fund and was very much to the individual taste of the young man, as well as fulfilling his specific disability needs and maximising his independence.

It was important to discuss the project with the trust fund at the planning stage to ensure funding was available and to keep the trust informed of the cost of the project, throughout the process.

## What are the housing needs of disabled people?

When choosing a home, everyone is restricted to some extent by what is affordable, their place of work, family commitments and the availability of suitable housing. Within these limitations most able-bodied people have some choice. Disabled people currently have the added restriction of having to ask, 'Is the property accessible to me?', 'Can I live there?', 'Are the local services and facilities accessible to me?'. The barrier free environment is not yet here.

New build developments need to achieve a wide range of housing which is accessible to all people. At various stages of life housing needs change. The Lifetime Homes concept, which is dealt with in detail in Chapter 5, has evolved with the aim that people should not have to move house because of the built environment when their circumstances change; all new build housing should be able to cater for any persons changing needs or abilities throughout their lifetime.

In the author's experience, disabled people choose to move for various reasons such as a change of job or family breakdown. Disabled people require housing appropriate to their lifestyle, and which enables rather than disables.

## The role of the local authority

### The local authority as an enabling agency

The Housing Act 1996 emphasised the need for local authorities to change their role as landlords and providers of housing to enablers.

The future role of local authorities will essentially be a strategic one, identifying housing needs and demands and encouraging innovative methods of provision and new interest in the revival of the independent rented sector.

Local authority housing departments have been assuming an enabling role for many years, in addition to their role as housing providers. The increased emphasis which is now being placed on the enabling role has led local authorities to develop their existing planning strategies. The government has not clearly defined the enabling role and has only stated that it is desirable for local authorities to develop the role.

### The local authority strategic planning functions

The enabling concept addresses these functions which, once identified, can be formulated into a strategic planning policy by the local authority and the information used for their annual capital spending bids. The functions are to:

- identify shortfalls in housing provision
- forward plan to ensure future housing needs can be met
- consider the geographical location for future development
- establish an order of priority for meeting identified need
- select the method of meeting the need: social housing or private sector
- address the funding implications
- monitor and assess all changes to existing housing provision which could influence the overall planning strategy.

The strategic policy should also consider in detail the specific needs of disabled people, ethnic minority groups and other minority groups in the local authority area. This is to ensure that the needs of all groups will be fully integrated into the planning strategy and not treated in isolation or as an afterthought. Where there is a local authority access officer they have an important role to play in ensuring that high standards of access are part of the local authority's policy and these are properly implemented.

The strategic planning policy may include a policy design guide, setting out criteria to be used in all new build developments. For example, it could state that all new housing will need to be built to visitability standard. All planning applications would then need to adhere to this standard.

The local authority has the ability to facilitate initiatives and opportunities for local housing providers by identifying housing need and by forward planning what it requires to achieve in a given period. The following is an example of one local authority's identified new build requirements.

1. To provide a total of 200 new homes within the local authority area, during the next 12 months.

    - 100 to be three-bedroomed houses for rent in area X; 10 of these to be wheelchair standard.

    - 25 to be one-bedroomed single person units for rent in area Y; to accessible standards.

    - 75 to be family housing for sale in areas X and Y.

2. To provide 30 residential care places in area X during the next 18 months.

3. To provide four group homes for people with learning difficulties during the next two years.

*Creating new communities*

The author's experience of working with a number of different housing associations has shown that the strategic planning policy should not only address the provision of housing stock, but also the importance of creating new community facilities. There is no point in building houses in an area where people do not wish to live because there has been no planning strategy to provide shops, schools and other facilities.

For example, several years ago, a housing association built a large development of flats. The scheme was well-planned and attractive. The external appearance was of two-storey houses with green areas and court-yards. However, the flats have always been difficult to let, especially to disabled people, because they are situated on the edge of a city, some distance away from any shops and other facilities, and not on a bus route.

*How can the local authority enable the housing process?*

As the enabler, the local authority can create opportunities for and encourage others to work together and provide a forum for consultation.

*Communication is vital to the process.*

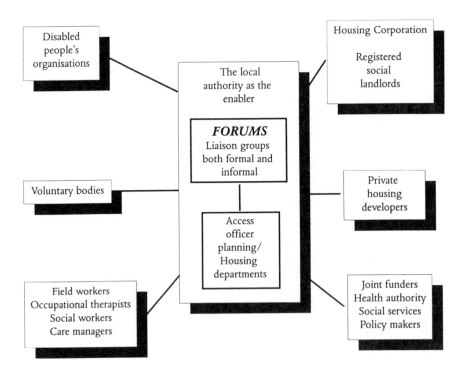

*Figure 6.2: The local authority as enabler*

Ideally, the strategic planning process should involve the local authority, housing and planning departments, organisations of disabled people, access officers, access groups, occupational therapists, housing association development and housing managers and representatives of social services and the health authority who are able to affect policy making as the result of their own planning and policy decisions.

Although inter-agency working between health and housing is recognised as being very important, research findings published by the Joseph Rowntree Foundation (November 1995) find that in practice it is very limited. There is a lack of common understanding of the constraints experienced by both, although the introduction of unitary authorities in Scotland, Wales and parts of England is bringing together housing and social services agencies and assisting in establishing links between health and housing agencies.

A unitary authority combines all services in its area resulting in housing and social services being within the same operational department. In the areas where unitary status is not in force, the two tier system of separately operating departments still exists.

Throughout the United Kingdom there are different ways in which local housing provision systems work. It is essential that on a local basis all departments and groups of people who have input into the provision of new housing share aims, objectives, strategies and implementation of policies on a long term and day-to-day basis.

It is important for occupational therapists to have input into the management and policy making procedures within social services and the health authority and that they are represented formally on local authority planning and housing committees. It is essential that occupational therapists explain their role and skills in analysis of function, lifestyle and care needs. These skills can be used to enhance provision in all types of accommodation. In the author's experience, with a co-ordinated and consistent approach occupational therapist input can be far reaching in supporting the housing needs of disabled people. Failure to get things right first time is costly for the provider and frustrating for the user. By promoting established standards of good practice, occupational therapists can influence local housing developments and facilitate independent living opportunities for disabled people.

It is equally important that disabled people are represented on local authority committees either as individuals or representing disabled people's action groups, to put forward their views and expertise on behalf of all disabled people. They can give practical first-hand information of what problems they encounter and are an essential part of the process to achieve a better understanding of disabled people's needs.

Many local authorities now have access officers whose specific role is to ensure that disabled people's housing needs are considered. The access officer will liaise with groups of disabled people and will often form an access group which brings together disabled people and professionals on both an informal and a formal basis.

Disabled people, occupational therapists, access officers and local voluntary bodies all working together can encourage local commitment to a holistic view of housing for people with mental health, learning, physical and sensory disabilities.

### Planning and building regulations

The local authority is legally bound to ensure that all new build developments meet current planning regulations and building regulations.

#### PLANNING REGULATIONS

Planning permission is required under the Town and Country Planning Act 1990. This is about the use of land and what a building will look like. There are two stages, both of which have to be satisfied:

Stage 1     Outlined planning permission which determines the use of the land.

Stage 2     Detailed planning permission confirming the scheme design meets local standards of appearance and light amenity for neighbours.

#### BUILDING REGULATIONS

The Building Act 1984 and regulations made under it apply in England and Wales. They cover the way in which a building is constructed to withstand the weather and to protect the health and safety of the occupants and others.

### The process of new build developments

Understanding the process of new build will enable occupational therapists to be aware of the relevant stages at which they could have input. This is equally important for everyone involved in the development process.

There are several stages to the process:

Stage 1     establishing the need

Stage 2     acquisition of land including funding

Stage 3     design and detailed planning

*Stage 4*        construction

*Stage 5*        occupancy

These five stages are common to all types of new build development. The process will be dealt with under the two previously defined housing sectors, the public sector and the private sector.

### *Stage 1: Establishing the overall needs of disabled people in a geographical area*

Each local authority in its enabling role has a statutory obligation under the Housing Act 1996 to provide information on disabled people's needs through its strategic planning policy. The Joseph Rowntree Foundation (September 1995) found that disabled people were not involved in planning processes for housing and community care in any systematic way, and that where there was involvement, it was at the lowest tier and on a single impairment basis.

The author has frequently worked with developers who are reluctant to look at specialist accommodation unless they are given good information to show there is a need. It is vitally important that housing developers communicate with all relevant organisations who can provide substantiated evidence of need. A specialist housing occupational therapist post can co-ordinate this process by keeping records of the available housing stock for disabled people and advising on the demand for different types, locations and sizes of property. The information can then be fed into the planning/negotiation process. The following example shows how need was identified and fed through the system, resulting in a housing association taking on a

---

### Example

Three large families all required rehousing in wheelchair standard property within an inner city area.

The housing need had been established by an occupational therapist working with the disabled people. The occupational therapist passed on this information to the local authority housing department. The local authority had been aware of a general housing need in the area, but not of the specific need of wheelchair users until this information was made available.

The local authority housing department worked with the occupational therapist and a registered social landlord to establish funding through the housing corporation. Three separate sites were identified, each one had a small frontage on to an existing street of terraced houses.

---

### Example (continued)

The specific needs of the disabled people and their families were identified. All three families were of ethnic minority origin. Two of the families had a child as the wheelchair user. Two sites were designed to accommodate three-bedroom, six-person properties and one site was able to achieve a four-bedroom, eight-person property for the largest family, which had six children. Because of the limited space available, two-storey houses were designed. The design brief was difficult to achieve on the narrow sites but the housing association and architect worked closely with the occupational therapist to achieve house designs which were practical for wheelchair users and acceptable to the families. Each design varied because of the restrictions of the site. Two sites were able to achieve carports, but the third had to rely on street parking. One site had a very small garden, but these compromises were thought to be worthwhile in view of what was being achieved.

Each house had a through floor lift installed and achieved full wheelchair access. The disabled person's specific needs were met with features such as ceiling track hoists and adjustable height kitchen units, clos-o-mat toilets, showers and so on. The project was costly but fulfilled an important housing need. It allowed two families to remain in their existing ethnic community and a third family to move to an area in which they wished to live.

---

highly complex project, whilst feeling confident that a need had been established.

*Stage 2: Acquisition of land*

When the need to increase the housing stock has been identified by the local authority strategic planning process, there will be negotiation between the local authority and prospective developers.

THE PROCUREMENT OF PUBLIC SECTOR SOCIAL HOUSING

The enablers = The local authority

The providers or developers = Registered social landlord (RSL)

The regulators = The housing corporation (who are also 'providers' of funding).

A) ACTION BY THE RSL

The RSL will go through the following stages of core social housing operations:

- *Finding a site*

The site has to be chosen with consideration to the local authority policy. This might result in developers having to build on difficult, inaccessible sites because housing is required in that area. The surrounding area
and availability of services all have to be considered. On occasions developers will put forward a proposal to the local authority for developing a site in an area not included in the planning policy, to test if this is
acceptable.

- *Employing an architect*

This is to draft an outline scheme based on the design brief. The architect will look at how to achieve the best use of the land and could produce several options for the RSL to consider.

- *Planning requirements*

Apply for outline planning permission only at this stage.

- *Carrying out a feasibility study*

The developer needs to be sure that the site is right for the purpose and
that the project will be cost effective. Before proceeding further with
the scheme, the developer will commission a feasibility study. This is an
outline assessment of the scheme as a whole and includes a survey of the
land and general design construction costs set against the likely financial return on the completed homes.

- *Securing funding*

When satisfied with the feasibility of the scheme, the RSL prepares a
funding bid which is made to the housing corporation or regulator
(only RSLs have access to this funding). If an RSL can show that they intend to provide good social housing built to a standard of identified
need, funding is more likely to be available.

B) ACTION BY THE REGULATOR

The Housing Corporation consider the bid and decide on the level of social
housing grant (SHG) that it will provide for the scheme. The level of grant
will be linked to the type of housing being provided. (This grant was
previously known as housing association grant or HAG.)

There are two types of regulatory standards required by the Housing
Corporation for new build development: performance standards and scheme
development standards.

Performance standards were introduced by the Housing Corporation in
1994 as part of their regulatory mechanism for all RSLs. They look at the

overall management, financial management, housing management, property maintenance, access and development of the RSLs.

Scheme development standards were introduced by the Housing Corporation in 1993 and revised in 1995. They set out requirements for all new build housing developments which are funded by the Housing Corporation and include wheelchair user requirements, housing for the elderly and special needs housing. They cover the following aspects:

- external environment
- internal environment
- accessibility
- safety and security
- energy efficiency
- building practice.

It is essential for RSLs to meet the required standards if their scheme is to be eligible for SHG, and they are notified of the level of funding which the Housing Corporation will provide.

Grants will not cover the full costs of the scheme, and an RSL now has to look at additional methods of raising money. This can be achieved in several ways, described below.

C) SPECIAL NEEDS FUNDING

Special needs schemes are projects where a health authority and social services department jointly wish to achieve accommodation for disabled people who are moving from a hospital setting into the community, for example small group homes for people with learning difficulties.

---

### Example

This example is of a development in which the author worked with a voluntary organisation who wished to rehouse the eight occupants of two group homes into new build property. An RSL and an architectural practice designed a scheme for both groups to live on one site in two semi-detached houses. The occupational therapist worked with the architect to advise on design and also acted as the liaison person between the architect and the eight people in the two existing group homes to ensure their individual and group living needs were met. These varied from the need for bath rails, toilet rails, shower trays and stair rails to certain kitchen design features. Several people had limited mobility or sensory impairment. Consideration of their views and involvement in the process was essential to overcome their anxiety.

---

---

## Example (continued)

By working with the occupational therapist the architect was able to understand the importance of creating a group home which would also meet the needs of the individual people.

---

## Example: The funding of one property on a new build scheme

| *Cost* | | *Cost* |
|---|---|---|
| Land | | £8,000 |
| Construction | | £30,000 |
| Costs – (legal fees, planning, building regulations, insurance) | | £5,000 |
| Total Cost | | £43,000 |
| | | |
| *Sources of funding* | | *Funding* |
| Housing corporation grant | | £13,000 |
| Mortgage | | £20,000 |
| Non-recoverable subsidy provided by RSL | | £10,000 |
| Total Funding | | £43,000 |
| | | |
| *Funding implications for the RSL* | *Income* | *Expenditure* |
| The rent is set at | £60 a week | |
| Management and maintenance costs | | £20 per week |
| Mortgage | | £40 per week |

The RSL will need to establish with the joint funders their level of contribution. A special needs project could be funded 50 per cent by the Housing Corporation using SHG and 50 per cent by social services joint funding to achieve the new build property. Working in partnership with a local authority is an asset to an RSL in terms both of securing funding and in targeting potential tenants, hence there is likely to be competition by RSLs for preferred partner status with an authority.

D) GENERAL HOUSING FUNDING

The additional funding for general housing projects usually has to be raised by the RSL through a loan or mortgage.

The following example from the author's experience of working with an RSL illustrates the complexity of funding a new build house and the subsidy, or non-recoverable cost which the RSL will have to carry.

It shows the costs that the RSL has to consider in building the housing, set against the revenue that the rented housing will generate. The rents have to be cost effective and need to cover housing management and maintenance costs, insurance and voids (loss of rent on unlet property).

THE PROCUREMENT OF PRIVATE SECTOR HOUSING FOR SALE OR RENT

The provider is usually a large private house builder who needs to achieve housing which will sell and still make a profit.

| | |
|---|---|
| The enablers = | The local authority |
| The providers = | Private house builder |
| The regulators = | NHBC (The National Housebuilding Council) and local authority. |

A) ACTION BY THE HOUSE BUILDER

- *Finding a site*

  The house builder will need to consider the market potential when looking for a site, and the quality and appearance of the proposed housing. Is the building to suit the needs of people on modest incomes who are first time buyers, or more expensive housing with large gardens and individual style?

- Production of outline scheme

- Planning requirements

- Feasibility study

- Raising funding

  This will be done on a commercial basis, with the house builder looking at the expected returns for the necessary outlay. In many cases it will involve negotiation with banks and other prospective investors to convince them of the viability of the scheme. Both investors and the house builder need to make a profit.

B) ACTION BY THE REGULATOR

The National House Building Council (NHBC) was set up to act as the regulatory body for private housebuilding development.

A technical and financial check is made on house builders who apply to be registered with the NHBC. Once accepted, the builder is then under an obligation to abide by the NHBC's rigid rules and to meet their technical standards on workmanship, design and materials used.

Spot-checks during the construction of a development are made by the NHBC's own inspectors. Once a home is built to the exacting standards, the NHBC awards its ten year warranty, called the buildmark.

THE PROCUREMENT OF PRIVATE SECTOR ONE-OFF DEVELOPMENTS

| | |
|---|---|
| The enabler = | The local authority |
| The provider = | Small building firm<br>The landowner |
| The regulator = | Building society – conditions of mortgage<br>Local authority planning and building<br>regulations |

The enabling role of the local authority is limited to planning permission and building regulations. It is unlikely this kind of development will be covered by the strategic plan.

If the provider is already the landowner and providing for their own use the following stages are required:

- produce a design
- obtain outline planning permission
- carry out a feasibility study
- find funding – this could be a mortgage.

*Stage 3: Design*

Clear information is required on what the design is intending to achieve. The process of design will vary considerably between developers. In general, if the design of a property is to be influenced by a particular identified need it is essential that it is incorporated as early as possible into the process and should be included in the feasibility study of the scheme.

The following example illustrates the author's experience of what can be achieved by an occupational therapist and RSL working together.

---

### Example

The RSL had obtained outline planning permission to build a large development of social housing.

An occupational therapist approached the RSL with a requirement for new wheelchair accessible accommodation for a child and his family. Their existing accommodation was unsuitable and not adaptable to the needs of a wheelchair user. The RSL looked at the possibility of alterations to the design of the proposed development, which was still at the feasibility study stage. It was agreed that it would be possible to build a four-bedroom family house with two bedrooms for the disabled child and his parents provided on the ground floor and wheelchair access achieved throughout the ground floor.

It was possible to influence the design because negotiations were at an early stage. There was sufficient land to enable the house to be included in the scheme. The RSL was able to fund the additional work. The occupational therapist was able to identify the need and provide a detailed design brief at an early stage.

---

ARCHITECT'S DESIGN BRIEF

Before an architect can design anything, a clear brief of what is required needs to be compiled by the house provider. Without this, misconceptions can occur. The brief needs to consider such points as:

- What the future tenant requires
- The number of people to be housed. For example developers talk in terms of a two-bedroom, three-person property, meaning there will be one double and one single bedroom.
- Whether a standard single bedroom will be of adequate size for a disabled person.

The architect could be using a book such as the *New Metric Handbook Planning and Design Data* as a reference (Tutt and Adler 1979). Space standards need to be clearly defined to avoid confusion. Standard bathrooms in new houses are usually very small.

Designers and developers often find it difficult to comprehend the requirements of disabled people who are not wheelchair users, but there are many issues to be considered. For example:

- Specific features such as flashing light doorbells for those with hearing impairment can be added to the design, as can additional stair rails and grab rails if the construction of the property is capable of supporting these in the first place.

- Top hung windows which are easily operated and have accessible catches, and properly illuminated houses are useful for all people, as are properties with level access and accessible car parking.

- Houses with ground-floor toilets are not only an advantage to disabled people but also mothers of young children.

This is not a comprehensive list but merely highlights the need to establish the brief.

Once the house design is established, the second stage of planning permission is required to confirm the design is acceptable. Also at this stage, building regulation approval needs to be obtained. The design stage is concluded when all details of the scheme are agreed and a contractor is ready to start on site. Beyond this stage it is difficult to make any major changes to design of the scheme.

It is important that if the disabled person has already been identified for a property they are included at this stage and the final plans are seen by and agreed with them. (Chapter 5 looks specifically at design guides and standards.)

FLEXIBILITY OF DESIGN

Occupational therapists should work with developers and architects in the early planning stages of schemes to ensure that the basic design will meet the needs identified in the design brief. With good design a property can result in a flexibility which only requires adjustments or fine tuning for subsequent occupants.

In the author's experience a common problem is that of trying to fit a stairlift on staircases within general housing stock. These could be built to a standard which would enable a stairlift to be installed in the future. Designers need to achieve unobstructed and adequate space for transferring at both top and bottom of a straight staircase. By ensuring the stairs are straight and radiators are not fitted on the wall at top and bottom of the stairs it would be simple to install a stairlift if it should be required.

THE DESIGN PROCESS TO ACHIEVE PUBLIC SECTOR SOCIAL HOUSING

*Design and build*

Most new build social housing is achieved using 'design and build'. This is a process by which the RSL employs an agent ('employer's agent') to oversee the process of design and construction.

The employer's agent will obtain tenders from design and build contractors. This means that the contractor is responsible for producing a detailed design of the scheme, the individual house design and the construction of the housing. The contractor will employ an architect to produce working drawings detailing the scheme. The contractor will liaise through the employer's agent with the RSL on all aspects of design, cost and construction. The importance of full consultation with disabled people, at all stages of the planning process cannot be over-emphasised.

The design and build process results in the following chain of command.

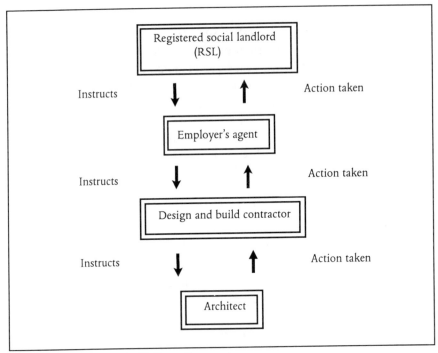

*Figure 6.3: The design and build chains of command*

The design and build process will have to consider the design brief. For example, if the housing is to include three wheelchair accessible bungalows on a scheme of 50 houses, this will have design and cost implications. Occupational therapists will be able to provide an on-going contribution to the design process, specification of fixtures and fittings, and detailing to meet individual needs, once involved in the chain of events. This is preferably achieved by direct contact with the RSL, who is responsible for the initial design brief and for instructing the employer's agent. No changes can be made to a scheme without the agreement of the RSL or other housing provider.

## 'TRADITIONAL' BUILDING PROCUREMENT

The traditional method could be employed when developing a small specialist scheme.

The RSL will commission an architect, who will produce a detailed specification and go out to tender. Several building contractors are asked to price a specification within a given tender period. The tenders are returned to the architect in sealed envelopes and opened on the last day of the tender period. The lowest-priced contractor usually wins the tender and is appointed to carry out the work. The architect oversees the work as the RSL's consultant.

## TENANT SPECIFIC DESIGN

At the stage of identifying disabled people for specific new build social housing, the disabled person now becomes paramount in the process. The occupational therapist's role is to facilitate their independent living opportunities by ensuring that all identified specific features are incorporated into the property. This can be as simple as the positioning of the sink taps, or could involve the assessment of need for a ceiling track hoist and recommendation to the developer for provision of this specialist equipment to be included in the design.

The allocation of a property to a disabled person has to be achieved early in the new build process to ensure their additional individual needs are built into the design. This is the most cost effective way to achieve what is required. If the allocation is not achieved early, the property will be built to the general agreed standards. The delay in allocation also leads to frustration and misunderstanding between occupational therapists and the developers.

The processes of design and build should allow for the disabled tenant's specific needs, the funding of which has to be achieved within the project, either by establishing initial funding for the anticipated costs or applying to the housing corporation for extra funding for adaptations. The latter is specifically for works required by the prospective tenant and is not always successful.

## TRANSLATING ASSESSMENT INTO DESIGN

The disabled person may have gone through a long period of self-assessment before all his or her needs are identified. This is especially important where disabled people are leaving residential care or a parental home to live independently in the community.

The occupational therapist has to consider the disabled person's needs. Is it likely that skills will improve or deteriorate? Will care support be required or can the desired level of independence be achieved with the right property and appropriate equipment?

To promote useful dialogue between the occupational therapist, disabled person and the developer it is essential for all to have the relevant material. This should include a site layout identifying the plot and all external works, elevations of the building, a 1:20 scale working drawing of the property which includes details of plumbing and an electrical layout showing position and heights of switches and sockets. It should also include information which is contained in the building contract, particularly details of kitchen and bathroom fittings and specification of windows, doors and floor finishes.

In addition, information on any specific design features which are already in the contract needs to be made available, such as wiring installed for a door entry system or ceilings reinforced for overhead tracking.

If all this information is available to the occupational therapist it is possible to identify what is already provided within the building contract before making any specific recommendations. It will also assist in ensuring the disabled person is fully aware of the end product and overcome any misconceptions as to the finished effect.

THE DESIGN PROCESS TO ACHIEVE PRIVATE SECTOR HOUSING DEVELOPMENTS FOR SALE OR RENT

Large, private house builders are usually building to standard specifications and standard house types. They will either have an architectural/technical department or buy in these services. They are unlikely to employ architects to design individual housing.

The basic cost of the housing will be increased if any variations are requested. The purchaser will be expected to pay these costs. Most disabled people are unable to commit themselves at the design stage and are likely to purchase a standard house which could then require adaptations or fine tuning to meet their specific needs.

THE DESIGN PROCESS TO ACHIEVE PRIVATE SECTOR ONE-OFF DEVELOPMENTS

The landowner could employ an architect to design a property, or alternatively employ a small builder to design and construct. The design and specification can change if the landowner wishes to do so, but must adhere to the planning permission. If the basic design criteria is not clearly defined a 'house' will be built which might not fulfil the intended purpose. The following example from the author's experience highlights the point.

---

### Example

---

David Walton sustained severe head injuries in a road traffic accident and was granted a substantial compensation award. This was intended to cover his care needs for the rest of his life and enable him to achieve suitable housing.

He bought a piece of land and approached several local builders to give him quotes for the building of a bungalow. A three-bedroom bungalow was built but it soon became apparent that it was not practical for David's specific needs.

No design brief had been established and no thought given to his method of transferring and achieving maximum independence, which affected the space required.

At this stage an occupational therapist working with a local architect designed adaptations to the bungalow, having established a design brief which took account of David's specific needs. A new bathroom had to be created with space allowed for transferring on to the toilet, a level-access shower replaced the step in shower cubicle and an accessible kitchen was designed to enable him to assist in cooking his meals. All these features could have been included at the initial design stage and would have saved a great deal of time and expense.

---

*Stage 4: Construction*

THE PROCESS OF CONSTRUCTION

There are several stages to the construction process:

- marking out the site to ensure all buildings, boundaries, roads and services will be in the correct position
- laying the foundations and the installation of services
- completion of the shell of the building
- first fixing – wiring for electrics and pipework for water drains and gas supplies
- second fixing – installation of kitchen and bathroom fittings
- snagging by the architect or agent to ensure the building is to the agreed specification.

During the stages of construction the architect or clerk of works will visit the site to oversee the progress of the work. The local authority will also carry out inspections to ensure that planning standards are adhered to. Building control will monitor the implementation of building regulations. The site foreman or manager is responsible for the daily operations and organisation of the site.

All relevant design information is given to the contractor before the construction process commences. The contractor will be working within his contract to provide housing to a certain standard at an agreed cost. Any deviations or additions to the scheme will now require agreement between the developer, contractor and local authority. It is likely that any changes will increase the cost to the developer and result in delays to the progress of the scheme.

CONSTRUCTION OF PUBLIC SECTOR SOCIAL HOUSING

The construction of social housing has to adhere to the scheme development standards laid down by the housing corporation.

### Involvement of the occupational therapist

When it becomes necessary to change the plans because of unforseen work it is important that the occupational therapist involved is notified. The smallest change in detail can significantly affect the use of a building for disabled people, as the following example illustrates.

---

### Example

A RSL incorporated several two-bedroom wheelchair accessible bungalows into a large housing scheme. An occupational therapist was involved at the design stage and in identifying the disabled tenants. A great deal of thought had gone into the design of the kitchen – it had adjustable-height units and the need to keep the space under the sink clear had been discussed. At first fixing the drains from the kitchen sink went straight through the floor immediately below the sink, thereby blocking wheelchair access. Fortunately, this was picked up by the occupational therapist at an early stage in the construction when it was still possible to modify the drains.

---

### Involvement of the disabled person

Once the disabled occupant has been identified for a property it is important that he or she is kept informed by the occupational therapist during the stages of construction. It is unlikely that the disabled person will be able to visit the site until it is at a late stage. Safety regulations and the conditions of the contractors insurance will only allow authorised people on the site. Anyone visiting the site to attend multi-disciplinary site meetings, must conform to safety regulations by wearing a hard hat and appropriate hard-toed footwear.

It is vital that the occupational therapist attends these meetings to act as the liaison point for the disabled person.

Special arrangements for access need to be made with the site manager for both the occupational therapist and disabled person to visit the site when it is agreed that it is safe to do so, usually after second fixing.

The site visit gives an opportunity for the disabled person to try out bathroom and kitchen fittings and other particular design features. Any final adjustments can then be identified before the snagging stage. Some contractors will include a contingency sum in their costs to cover small adjustments to the specification detail. This is not always the case, however, and extra funding could be required from other sources. It is important to establish how to achieve this.

On the occasions when a disabled occupant is not identified until the property is nearing completion, his or her specific needs will not have been included in the contract.

Any identified need not included in the property will have to be incorporated as an adaptation. Some specific individual requirements of the identified tenant can be funded through the housing corporation adaptations budget.

CONSTRUCTION OF PRIVATE SECTOR HOUSING DEVELOPMENTS

The construction of private sector housing is not controlled in the same way as social housing. Most large private house builders will be constructing to a basic design and as inexpensively as possible within the local authority planning regulations. It is often difficult to convince house builders to give thought to specific features such as access. This is highlighted in the following example from the author's experience.

---

### Example

A local authority with a policy to try and achieve level access in all new build housing gave planning permission to a private house builder on the condition that houses with level access were built. The housing development extended on to an adjoining authority's land where there did not appear to be a similar policy. The house builder could not understand the need to build houses with level access because it had never been needed previously. The builder complied with the authorities wishes and built houses with level access, but once over the boundary onto the adjoining authorities land, the builder reverted to building houses with doorsteps. The house builder was still convinced that this was the right way to do it, because this was the traditional way to keep water out.

---

### Example (continued)

---

Building with level access had not affected the cost of the houses and would be of benefit not only to disabled people, but also parents with prams and pushchairs. Because of entrenched attitudes the house builder insisted on building the inaccessible unless forced to do otherwise. Many local authorities have incorporated a level access policy in their development plans, but this is being challenged by private developers who wish to build traditionally.

---

ONE-OFF DEVELOPMENTS

The construction of a one-off property is again bound by the local authority planning regulations. The disabled person as the identified occupant has much more control over the process especially if he or she is funding the development. Advice from architects and occupational therapists is valuable but the final decisions on construction costs are made by the funder.

It is still important that the agreed scheme is adhered to, as any changes will affect costing and possibly the use of the property by the disabled person.

The construction of one-off properties will be more expensive than a property on a large housing scheme, because materials are purchased in small quantities and labour is not as cost effective. However, the finished results for a disabled person can be so effective that the extra cost is worthwhile, especially if long-term needs have been considered.

*Stage 5: Occupancy*

THE OCCUPANCY OF PUBLIC SECTOR SOCIAL HOUSING

This is the stage at which the property is formally 'handed over' from the contractor to the RSL. Prior to handover the architect or employer's agent has completed the snagging stage and is satisfied that the property meets the specification. A certificate of practical completion is then issued.

It is important for the occupational therapist to snag their specific design brief with the architect. This will ensure that the disabled person does not have a problem when they move in because a grab rail has been incorrectly sited or a door entry phone is not working.

The contractor has to complete the scheme within the contract period; if this deadline cannot be met and there is no justification for the delay the contractor starts to forfeit money from the contract. The architect will have issued interim certificates at the various stages of construction to enable the contractor to receive interim payments, but the final payment is dependent upon completion and the snagging by the architect.

Any uncertainty over the handover date leads to difficulties for the RSL and the identified occupants. Disabled people require as much advance notice as possible of the completion date, especially if a care package needs to be arranged. The care provider will also require adequate notice. Some disabled people will need a great deal of support at this stage. The occupational therapist can assist by ensuring that all agencies are kept informed and by taking the new tenant around the property as soon as possible after handover. This is especially important if a visit has not been achieved during the construction process. The disabled person might require some training or assistance in the use of new equipment such as a clos-o-mat toilet or kitchen equipment.

### Social housing for rent

Ideally the tenants will have been identified at an early stage and all their requirements built into the property. On occasions when a tenant has not been identified before handover, the RSL is under pressure to let the property. A 'void' or unlet property produces no rent. The RSL cannot financially support a long void and could be forced to consider inappropriate tenants to fill the property. Chapter 4 deals with the housing register and ways to try and overcome this problem.

### Social housing for shared ownership

The RSL has to sell the properties and will often have a show house and produce packs of publicity information. This is an opportunity for disabled people who are interested and able to afford the purchased 'share', either through a mortgage or the sale of an existing property. The disabled person can work with an occupational therapist and the RSL to achieve modification within the property and ensure it meets their needs. The disabled person has to make a commitment to purchase at an early stage in the construction to ensure that such detail as the toilet being the correct height and type is achieved. Further detail such as the height of the kitchen worktop and position of units could also be adjusted.

If the disabled purchaser has very specific needs which have not been incorporated in the property such as a ceiling track hoist, these could be met by a private advance payment to the RSL who will then provide them. Alternatively, the disabled person can purchase the property and then apply to social services and the local authority for adaptations funded by a disabled facilities grant. Details of this are explained in Chapter 3.

Shared ownership property is the responsibility of the purchaser and is not maintained by the RSL.

Some shared ownership properties do have services such as a warden or caretaker which are paid for under a service agreement in addition to the rent.

THE OCCUPANCY OF PRIVATE SECTOR HOUSING

### Private housing developments

A private house builder needs to sell property at an early stage in the development and will often have a 'show home' to enable potential buyers to see the finished product. Disabled people who require any changes to the basic design need to be clear how this will be achieved. It is important to be fully aware of what is to be provided in the property before the purchase is completed, as illustrated in the following example from the author's experience.

---

### Example

A private house builder developed a scheme of luxury flats for elderly people to purchase. Each block contained six flats on three floors. The first- and second-floor flats had access by stairs and a lift large enough for a wheelchair. Each flat was linked to a warden service and the occupants paid a yearly service charge for maintenance.

This seemed like the ideal setting for elderly people who wished to sell their existing house and move to a sheltered environment whilst remaining owner-occupiers.

For most people this did work well, but it presented problems for one elderly lady with limited mobility. She decided to buy a flat on the second floor because it would be quieter with no one above her, and also the view would be better. She saw a ground-floor flat before purchasing and was assured that the flats would 'all be the same'. The flats were alike with the exception that door closers were fitted on all the internal doors of her second-floor flat. This was to comply with fire regulations, which apply in certain circumstances to all flats above the first floor in multiple occupancy buildings. The elderly lady could not get through the doors with her walking frame and had to wedge them open. The entrance door to the flat also had a door closure fitted which she found very difficult to use. There are timed closers available which can be fitted to doors but these are expensive and not always a satisfactory way of trying to overcome this problem. If this elderly lady had been aware of the necessity to have the door closers on the second floor, she could well have chosen to buy a ground-floor or first-floor flat where this restriction did not apply.

The house builder did not seem to appreciate that door closers could restrict access for disabled people and did not show any interest in helping her to overcome the problem once she had bought the flat.

---

ONE-OFF DEVELOPMENTS

When the property is for the personal use of the disabled owner, they will have decided details of specification as the property was constructed. So long as the property meets required building standards and is inspected by the local authority on completion, the owner can move in when they are ready to do so.

If the property is to be privately rented by a disabled person, hopefully all their needs will have been considered. If they or subsequent tenants should require adaptations, these could be achieved through the disabled facility grant system, with permission of the owner.

## Conclusion

New build housing development is a complex process involving many different agencies and disciplines. This chapter has tried to highlight the problems which could be encountered and to raise awareness of the need for professionals to communicate with each other and with disabled people. The following summary identifies the stages at which it is useful for disabled people and occupational therapists to have involvement:

- Identifying need, by compiling a register of disabled peoples housing needs.
- Development of planning/management strategies by social services and the health authority working with local authority housing departments.
- Initial design of scheme working with developers and architects at the early design stage.
- Tenant-specific needs, to ensure that individual needs are identified and funding is available.
- First fix – the building stage when electrics and plumbing are installed as it is costly to change these later.
- Second fix or half-way snagging – the building stage when bathroom and kitchen fittings are installed and minor adjustments might need to be made.
- Snagging – when the building work is completed, before the contractor hands over to the provider. It is important to check that all identified requirements are not only included but securely fitted in the correct position.
- Tenancy – moving into the property. Training on the use of equipment and possibly care staff involvement.

- Final snagging – at the expiry of the defects liability period. This is usually six months after the official handover.

It is very important that all policies relating to the provision of new build housing, especially social housing, are made public, agreed at high managerial level and are seen to be adhered to in practice.

## Glossary

| | |
|---|---|
| *Approved costs* | Development costs approved by the Housing Corporation. |
| *Architect's appointment* | The terms under which an architectural consultant is appointed. |
| *Architect's brief* | The instructions given to an architect which describe the client's design requirements. |
| *Architects interim certificate* | The certificate issued by the architect at various stages in the building process. The client then pays the contractor the due amount. |
| *Bids* | The annual process by which an RSL makes a bid to the housing corporation for the following year's development programme. |
| *Building regulations* | The minimum construction standards required. Formal approval is required by the local authority. |
| *Certificate of practical completion* | The certificate issued by the architect on completion of the work (handover). |
| *Clerk of works* | Employed by the architect to inspect the building work at various stages. |
| *Competitive tendering* | Pricing on the common information supplied for building contracts. |
| *CDM* | Health and Safety Regulations 1994 applying to Construction, Design and Management. |
| *Contingency* | A sum included in the building contract for unforseen work. |
| *Defects liability* | The period, usually six months after practical completion, when a contractor is financially responsible for rectifying any defects. |
| *Density* | The number of units to be fitted on to a scheme. |
| *Employer's agent* | The client's representative for design and build schemes. |
| *Exchange of contracts* | Legal commitment to purchase. |

| | |
|---|---|
| *Extension of time certificate* | Issued by the architect allowing an extension to the contract without a penalty to the contractor. |
| *Feasibility study* | An assessment of viability at an early stage of the project. |
| *Handover* | The formal stage of handing over the property from the contractor to the housing association. |
| *Housing Corporation* | The body responsible for supervising and controlling registered social landlords in England. |
| *On Site* | Building work started. |
| *Performance review* | The Housing Corporation monitoring of performance standards. |
| *Prime Cost (PC) sum* | A provisional sum included in the tender for unforeseen circumstances. |
| *Quantity surveyor* | A consultant responsible for calculating the costs of a development. |
| *Retention* | Money kept back to ensure the contractor completes defects. |
| *Service charge* | A charge for communal costs incurred by a development, such as provision of a warden. |
| *Scottish Housing* | The national housing agency in Scotland – the equivalent of the English Housing Corporation. |
| *Shared ownership* | Housing to part purchase, part rent. |
| *Site report* | The survey of the site, particularly the ground condition, prior to purchase. |
| *Sketch scheme* | Initial design sketches to look at the feasibility of a scheme. |
| *Snagging* | The inspection of a property by the clerk of works, architect or the employer's agent before handover of the property. |
| *Tender period* | The length of time which a contractor is given to submit a written, priced tender for a particular job. |
| *Tranche agreement* | Fixed payments at set stages, usually exchange of contracts, start on site and practical completion. |
| *Valuer* | The consultant who assesses the price of new sites and properties. |
| *Working drawings* | The detailed architect's drawings used by the contractor on site. |

# References

*The Building Act* (1984) *The Building Regulations (Amendment). Approved Documents A,B,C,D,E,F,G,H,J,K,L,M,N and Regulation 7.* London: HMSO.

*Housing Act* (1996) *Section 162, Allocation of Housing Accommodation.* London: HMSO.

The Housing Corporation (1993) *Scheme Development Standards.* London: The Housing Corporation.

The Housing Corporation (1994) *Performance Standards.* London: The Housing Corporation.

Joseph Rowntree Foundation (1995) *Health and Housing: The Extent of Inter-agency Working.* Findings Fact Sheet 74, November. York: Joseph Rowntree Foundation.

Joseph Rowntree Foundation (1995) *The Effect of Community Care on Housing for Disabled People.* Findings Fact Sheet 115, September. York: Joseph Rowntree Foundation.

*Town and Country Planning Act* (1990) *The Planning Acts.* London: HMSO.

Tutt, P. and Adler, D. (1979) *New Metric Handbook: Planning and Design Data.* Oxford: Butterworth Architecture.

# CHAPTER 7

# Living Independently

*Veronica Watts and Christine Galbraith*

This chapter looks at how three different groups of people can achieve or may progress towards greater empowerment and/or independence in their lives in the domestic context: people with physical disabilities, people with learning disabilities, and people with mental illness.

Each section is written from the experience of the authors in working with disabled people, as well as from published research. The groups have different needs and solutions, and different options for achieving their objectives. It is acknowledged that some people's needs will fall into more than one group. Achieving independent living in relation to housing is a complex process and involves not only the removal of physical barriers but should also satisfy needs which include 'privacy, security and safety, affiliation and belonging, recognition and status and that these basic needs vary with age, culture and psychological make-up of the individual' (Kestenbaum 1996, p.7)

Acknowledgments

The contributions from the anonymous interviewees were invaluable. Also drawn upon was the experience and knowledge gained directly from the many disabled people I came in contact with while writing this chapter and during my working life. Special mention is given to the following disabled people – Ken Davies (Chair, Derbyshire Coalition), John Evans (Chair, BCODP Independent Living Sub-committee), Carl Ford (Disability Consultant) and Neville Simpson. Occupational therapy colleagues have contributed both spoken and written comments. Many housing associations and organisations of disabled people gave information on the services they offer. *Veronica Watts*

To those people with and without learning disabilities who gave me the greatest challenges of my career – thank you. In particular Janet and the late Iris, Ivy, Val, Gary and Gary, who among many taught me to reflect critically on my work. My reward was immeasurable when you approved of my efforts. *Christine Galbraith*

## People with physical disabilities

### Introduction

The previous chapters have looked at the people, professionals and agencies that disabled people may need to involve to work out solutions to their housing problems in progressing towards greater independence or choice in their lifestyle. When continuing support is required in the form of personal care or assistance and/or professional services, the availability of that support, where it comes from and who directs it is of crucial importance to the disabled person concerned. In the past, residential or hospital care was for many the only place for such care to be delivered, if living at home with the family as informal, i.e. unpaid, carers was not a possible or chosen option. This chapter will show how the present statutory services and changes in the social structure are gradually enabling more disabled people to have control over the services they need, although scarce resources can still present real and frustrating difficulties.

During the 1980s disabled people put well-organised pressure on national and local government to bring about policies and legislation towards improving their civil rights which became known as the Independent Living Movement. John Evans, chair of the British Council of Organisations of Disabled People (BCODP) Independent Living Sub-committee gives this definition of independent living:

> Independent living is the ability to choose what a person wants, where to live and how, what to do, and how to set about doing it. These goals or decisions about a person's life and the freedom to participate fully in the community have been and will continue to be the essence of Independent Living. It is also the taking and establishment of self control and self determination in the total management of a person's everyday life and affairs. (Laurie 1991, p.2)

On the international scene, the European Network on Independent Living (ENIL) agreed the principles of independent living in the 'Strasburg Resolutions', (ENIL 1989; Barnes 1993) and the 'Definition of the Term "Independent Living"' (ENIL 1992; Barnes 1993).

In this country, the Housing, Independent Living and Disabled People conference in 1990 focused the attention of disabled people and service providers on the issues of independent living, and what changes were needed to give equal opportunities to all disabled people and the progressive removal of all discrimination. Rachel Hurst, a founder member of Greenwich Centre for Independent Living and BCODP representative for Disabled People International (DPI), made a keynote speech at that conference. She argued 'that the whole question of independent living as the tool for our empowerment is part and parcel of our struggle for equal opportunities' (Laurie 1991, p.9). However, many disabled people may consider that choice and empowerment have just not happened.

People who consider independent living as a way of widening their opportunities in life require the following (Ford 1996):

1. Information
2. Counselling and peer support
3. Personal assistance
4. Technical aids
5. Housing
6. Education
7. Transport.

### Profiles of users

The profiles below show how some individuals with a need for assistance during the day and night can employ or control their own assistance, and to what extent the above components were available to them or otherwise. They show some of the advantages and difficulties involved. Contact was made with some of these people through BCODP – the umbrella group for all the local centres for independent living (CILs) – while others were approached through the occupational therapists involved. They were interviewed in the latter half of 1996.

#### PROFILE I: NEIL

> Neil became disabled at the age of 28 following a car accident. He broke his neck at level C5/6 and now needs full 24-hour care due to almost complete paralysis below his back. After one unsuccessful attempt at moving out of the 'horrors of institutional care', he had a second chance, and moved out in 1985.

#### Housing

The ground- and first-floor flats of a Victorian town house were in need of renovation. This allowed the design to accommodate Neil's needs. He was fully involved in the planning process, although with hindsight he would have made some different requests. Neil was to live on the ground floor, while his carers would have the first-floor flat, licenced and furnished by social services. This allowed Neil his much-valued privacy while maintaining easy access to his carers when required via an internal communication system.

### Personal assistance

The building work took three years, allowing plenty of time to organise the support required. At first community service volunteers were used, but later volunteers were recruited. Advertisements were placed in the national and local press, and applicants were interviewed by the local authority social services (LASS) and Neil, which gave him more control over his life. Approved applicants work for 6–12 months and are paid expenses and pocket money plus food when on duty. Neil explains 'they are resourceful people who come because the experience will stand them in good stead for their chosen career. Most have proved very reliable'. An emergency cover system from LASS is in place, and is available to users in the borough who employ their own carers as well as those using volunteers.

### Funding

This comes from a combination of local authority funding and benefits, including domestic care allowance (not now available).

### Transport

Neil uses indoor and outdoor electric wheelchairs. The immediate environment is level and centrally situated close to all facilities.

### Outcome

Neil says that 'independent living suits me and my present model offers me as much flexibility as I require and avoids some of the disadvantages of an employer/employee relationship'.

PROFILE 2: BETTY

> Betty was born disabled and became involved in the first independent living research group in the country, started in 1979 by a group of young residents in a Cheshire home. She was supported by her peers, as IL was unheard of at this time. The group felt 'they had to prove themselves'.

### Housing

A housing association owns Betty's bungalow which 'is very suitable to my needs as I chose it and negotiated with the association to buy it'. She was involved in the plans for alterations. The initial alterations to the bungalow, using the old grant system, took about a year. This she found difficult as she 'had to try and get everything in place – benefit changeover, employment of staff and so on, all with no definite removal date'. She moved in before all the alterations were complete as 'the person I had hired was on a fixed time scale' and had to be employed. More recently a disabled facilities grant (DFG) and other financial assistance for equipment and adaptations have been provided.

### Personal assistance

Betty employs local people and has total control over who she employs, their wages and their rota of duty. Her staff do the physical tasks 'that I am unable to do'. The most common problem is sickness – 'short notice absence is hard to cover for', and another problem can be sociability as she expects her PAs to mix with friends and family on an informal level. In the beginning she employed foreign people who lived with her, but she found that this did not work and now employs people who can go home or to stay with someone else in their off-duty time. She prefers the person who is going to get her up in the morning to be on the premises then, 'I know I will definitely get up even if I have to wake them when they oversleep!'

### Funding

Her rent is paid by housing benefit and since June 1995 funding for personal assistants has come from the local authority social services (LASS) user-operated care scheme, the Independent Living (1993) Fund and a 'large amount of my income support!'

### Transport

A Ford Escort van driven by her PAs.

### Outcome

Betty has a leading role in the disabled movement and frequently gives the peer support offered by her local centre for independent living to those wishing to set up their own IL project.

PROFILE 3: DONALD

> Donald is 49 and has become progressively disabled from 1984 when he was employed as a Royal Navy diver. He was retired early on medical grounds in 1985. After divorce and a short-term admission to an old people's retirement home, he transferred to a residential home where he stayed for four years.

### Housing

The home was planning a group of eight wheelchair accessible flats on a vacant site nearby. Those residents who expected to become tenants were fully involved in all aspects of the planning procedure, and an occupational therapist was also closely involved. The building was funded by the home and a housing association. The flats took 18 months to build and most of the future residents' requirements were met. These included level access, under-cover garaging and lift access to their front doors. All communal doors open automatically. The flats are well equipped and have an oval or lozenge shape with open plan design. The sleeping and washing area is shielded from the living and kitchen area by a high screen. The flat is wired for an infra-red environmental control system and there is ceiling mounted tracking for a hoist from the bedroom, through the shower/toilet room (no bath) into the hall. The kitchen has wall hung units and an adjustable-height ironing board that doubles as an occasional table. A spacious balcony leads off the living area.

### Personal assistance

Donald has organised the help he needs. This is a mixture of paid assistants, who are paid a retention fee plus an hourly rate when called out sometimes at short notice, a residential home warden service from LCF and family and friends. He can do his own shopping, weather and assistance permitting, but also uses taxis, friends and various delivery services. The shops are some distance from his home but accessible by electric wheelchair in good weather.

### Funding

This comes from his war pension, the Independent Living (Extension) Fund (ILF) and his occupational pension.

### Transport

He uses a manual wheelchair indoors, an electric wheelchair outdoors (transferring independently), and his own car which is driven by another person.

### Outcome

Donald describes himself as 'very lucky'. Being able to shut his own front door – privacy – is the biggest bonus. He accepts that he can and does fight for what he needs, and feels in control.

PROFILE 4: ANDREW

Andrew is a quantity surveyor who became disabled ten years ago. He has needed personal assistance for two years.

### Housing

With his family, Andrew moved to a smaller house on a sloping site before considering adaptations. A ground-floor bedroom and bathroom with access and circulation modifications designed by himself were funded by a DFG.

*Personal assistance*

An occupational therapist was involved in the modifications to his house, who introduced him to the local centre for independent living (CIL) and the social services user operated care scheme. They drew up an assessment of need together. His personal assistants are from the local CIL register, twilight nurses, care assistants from social services together with locally recruited people. His wife works full time, so he tries to make sure she doesn't have to assist him as well. He has some control over when the care assistants and twilight nurses come and complete control over the personally recruited staff during the day. Changing staff is difficult, but he finds university students and some of the people from the local CIL register are the most adaptable.

*Funding*

The local authority money is given at a fixed hourly rate which includes an allowance for emergencies and administrative costs. In Andrew's opinion it is not sufficient to pay his staff an adequate wage and it doesn't cover many of the household tasks that are needed to relieve the burden on his wife. He is working part time doing consultancy work which, with his wife's earnings and his disabled living allowance, helps to make ends meet. He can ask for a review of the assessment at any time.

*Transport*

He doesn't drive himself now, but he works for a local school for multiple handicapped children on their building development programme, and he can borrow their vehicle to be driven by one of his personal assistants.

*Outcome*

Andrew feels his lifestyle is fairly satisfactory, but regrets many of the things he can no longer do, such as having access to the first floor. He and his wife have had to make many adjustments to their relationship and his wife still finds it difficult to cope with other people 'interfering' in her home.

PROFILE 5: ELLEN

Ellen has become increasingly disabled over the years, and was medically retired as unfit for work ten years ago. She was living alone in an upper-floor flat where the access lift was often broken down. It was not until she herself heard of a suitable flat and asked for the tenancy that she was offered the flat she had identified.

*Housing*

Around 1992 she moved into a council, ground-floor flat, built in 1979. She was told it was built to wheelchair standard, but inspection by the author revealed that her flat is not to the Department of the Environment (DoE) space standards. She still does not have wheelchair access to the airing cupboard and wash hand basin. The toilet was altered to suit her but all other adaptations other than repairs, such as level access patio doors, extra storage in the kitchen and changing the position of the oven unit, she had to pay for herself. She has recently had a shed provided for the storage and charging of her electric wheelchair. She has a second bedroom for overnight assistance if this becomes necessary, which at present is used as a study.

### Personal assistance

Ellen's assessment or care plan allows her 35 hours per week. This covers washing, dressing, getting up and putting to bed, with some shopping, preparation of meals and gardening or clerical work, but not social events. These tasks are carried out by care assistants (CAs) from the local authority and privately recruited personal assistants (PAs). She is happy with the degree of control and choice that this gives her, although the private PAs sometimes take advantage of her vulnerability and she is afraid to speak up for fear of losing them. She was once let down when they forgot to turn up – she sat up all night. She has tried private agencies but they 'tended to use me for training purposes'. Emergencies are covered by district nurses or, with her agreement, admission to hospital.

### Funding

It was not until the nursing service was withdrawn because they were providing 'social care' not a 'nursing service', that she was offered the LASS user operated care scheme. This now pays for all CAs and PAs. She has a 100 per cent war pension, disabled living allowance, and an occupational pension. She pays her own rent. The present hourly rate for carers doesn't cover the extra costs of employing people during unsocial hours. She finds she must pay her PAs below the LASS rate to have a reserve for emergencies and to offset costs.

### Transport

She has a car which will accommodate her electric outdoor wheelchair and a manual chair for indoors.

### Outcome

Ellen first heard about independent living from another disabled person, after being advised by her consultant to consider residential care. She finds interviewing future employees very difficult, and appreciates the advice, training and support given by the local CIL.

*The process*

Local authorities have a duty under the National Health Service and Community Care Act 1990 to carry out an assessment of need and design a package of care and services to meet those needs. Therefore each authority must have an assessment procedure and agreed criteria for eligibility in place. This assessment is an important contract which identifies the needs. It is usually carried out with the user by a social worker, occupational therapist or care manager. It is important that the disabled person is given information on the assessment process so they can be prepared and know who will be involved. Personal, domestic and social needs on a daily and occasional basis will be considered. This is the point where peer or advocacy support is most useful if available. The assessment should truly reflect the needs of the user, not the ability of the local authority to provide the service (see Chapter 1). Adaptations and/or equipment may be required to increase the independence of the user and/or reduce the need for assistance or make the personal assistant's job safer and easier. Many schemes are precarious, in that a break down of the support system puts the user at considerable risk; a viable emergency system that gives the user confidence needs to be in place.

WHO MIGHT BENEFIT FROM AN ILS

The user of an independent living scheme (ILS) is no different from any other disabled person who uses the statutory authorities and legislation to gain support, advice, equipment and adaptations to enable them to live independently in their own homes. Independent living schemes offer disabled people in need of a high level of care or support, and who feel capable of doing so, the opportunity to exercise complete or greater control over who meets their personal care needs and when and where they do so. If disability prevents or threatens the independence of a person aged 18–65 years, and that person is in receipt of the top care rate of the disability living allowance (giving access to Independent Living Fund – ILF – funding), or the attendance allowance, (which meets the criteria for other sources of funding), setting up an ILS is an option available to maintain or attain an independent lifestyle. Such an option is now available to people with disabilities, people with learning disabilities and people with emotional or mental distress, at the discretion of the local authority concerned. An ILS can be set up in many different ways, some with peer support and others with help from statutory services, or a mixture of the two. It is an option for many disabled people, but not all. It should be remembered 'that the fundamental philosophy of independent living is the right to choice as a civil right. That includes the right to live in an institution'. (Ford 1996, p.7)

WHERE TO FIND SUPPORT AND INFORMATION

1. *The local authority.* Social services have the statutory duty to make public the services they offer and the criteria for access to those services. Multi-disciplinary, multi-agency teams are required to co-ordinate the different factors. For all potential users access to information is essential and not always easy to achieve (Heaven 1996, p.6).

2. *Advocacy.* This can take many forms but is 'essentially about the effective representation of the interests of people who are disadvantaged or discriminated against and who need support to make their voices heard' (Kestenbaum 1996, p.28). Such support may come from either professional (e.g. an occupational therapist), peer advocacy (a lay person with similar personal experience) or citizen advocacy (e.g. one-to-one relationship with an unpaid volunteer). Non-professional advocacy is being promoted by disability groups and is 'linked closely with Independent Living as that idea has extended to other than young, assertive people with only physical impairments' (Kestenbaum 1996, p.28). The report of a project which aimed to encourage Independent Living among disabled people from minority groups, found that a care management advocacy service employing people from the same culture as the disabled person, helped to overcome many problems of lack of information (Kestenbaum, 1996 p.34).

3. *Organisations of disabled people (e.g. CILs).* These are set up, staffed and controlled by disabled people, and funded in a variety of ways. They have political, advisory and service functions. They are increasing in number and offer a wide range of information, support, training and services accessible to people with disabilities in the areas in which they operate. By 'networking' information can be disseminated countrywide. In general coalitions of disabled people campaign for anti-discriminatory policies both nationally and locally and CIL's provide advice and services for their members and other organisations, such as a deaf signing/interpretation service. Most are registered charities and companies limited by guarantee.

FUNDING

Choice and control are central to the principles of IL and it is not difficult to see that having sufficient money greatly increases the chance of these aims being achieved. Listed below are some sources of income other than Department of Social Security (DSS) benefits:

1. *Local authority social services.* When services reach the value £200 per week other sources of funding come into play.

2. *Independent Living (Extension) Fund.* A government charity for existing users of the original independent living fund.

3. *Independent Living (1993) Fund.* This will pay up to a maximum of £300 per week to new applicants who are already in receipt of £200 worth of services per week from their local authority.

4. *User operated care schemes.* These give cash payments from the local authority via an agency or third party to meet assessed needs. (These may be affected by the new 'direct payments' – see below.)

5. *Compensation after injury or disease.* Any court settlement/award will take into account a full and detailed assessment with costing of all adaptation and support needs. This is only open to those who can successfully sue through the courts. In the absence of a no-fault compensation system 'there will be vast differences of personal income between disabled individuals' (Ford 1996, p.5).

6. *Direct payments.* The Community Care (Direct Payments) Act 1996 was implemented in April 1997 and gives local authorities the power, not the duty, to make direct payments to disabled people aged 18–65, in lieu of services. The aim is to 'increase user's independence by giving them more control over the way the community care services they receive are delivered' (Department of Health 1996a, p.1).

The local authority has a duty to ensure that:

- the user understands his/her obligations, responsibilities and accountability before giving consent
- the level of service agreed is cost effective
- carers' needs are taken into account
- assessed needs are being met
- users financially contribute if appropriate
- a continuing monitoring system is in place
- a complaints procedure is available.

The National Centre for Independent Living (NCIL) has been set up by BCODP, with funding from the Department of Health, to work with local authorities and groups of disabled people to assist in the implementation and development of the 'direct payments' legislation.

## WHAT NEEDS FUNDING?

Primarily, the wages of the personal assistants/care assistants employed and the administrative costs of recruitment and interviewing. The housing costs of the user may be covered by DSS benefits or other income. The costs of being a good employer of full-time staff, such as national insurance, holiday pay, employers liability insurance, statutory sick pay and maternity leave entitlements are not always adequately funded by the options for funding listed above (compensation excepted), although local authorities may use their discretion to support these costs through schemes set up under the direct payments legislation.

## TRAINING

Some training for new skills or updating of existing knowledge/skills will be required by most people who are contemplating independent living for the first time, and may be achieved formally or informally. Some courses are available locally (e.g. social skills courses at a college of further education), while others may be part of the 'in-house' service offered by CILs or through peer counselling. As direct payment schemes are implemented, training for disabled employers, their employees and their care managers is improving the quality of independent living. Individual users' needs will vary enormously but may include a wide variety of personal, social, business and administrative skills.

## HOUSING

### *For the user*

The challenge of any new IL scheme is to have the funding, housing and PAs available at the same time. Planning and applying for the finance and support required can only be done once a property has been identified. Many users have experienced the frustration of having an unfinished property and PAs ready to start work or *vice versa*. The user may consider a variety of options.

- *Transitional or 'move on' housing.* Sometimes it may be appropriate to have temporary or transitional housing while a more permanent solution is found. This can also help to identify what exactly is required. Some housing associations and local or health authorities may have 'trial flats' where equipment and layout of the property can be evaluated. Planning and management of such properties requires team work to co-ordinate housing, social capital and revenue costs such as who pays for furniture and rent. Transhouse (Oswestry) Ltd, a new project for spinal cord injured people, for example, provides short-term accommodation with the opportunity, on discharge from hospital, to acquire the independent living skills they need to regain control of their lives. This prevents even temporary inappropriate admission to institutions which can demoralise the disabled person. The project has an independent living advocate as a facilitator and also gives direct access to the experience of other disabled people.

- *Adaptation.* If the user wishes to return to existing housing and this is adaptable and suitable in other ways this may be the preferred option; finding other adaptable or accessible housing is the alternative (see Chapter 4).

- *Homelessness.* The disabled person has to qualify as unintentionally homeless and vulnerable if leaving hospital, residential care, temporary housing or leaving existing home after a relationship breakdown. If priority is not sorted out correctly, opportunities may be lost (see chapter 8).

### For the Personal Assistants

Increasingly, with the employment of PAs living locally, housing for PAs is not such a problem. If a user needs attention at night, or requires going late to bed and getting up early, however, it is essential to have a room in the user's home where the PA can sleep over. They should also have access to toileting facilities that do not disturb the user.

### Conclusion

The reality of disabled people being independent and taking a full part in society – their civil right – is more likely to occur if the disabled person has control of his or her personal assistance requirements. Any reduction in control over when or who performs that care will reduce the ability of the user to exercise the right to take up employment, or any other chosen activity, inside or outside the home. Some disabled people may be quite content with some of their care being provided by statutory services such as the local or health authority, for a variety of reasons. Some find that residential care as a permanent solution meets their needs most appropriately (Morris 1993, p.55). The important thing is that the disabled person is happy with his or her solution and that he or she has been able to exercise well-informed choice in the matter. All the people interviewed considered their quality of life had been enhanced, although not all were in receipt of funds which enabled them to directly control all the assistance they needed – the criteria of the independent living movement. Public and corporate opinion generally is recognising the need for equality of opportunity in all walks of life. The recent Disability Discrimination Act implemented in December 1996, and the Community Care (Direct Payments) Act 1996 are steps in the right direction in giving disabled people equality of opportunity. However, this book is primarily concerned with housing for disabled people. In the absence of sufficient identifiable, suitable housing and the failure to build new properties to an accessible standard, genuine choice in where to live will remain a lottery.

## People with learning disabilities

*Introduction*

Independent living for people with learning disabilities is achievable but not yet the commonly held expectation. Any of the personal accounts in the previous section could have been from people with learning disabilities, and if they had been it would have been a testimony to the equality of access to a normal life. Unfortunately, however, the belief that no matter the degree of psychological, emotional or physical support needed, all people with learning disabilities have the same right to an ordinary, normal life and all the roles and responsibilities that this brings with it, is a concept that continues to challenge many people – family, carers, friends, service commissioners, planners, providers and people with learning disabilities themselves (Collins 1996). Consequently, similar accounts describing life for people with learning disabilities are all too rare. This section aims to present the influences that hinder or assist the move towards independent living.

To see people with learning disabilities as people first, their disability as an integral part of them, and help them to realise an ordinary lifestyle as of right, has required fundamental changes in the assumptions and beliefs that are attributed to them. As with people who are labelled as having mental health needs, people with learning disabilities are greatly stigmatised by the rest of society. Although described as vulnerable, collectively people with learning disabilities are often thought of as dangerous and at best as bizarre or to be pitied. People with learning disabilities have to prove their worth and readiness in order to be granted any valued role in society. With these attitudinal barriers, the majority of people with learning disabilities have always lived in the community and not in institutions (Collins 1996). However, prior to the 1970s services did not extend into the community. Unless family and friends enabled the people with learning disabilities to live life in a manner that was contrary to the commonly held expectations, people with learning disabilities were not afforded the same experiences and opportunities that non-disabled people expect as of right – to have a home of their own, to further their education, to work, to form relationships, to have a family of their own. By far the most typical experience was that people with learning disabilities found themselves separated and segregated whether by being sheltered in the family home or in the large institutions (Sperlinger 1994).

Services today are challenged to discard the old ways of 'doing to' people with learning disabilities and adopt the new ways that demand a change in the philosophy, requiring providers to 'work with' their users. These new beginnings were seen in the 1970s with the development of the principle of normalisation. Normalisation continues to be used to challenge the worth of traditional provision. It is about giving people with disabilities the patterns and conditions of everyday life which are as close as possible to the norms and patterns of mainstream society (Nirje 1970). Another way of describing what normalisation seeks to achieve for people with learning disabilities is to call it ordinary living. The ordinary living initiative set in motion changes to services along a continuum that has as its consequence independent living.

### The ordinary living initiative

By the 1980s O'Brien (King's Fund 1980) had identified five areas for services to consider when attempting to improve a person's quality of life. These are known as the five service accomplishments of normalisation, sometimes referred to as 'social role valorisation'.

1.  *Community presence.* The right to take part in community life and to live and spend leisure time with other members of the community.

2.  *Relationships.* The right to experience valued relationships with non-disabled people.

3.  *Choice.* The right to make choices both large and small, in one's life. These include where to live and with whom to live.

4.  *Competence.* The right to learn new skills and to participate in meaningful activities with whatever assistance is required. Also for the competence of the community to provide emotional and practical support.

5.  *Respect.* The right to be valued and not to be treated as a second class citizen.

These principles are in keeping with the aspirations of the independent living movement of disabled people in general, and indeed people with learning disabilities themselves are working within user organisations of disabled people to ensure change continues, to enable people to take control of their lives. People with learning disabilities and their carers can request assessment, help and advice from mainstream as well as specialist services such as community teams for people with learning disabilities. The composition of these teams varies from locality to locality, but it is likely that the specialist knowledge and skills of nurses, occupational therapists, physiotherapists, psychiatrists, clinical psychologists, social workers, speech and language therapists, from both health and social services, can be accessed. Nearly all specialist services will claim to be working in ways that enable people eventually to lead ordinary lives. However, the fact that nearly two decades have past and the main objective of supported independent living is still not the usual expectation of people with learning disabilities, serves to illustrate the complexity and depth of change required of attitudes and traditional services providing housing and support.

### Advocacy

Since the early 1980s self-advocacy by people with learning disabilities has been an important force for ensuring society increases the opportunities and resources necessary for independent lifestyles. Accessing mainstream services as well as specialist services is crucial (Collins 1996). People First is such a self-help group run by people with learning disabilities. As an advocacy organisation People First now have experience of evaluating service provision, enabling individuals and groups and providing education and training for disabled and non-disabled people alike.

However there remain many people with learning disabilities who have not yet been enabled to learn to speak up for themselves. Often these are people for whom formal communication such as speech and sign are not possible; they communicate their needs through their actions and reactions to specific situations. For these people peer advocacy and citizens advocacy must be seen as essential to ensure the individual's needs are not compromised in the push for service efficiency. Also seen as crucial is that people who work with and care for people with learning disabilities are informed of the possibilities that make independent living attainable. It has long been recognised that it is these people who make changes happen because they believe they can happen, even if the know-how is not yet in evidence.

But perhaps it is how non-learning disabled people perceive the capabilities of people with learning disabilities to express their own opinions, that hinders or helps with shifting the balance of control in working and caring relationships with people with learning disabilities. It is as if intellect is a pre-requisite to having rights. There is still a vestige of the assumption in society that says people with learning disabilities are so different that the difference means they are not capable of benefiting from the same rights as non-learning disabled people. In opposition to this viewpoint, as evidenced by the fact that they exist, are examples of how people with learning disabilities have been supported to achieve independent living. (The reader is directed towards Ken Simon's book *My Home, My Life* (1995) and Fitton, O'Brien and Willson's book *Home At Last* (1995) for in-depth portrayals of innovative approaches to housing and support for people with learning disabilities.)

*Housing and support*

These services have historically been provided separately from those for other groups of disabled people. Indeed the fact that a person has a label of learning disabilities has in the past been reason enough to deny them access to mainstream services even though they may have needs arising out of an additional disability such as a physical or sensory impairment, being elderly or experiencing poor mental health (many learning disabled people do have additional disabilities). This situation is changing with some existing service providers acknowledging their responsibility to be accessible to all disabled people. These providers train staff to respond appropriately to people with learning disabilities.

The perceived accumulative effect of any disability in addition to learning disabilities is also one of the main reasons that some health providers continue to develop 'special units' especially those for people with learning disabilities deemed to have challenging behaviour, despite best practice guidance which warns against this (Emerson *et al.* 1987). Consequently this becomes the usual alternative for people with learning disabilities and challenging behaviour who are facing homelessness or receiving inappropriate support. Many of the innovative housing and support options have usually arisen out of the breakdown of more traditional residential care coupled with a determination not to fail the person with learning disabilities by reverting to an even more restrictive model of care: '...people with learning disabilities see moving into residential care, no matter how appropriate the support they receive, like a prison sentence. Not knowing if they are ever likely to get out' (Simons 1995).

People with learning disabilities in Britain today are living in hospitals, on residential campuses, in hostels, large or small group homes or adult fostering schemes – all commonly referred to as residential care – or in the family home (Fitton *et al.* 1995), or a home of their own, rented from mainstream landlords or as owner-occupiers, or as a member of a housing co-operative. It is all too easy to label institutions as all bad and other ways of living as desirable. The behaviour of attaching beliefs, funds and services to buildings and not individuals has been identified as one of the main reasons why change has been so drawn out. A better measure of having achieved independent living is to examine the ways in which a person has been supported to have the final say in any decision that shapes their life.

When a person is first referred, usually in a crisis because their housing and support is breaking down, it is now more likely that the initial response will be to meet the user's wishes rather than the perceived needs in the short term. Best practice aims to support the person in their own home through the crisis. Focus then shifts to exploring long-term plans with the person concerned and his or her carers, recognising that the current situation could continue or be radically changed.

PROFILE 6: HARRY

> Harry Benson, leaving residential school at 16 years old, returned to live with his father. After his father's sudden death, when Harry was 35 years old, his extended family requested an assessment of need for him. Harry had led a sheltered life; his father did everything for him. Despite being physically able, healthy and articulate, Harry, reflecting on his life with his father, said 'I know he meant well, but it was like being a prisoner in my own home'.

Harry knows that at times he has an uncontrollable temper which places those with him at risk. He says he does not know why he gets angry. His family cannot be specific either but they feel it has something to do with unexpected upsets to routine and the stress Harry experiences in social situations. Harry sees his greatest immediate need as having meals and heating provided. He does not want to leave his house, but he does not know how to use the appliances within it or how to light the open fire – which also gives him hot water – or organise and execute all the tasks that go with the role of being a home owner. Harry's care manager has arranged for essential services to enable Harry to stay at home – meals on wheels and someone known to Harry to visit daily to light the fire. As an interim measure Harry's cousins are able to support him in managing his finances and matters to do with his father's funeral and estate. Referrals were made to the occupational therapist and clinical psychologist on the team for adults with learning disabilities. Information from specialist assessment with Harry identified the minimum level of support needed so that Harry's daily routines are kept the same as they were before his father's death. As the provider and Harry's relationship develops an increased awareness of each other's strengths and needs will direct its development. This will be the starting point in fashioning a flexible package of care with Harry.

*Supported living initiative*

Building on the premises of normalisation and the five service accomplishments, the supported living initiative as a concept in the UK was developed by the National Development Team (an independent body who provide advice and consultancy services for people with learning disabilities). It too is based on five principles (Kinsella 1993).

### 1. SEPARATE HOUSING AND SUPPORT

The huge institutions provided an inflexible regime of accommodation and support intertwined. It is ironic that the most recent models of provision have the landlord also providing the support (even if to a smaller number of people). Providing these two functions in parallel means that the rights of people with learning disabilities are more likely to be compromised as they have to accept one with the other whether or not both are needed. Collins' *What's Choice Got To Do With It?* (1996) is a study of the consequences of the relationships between housing, support and people with learning disabilities in its multitude of configurations throughout the UK. She concludes:

> Where mainstream services are not available, or do not meet the specific requirements of the individual, the following three conditions should apply:

1. Housing and support should be provided by agencies which are totally distinct and separate.

2. Service users must be party to individual contracts with the providers of both their housing and support.

3. The agencies providing the housing and support must be explicitly committed to respecting the rights of people with learning difficulties. (Collins 1996, p.47)

### 2. FOCUS ON ONE PERSON AT A TIME

This is not as easy as it seems. Many services have been developed around the funding systems and structures which impede this way of working. Some of the tools initially developed to place the service user at the centre of provision have in themselves become inaccessible to people with learning disabilities and bureaucratic. Individual planning systems have been the focus of considerable criticism for this reason (Lindow and Morris 1995).

### 3. OFFER USERS FULL CHOICE AND CONTROL

People with learning disabilities should have the same autonomy as others in the community, for example, hold their own tenancy or mortgage and choose where they want to live and with whom. In law there is no reason why people with learning disabilities can not inherit estates. Currently in society it is thought that such people are not able to make decisions, and the usual course, therefore, is for trusts to be set up. However, these are usually unecessarily constrained and therefore offer little choice and control for the person with learning disabilities. A more contemporary way of safe-guarding the freedom of choice and decision making could be achieved where North American style 'circles of support' are created. This is where a group of people meet on a regular basis to help a person with learning disabilities to meet their life goals. These people are trustees, family friends, and members of the community who know the individual. Sometimes service providers are included but only because they know the individual (Simons 1995).

4. REJECT NO ONE
No matter how great the perceived impact of the person's disabilities, supported living should be available to them.

5. FOCUS ON RELATIONSHIPS
Building on and creating relationships with family, friends and the local community is vital if people with learning disabilities are to be valued citizens. A person with disabilities is less likely to be moved from his/her local community if he/she has established these links.

*Working towards self-determination*

Services that are attempting to improve the self-determination of people with learning disabilities are those that:

1. *Inform potential service users* in a way that is accessible to most people with learning disabilities about the services they provide and how to access them. People with learning disabilities find their community inaccessible to them in many formats but none more powerful than inaccessible information (People First 1994). The best examples of this are those where there is collaborative effort between the user led organisation and the service provider. (People First/Camden Social Services, undated)

2. *Develop assessment procedures* with people with learning disabilities. Securing the resources and additional support needed for the service users to have equality with service providers in the relationship is important (Lindow and Morris 1995). Ownership of the assessment process is seen by people with learning disabilities as crucial (People First, undated). A request for assessment though has to begin with a

perception of need. To this end the clinical psychology service of the Lewisham Adult Learning Disabilities Team has been developing an imperative method of enabling people with learning disabilities to express their level of satisfaction with their existing housing and support arrangements (Hughes and John 1996).

3. *Shift the contracting of services* from providing for large groups of people (also known as bulk provision or block contracting), to core funding and spot contracts (contracts relating to an individual or a small group of people). This is an attempt to bring the spending of resources closer to the control of the individual and therefore the meeting of their actual needs as it would be if they were given direct payments to purchase their own care. Existing services require two levels of funding: core funding to ensure its permanency and project funding attached to adapting services to an individual's needs. For many people with learning disabilities the Independent Living Fund is not an option on its own because their level of assessed need costs are greater than the current £500 per week limit.

4. *Provide flexible levels of support,* that people with learning disabilities can have the appropriate level of support they need whether they are becoming more or less able. This approach has the greatest impact for people as it can secure their home for as long as they wish. They need not move if their support needs change. Likewise if the people with learning disabilities need to move home then their support may be structured so that it can move with them, if they so wish.

PROFILE 7: MICHAEL

> Michael Hinds at 32 years of age had lived with his parents in their council property for 20 years. It no longer met his needs and, in fact, put his carers at risk as it could not be adapted further to ensure safe moving and handling of Michael. Michael, with cerebral palsy described as spastic quadraplegia, uses an individually adapted wheelchair and seating support much larger than the standard issue. He has received day services and respite care from the local learning disabilities hospital since the age of 19. He communicates by using his eyes to indicate yes or no, and understands what is being asked of him only when in the context of the subject.

The hospital was to close, the replacement accommodation being small group homes of up to four people dispersed throughout the borough. Although funded by the health authority, once built the houses would be the property of various housing associations and the people with learning disabilities living in them would be tenants in their own right. Michael was offered a room of his own, to be designed specifically to his needs, in such a house as close to the locality of his choosing as possible and with a limited choice of whom he could live with.

Michael's parents did not wish Michael to leave home and it was not feasible to assess whether Michael would want to move. To remain in the present home would be to put up with an unsafe situation in which paid additional support could not be expected to work. Michael's occupational therapist confidently suggested that the money be allocated to provide a new home for the whole family with a contribution from the council. Michael's family said they could not believe their preferred solution was being suggested by someone from a statutory agency – 'We will believe it when it happens.' It did! A new house was designed with Michael and his parents, in their existing locality and support network of friends and family and within easy reach of additional support from a small group home staffed by people who knew Michael. Additionally, his old home was allocated to his sister and family who play a crucial part in Michael's support. This helped the family emotionally as they had invested money and effort in improving their original council home which continued to benefit Michael and his extended family.

### Conclusion

Achieving independent living is a testimony to equal partnerships between those who ask for help and are enabled to buy the help they want and those who provide the help (Fitton et al. 1995). Not all but many people with learning disabilities want to be actively participating in shaping their services. Richard Maylin of Herts People First is quoted as saying 'We want to be more involved in our services ... to have a more powerful say in our lives' (Simons 1995).

The challenge for those of us who provide services is to ensure the person with learning disabilities and their advocates remain central to any decision making that shapes their lives.

The current social and economic climates in the UK mean that progress towards independent living for the majority of people with learning difficulties is slow. The impediments lie in the transition from large, inflexible institutions with provider led regimes to flexible personal solutions where the assessors recommend plans for each individual's needs. This requires a creative use of finite resources and a basic shift in the way society appreciates that people with learning difficulties have the right to as diverse and personal a life as anyone. The rate of progress is slow and varies across the country, but perceptible change is happening and with the circulation of ideas and sharing of experience it is hoped that this rate will gain momentum.

## People with mental illness

*Introduction*

The Key Area Handbook *Mental Illness* (DOH/SSI 1994) sets out many strategies for promoting mental health and supporting people with an enduring mental illness in the community. The success or otherwise of such 'care in the community' has been well publicised. Of concern to this chapter is the development of 'multi-disciplinary team working, and greater involvement of users and carers' (Department of Health/Social Services Inspectorate 1994, p.12). Services designed to meet the needs of users must always strive for a balance between user empowerment and choice and the safety of both users and society at large. The National Association for Mental Health (MIND) gives the core components for fulfilling the whole person as:

- opportunity for achieving life quality
- personal support during a period of distress
- support during a personal crisis
- practical help at home
- opportunities to assure income
- somewhere to live or stay
- access to paid or unpaid occupation
- access to information that supports fair treatment
- someone to talk to
- opportunities for assuring mobility and travel
- ways of improving access to and contact with services
- opportunities for taking a break.

(Perring, Willmot and Wilson 1995)

*Community mental health services*

The government identified mental illness as one of the key areas in their health strategy and the primary targets set in the White Paper are:

- to improve significantly the health and social functioning of mentally ill people
- to reduce the suicide rate overall

- to reduce the suicide rate of severely mentally ill people.

(DoH/SSI 1994, p.11)

In the housing context the first of these targets is relevant to this chapter, the success of which will affect the other two. Community mental health services are provided by multi-disciplinary teams based in health and/or the local authority and normally consist of:

- a nurse
- a psychiatrist
- a social worker
- an occupational therapist
- a psychologist.

(DoH/SSI 1994, p.141)

These teams have a remit (amongst others) to:

- promote joint working with other agencies
- consult widely with local groups
- implement the Care Programme Approach (CPA).

The essential elements of the CPA are:

- the assessment of health and social care needs
- an agreed care plan
- the allocation of a key worker
- regular review of the patient's progress.

(DoH/SSI 1994, p.126)

In 1996, significant extra money was allocated by the government to 'improve services for severely mentally ill people' which included housing support schemes, and outreach schemes to maintain contact with the most vulnerable people (DoH 1996b).

*Housing – general considerations*

Offers of housing for this group of people, as for other groups, will be dependent on national and local legislation and the degree of vulnerability. The type of accommodation that is most suitable will also be dependent on the stability of the mental health of the applicant and the quality and frequency of any health orientated or user controlled support. Any personal assistance needed is likely to be related to social and leisure activities and

---

### Example

A Health Care Trust Intensive Community Treatment (ICT) Project:

This outreach scheme aimed to provide an intensive service to an identified group of people with serious on-going mental health needs, and to evaluate this work in comparison with standard community care. The findings concluded that ICT increased clients' social and life skills but not their quality of life. Clients' satisfaction with mental health services was increased, and admissions, readmissions, length of stay in hospital and use of duty and out of hours services were all reduced.

---

general living skills which give the user more confidence and independence in their everyday lives. Support to carry out the duties of being a householder may be required, for example reporting or carrying out maintenance or repairs to the property occupied. Voluntary organisations and the private sector offer a number of complementary services to those of the health and social services. The success of any housing placement will depend on accurate assessment of the needs of the individual, delivery of the support agreed as necessary and in-built flexibility to take account of changing needs.

*Housing options*

Housing providers for this group are likely to be housing associations (registered social landlords), and local authority housing departments. Charitable organisations will usually form housing associations to further their concerns. Options are given below which can offer varying levels of support according to need, allowing those just discharged from hospital and those well established in the community the appropriate level of support. Provision, although varyable countrywide, can be described under the following broad categories (with the highest level of support first):

1. HOSTELS

Hostels offer opportunities for self-care in a large group while retaining mutual support of each other and the psychological and practical support of staff from the statutory services.

2. SUPPORTED ACCOMMODATION

This is the bulk of provision for those in a fairly stable situation. Most provide several houses and flats within easy reach of each other and a central office

## Example: 'Hostel in Bristol'

This was set up in collaboration with a housing trust. The building consists of bedsits with communal areas for shared living, blending privacy and independence with reduced isolation. Prior to opening potential residents met and, with keyworkers and the community occupational therapist, began the process of getting to know one another. Practical issues, such as choosing furniture, were managed together. Identifying specific support needs and thereby managing input of staff was evaluated by the community occupational therapist and presented to the management.

Linking residents to the management process was a fundamental goal of the ethos. 'User involvement' was approached by:

- developing the preparation group activities and meetings into weekly residents' meetings

- enabling residents to learn to chair meetings and take responsibility for the agenda

- facilitating user representation on the projects management group

- carrying out a residents' survey with questionnaire, designed by the residents, and with residents interviewing each other with support from staff

- producing a leaflet using a community-based print project, with wording in the 'first person' and containing a synopsis of residents survey.

This approach was possible because of the influence and emphasis of occupational therapy, reflecting the principles of O'Brien's 'accomplishments', also referred to in the previous section (King's Fund 1980), and the support of the housing trust, which had written a service philosophy with stated user outcomes.

staffed by a project manager who, with other staff, provides a flexible support service all or most of the day, with an emergency call system for parts of the day not covered. Sleep-over cover at night is sometimes, but not always, provided. The type of support given includes self-care, budgeting, shopping, cooking and food hygiene and so on. Emotional support and encouragement to participate in the local community activities is also included.

The 'core and cluster' model is used in some areas – usually this consists of dispersed one- and two-bedroom furnished flats within easy reach of a core support centre. All flats have payphones which are pre-programmed to facilitate emergency contact with the 'core' at all times. This requires a higher degree of responsibility from its residents and most are expected to be self-medicating. Residents may stay for a long or short period. They may move on to a more independent lifestyle or, if they become more dependent, to a more suitable establishment which meets their needs. A few housing providers offer flats with individual bedroom, sitting room and kitchen but shared bathroom with one other resident, and floating support which is flexible according to need is available, increasing or decreasing as necessary (see Hostels, above).

### 3. UNSTAFFED GROUP HOMES OR SHARED HOMES

These are usually small rented, furnished homes where each individual has his or her own bedroom, but shares kitchen, living and bathroom facilities. It suits people who get on well together, but probably a maximum of three in any one house is desirable. The tenancy is shared between the occupants. Support may be available on a regular basis from a designated worker, or group of workers, but no resident help is provided.

### 4. SUPPORTED LODGINGS, (OR ADULT PLACEMENT SCHEMES)

This type of scheme recruits and supports a local network of people willing to provide a room in their own home with varying levels of support for single adults. This option suits some single adults, as it can be tailored to meet the individuals' circumstances. Support is provided from statutory services ensuring that the landlords are registered with the authority if necessary.

### 5. SECURE TENANCIES

Many people who have established and stabilised their health and living skills will graduate to this option, although the shortage of available properties and the difficulties of having their needs recognised can mean long and frustrating delays.

## Mental health service user action groups

Also known as the 'Psychiatric system survivor movement', which aims to counteract the 'centuries of discrimination against people deemed to be mad and more recently mentally ill' (Lindow 1994, p.2). Lindow goes on to state that 'until recently, there has been no choice for people who have not felt helped (or indeed, have been harmed) by existing services'; and also 'while noting that the psychiatric system survivor movement has its base in protest, user controlled alternatives recognise that some people need temporary or on-going support because of severe emotional distress' (Lindow 1994, p.4).

The structure of user controlled groups is democratic with members drawn from mental health service users or ex-users. Some are run as charities, others as co-operatives. More have been set up over the last ten years, since the formation of Survivors Speak Out in 1986. Funding is mostly insecure and inadequate but may increase as they are able to demonstrate their effectiveness. Most groups are run on a voluntary basis as few have sufficient funds to allow for paid staff. The importance that all self-help alternatives to mental health services are completely user-controlled and independent of mental health services is stressed (Lindow 1994, p.7) The groups have a wide variety of functions:

- services and training, such as distress awareness training, crisis services, outreach services, housing support
- leisure activities, such as cafe facilities, music/art groups, survivors' poetry groups, holiday clubs.

### Support services

Multi-disciplinary teams and inter-agency co-operation are being encouraged by the government (Department of Health 1995). This means that services will come from health and social services to work together with voluntary organisations, users and users' friends and family. Some of these are developing very flexible services that enable a known person with a need, but not a crisis, to contact a known worker at any time of the day or night. Such services, which vary widely, may include the following:

SOCIAL SERVICES

- home helps trained to work with mental illness
- care plan
- 24-hour emergency duty service.

OCCUPATIONAL THERAPISTS

Usually from the health service, they:

- use analysis and problem solving skills to assess for the type of accommodation and support required to maintain a tenancy
- work to maintain individuals' mental health and their acquisition of social and practical skills to live successfully in the community
- contribute to the housing strategy planning for provision of appropriate housing.

COMMUNITY PSYCHIATRIC NURSES (CPN)

- supporting people in their own homes.

COMMUNITY MENTAL HEALTH CENTRES

These offer a base for the above teams to:

- assess health and social care needs
- carry out interviews
- run clubs
- provide adult education
- provide advice.

(Department of Health 1996, p.10)

HOUSING ASSOCIATIONS AND HOUSING DEPARTMENTS

- support workers with a variety of skills, such as counselling skills, nursing or social care
- support workers with experience in adult survivors of sexual abuse, drug and alcohol misuse and bereavement counselling.

Gaps in services is a risk that can occur in the community setting. Perring *et al.* (1995, p.20) maintain that 'the straight forward way of mapping the gaps and identifying priorities is to ask users what they want and need'. The most common need expressed was for 'someone to talk to, especially out of office hours'.

### Advocacy services

There are many types of advocacy. Such services are available from various statutory and voluntary bodies which may serve specific functions. Self-advocacy or peer counselling is the only form that is user controlled (Kestenbaum 1996, p.28; see also 'Where to find support and information', in the first section of this chapter). Occupational therapists may be the most user friendly of the statutory advocacy services. They always have a liaising role and can start and carry forward the process of integrating back into the community. Examples of advocacy groups from the voluntary sector include:

- Citizens Advice Bureau (CAB), which operates an advocacy scheme
- Kingston Advocacy Group, which uses volunteers to give support and representation on a one-to-one basis.

*Conclusion*

User empowerment in the area of mental health is being actively encouraged by government in the community care legislation. Occupational therapists have a positive role in promoting a return to meaningful employment (work and leisure) but are not always given the opportunity to do so (Munday 1997). A new initiative by a mental health NHS trust in London is combining the aims of making services more 'user orientated' and 'improving the prospects of ex-service users', by a selection criteria which encourages the employment of ex-services users in the trust (*Therapy Weekly* 1997). Will this be a suitable role model for other services? 'Care in the community is not merely the transfer of hospital type care into the community. It is about full integration of a range of services' (Perring *et al.* 1995).

The rate of change is variable with support, services and housing being dangerously below an acceptable level in some areas, leading to many single, mentally ill people ending up on the streets or in prison where their chances are poor to say the least. Full community participation may be a very long-term goal for some individuals, so any step, however small, towards this goal should be encouraged to increase self-esteem and valued roles.


## Useful addresses and sources of information

### Bristol Missing Link Housing Association
7 Pipe Lane, Bristol BS1 5AT.

Supported housing for single homeless women.

### British Council of Organisations of Disabled People (BCODP)
Litchurch Plaza, Litchurch Lane, Derby DE24 8AA.
(Can also provide information about all their member groups.)

### Circles Network UK
c/o Angela Angel, 35 Mangotsfield Road, Bristol BS17 3JJ.

Provide workshops, advice, consultancy services and information on interaction issues and circles of support origin from North America.

### The Independent Living 93 Fund
PO Box 183, Nottingham NG8 3RD.

### Joseph Rowntree Foundation
The Homestead, 40 Water End, York YO3 6LP.

### Leonard Cheshire Foundation
26–29 Maunsel Street, London SW1P 2QN.

### London Boroughs People First
Instrument House, 207–215 Kings Cross Road, London WC1 9DB.

**National Association for Mental Health (MIND)**
15–19 Broadway, London E15 4BQ.

**National Development Team**
St Peter's Court, 8 Trumpet St, Manchester M1 5LW.

**National Centre for Independent Living**
250 Kennington Lane, London SE11 5RD.

**Scottish Association for Mental Health**
Atlantic House, 38 Gardener's Crescent, Edinburgh EH3 8DQ.

**Spinal Injuries Association**
Newpoint House, 76 St.James Lane, London N10 3DF.

**Stonham Housing Association Ltd**
Housing with care. Octavia House, 235–241 Union Street, London SE1 0LR.

**Survivors Speak Out**
33 Lichfield Road, Cricklewood, London NW2.

**Second Step Housing Association**
9 Brunswick Square, Bristol BS2 8PE.

**Transitional Housing for spinal cord injured people**
For a report of Transhouse (Oswestry) Ltd.

Chichester House, Broad Street, Hanley,
Stoke on Trent, Staffordshire ST1 4EU.

**Values Into Action**
Oxford House, Derbyshire St, London E2 6HG.

## References

Barnes, C. (1993) *Making Our Own Choices: Independent Living, Personal Assistance and Disabled People.* Derby: BCODP.

Collins, J. (1996) *What's Choice Got To Do With It?* London: Values into Action.

*Community Care (Direct Payments) Act 1996.* London: HMSO.

Department of Health/Social Services Inspectorate (1994) *Key Area Handbook Mental Illness, 2nd Edition.* London: HMSO.

Department of Health (1995) *Building Bridges: A Guide to Arrangements for Inter-agency Working for the Care and Protection of Severely Mentally Ill People.* London: Department of Health.

Department of Health (1996a) *Community Care (Direct Payments) Act 1996: Draft Policy and Practice Guidance – Consultation Paper.* November. London: Department of Health.

Department of Health (1996b) *£30K in Grants to Improve Services for Severely Mentally Ill People.* Press release, September. London: Department of Health.

Department of Health (1996c) *Local Services for People with Mental Health Problems – The Health of the Nation. London: Department of Health.*

*Disability Discrimination Act 1996.* London: HMSO.

Dunn, P. (1990) 'The impact of the housing environment upon the ability of disabled people to live independently.' In *Disability, Handicap and Society 5,* 1.

Emerson, D. (1987) *Developing Services for People with Severe Learning Difficulties and Challenging Behaviour.* Canterbury: University of Kent, Institute of Social and Applied Psychology.

ENIL (European Network on Independent Living) (1989) *Strasbourg Resolutions.* Agreed 14 April. Copies available from BCODP, Derby.

ENIL (European Network on Independent Living) (1992) 'Criteria for the use of the term "Independent Living"'. In *Independent Living Newsletter,* 3 December.

Fitton, P., O'Brien, C. and Willson, J. (1995) *Home At Last.* London: Jessica Kingsley Publishers.

Ford, K. (1996) *Social Standards, Personal Assistance and Independent Living.* August, Sonnenberg Conference, Hanover, Germany.

Heaven, C. (1996) *The Ticket In: Access to the Welfare State for People with Disabilities.* London: The Leonard Cheshire Foundation.

Hughes, A. and John, F. (1996) *Needs Assessment: Rationing or empowerment?* Unpublished.

Kestenbaum, A. (1996) *Independent Living: A Review.* York: Joseph Rowntree Foundation.

King's Fund (1980) *An Ordinary Life.* London: King's Fund Centre.

Kinsella, P. (1993) *Supported Living: A New Paradigm?* Manchester: National Development Scheme.

Laurie, L. (1991) *Building Our Lives: Housing, Independent Living and Disabled People.* London: Shelter.

Lindow, V. (1994) *Self Help Alternatives to Mental Health Services.* London: MIND.

Lindow, V. and Morris, J. (1995) *Service User Involvement.* York: York Publishing Services.

Morris, J. (1993) *Your Rights to Housing and Support.* London: Spinal Injuries Association.

Munday, C. (1997) 'London's mental health'. *British Journal of Occupational Therapy 60,* 3, 101.

*National Health Services and Community Care Act 1990.* London: HMSO.

Nirje, B. (1970) 'The normalisation principle: implications and comments.' *Journal of Mental Sub-normality 31,* 62–70.

People First (undated) *Oi! It's my Assessment.* London: People First.

People First (1994) *Your Rights to Housing and Support.* London: People First.

People First/Camden Social Services (undated) *Helping to get the Services You Want.* London: People First/Camden Social Services.

Perring, C., Wilmot, J. and Wilson, M. (1995) *Reshaping the Future: MIND's Model for Community Mental Health Care.* London: MIND.

Simons, K. (1995) *My Home, My Life.* London: Values into Action.

Sperlinger, A. (1994) 'Changing services'. In H. Brown and S. Benson (eds) *A Practical Guide to Working With People with Learning Disabilities.* London: Hawker Publications.

Therapy Weekly (1997) April 17, *23,* 40.

## Further reading

Arnold, P., Bochel, H. and Brodhurst, S. (1993) *Community Care: The Housing Dimension.* York: Joseph Rowntree Foundation.

Collins, J. (1992) *When the Eagles Fly.* London: Values into Action.

Hampshire Centre for Independent Living (undated) *HCIL, Guide to Independent Living.* Hampshire: HCIL Books. (31 Churchfield, Headley, Borden, Hants GU35 8PF.)

Hudson, J., Watson, L. and Allan, G. (1996) *Moving Obstacles: Housing Choices and Community Care.* Bristol: The Policy Press.

KeyRing (1993) *Community Living for People With Learning Difficulties.* (Social Care Findings No.41)
York: Joseph Rowntree Foundation.

Mobsby, I. *A Guide to the Responsibilities of Occupational Therapists and their Managers in Regard to Homeless People who Use Their Services.*

*The British Journal of Occupational Therapy* (1996), 59, 12, 559.

# CHAPTER 8

# Specific Areas of Work, Research or Investigation

*Jan Jensen, Jenni Mace, Zeenat Meghani-Wise, Brenda Parkes and Jeremy Porteus*

## Introduction

The broad aim of research is to gain knowledge and insight into specific areas requiring investigation. In this chapter, five specific areas have been used to illustrate examples of research or investigations recently undertaken by five different people where disability and housing feature. These areas are as follows:

- the issues influencing the decision to adapt a home for someone suffering from multiple sclerosis
- homelessness
- the impact of culture on housing adaptations
- housing for elderly people
- designing housing for people with a visual impairment.

Although the topics are diverse, they all seek to portray the users' perspective and avoid being too prescriptive. The sections on adaptations for people with multiple sclerosis and housing for frail elderly people address fairly common problems. These two studies have investigated the views of the user and have adopted a holistic approach. The sections on minority ethnic groups and visual impairment have been included to show two areas which may not be familiar to the reader.

## Exploring the issues influencing the decision to adapt a home for people with multiple sclerosis

*Background*

Working with people with multiple sclerosis (MS) to obtain a satisfactory adaptation to their home requires a wide range of skills on the part of the occupational therapist. While the occupational therapist will have considerable knowledge of equipment or structural changes that may assist the client to utilise their abilities and minimise the structural limitations of their domestic environment, frequently, considerable time needs to be spent in exploring the options and the impact on the family unit. Clients who have apparent functional difficulties often seem unable to accept the need to plan for future changes. MS is characterised by a variable onset of symptoms with no known cause. This results in difficulty in arriving at a definitive diagnosis until properly investigated. The prognosis is uncertain and there is no known cure or effective treatment at present. The course MS takes differs between people and is unpredictable – it may range from being relatively benign throughout life to causing intermittent symptoms over many years. It may be rapidly progressive. Physical symptoms may be obvious, while others, such as fatigue, sensory disturbances, pain and concentration problems, are less evident. People with MS and their families need to determine their own understanding of and develop their own ways of managing the effects of the disease on their lives (Robinson 1988).

*The purpose of the research*

People with MS, when faced with functional problems in their domestic environment which they are not able to solve, may seek assessment and advice from a social services department occupational therapist. Often their functioning, or the ability of their carer to assist them, is restricted by the physical limitations of their domestic environment. In the experience of the author and her colleagues it is not infrequently found that people with MS struggle to carry out activities of daily living without the use of equipment or modifications to the environment and seemingly put themselves and/or their carers at risk. The decision to make a structural alteration such as adding a lift to gain access to an upper floor would appear not to be made simply on the basis of enhancing independence. A small qualitative study using content analysis was carried out by the author to explore what meanings adapting a home had for people with MS and their carers. Participants were identified over a two-month period from the occupational therapy waiting list requesting assessment for adaptations (Jensen 1993). Three men and four women, aged between 33 and 63, agreed to take part with their support carer. Diagnosis had been made three to thirteen years previously, and individual analysis reflected a range of issues.

### Range of issues reflected in the study

MOVING HOUSE

All the participants had considered moving house. For local authority tenants there were few options. Several authorities had a policy of rehousing rather than adapting properties.

> They [the local authority] talked about putting me in a bungalow some-where ... I didn't want to be stuck in with a load of old people ... I like to stay with people my own age.

One tenant had already moved from a town house with her three children and new husband.

> I just don't want to move again. I just haven't got the energy. It's not just the packing, it's all the sorting out ... even if it came to putting a bed in the dining room, I'd rather do that than move.

For owners, financial and locality constraints were expressed.

> It was our ideal home. We took a long time choosing where we were go-ing to move to. It suits my husband and it suits my children. We thought about moving to a bungalow ... there's just no physical way we can do it. Not on one income.

And design of houses caused problems, too.

> And of course this wretched house is not designed for people who drag their feet like I do.

OCCUPATIONAL THERAPY SERVICE

Participants had various experiences of occupational therapy services.

> I'd never heard of an occupational therapist before ... my doctor said he thought it was time I saw an occupational therapist. I thought, 'What work do they think I'm going to do? Sit at home and knit?' And she popped into the surgery, and within a very short time, bless her, there was a bloke here screwing the handles on the wall. I was so impressed.

This man worked for the local MS group. He was less impressed when the oc-cupational therapist was not able to action more structural work and he had to wait for several months for assessment by a social services occupational therapist. Some clients who had previously been seen by an occupational therapist were very pleased with the service and had found equipment supplied to be helpful. Others were less impressed, especially when their condition was changing quickly.

> We still don't know everything the occupational therapist can provide … I had an assessment last year and all I ended up with was two grab rails. And that was only because I asked for them!

### ADAPTATIONS

Most clients considered that a stair lift or an extension would solve their difficulties but still had reservations about how this would affect other family members. Few knew about through floor lifts.

> I don't want the house to become only for me. They have to live here as well. My wife likes a bath and she would like to keep a bath. If you put a stair lift in you're going to mess the house up. If you spent that much money [extending] you might as well move somewhere that gets to suit me.

### COPING STRATEGIES

Analysis of the data showed that the main issue was coping with the effects of MS. While most participants were aware that their functional abilities were lessening, this was not of paramount importance. Life had to be lived. Most lived only one day at a time, tried to minimise their difficulties and live a 'normal' life.

The theory that appears to explain this finding is that of normalisation, based on work by Strauss (1984). Wiener (1984) has used this concept to explore ways that people with rheumatoid arthritis cope with their disease. There are some similarities between the two diseases in that they are both chronic illnesses characterised by fluctuations in symptoms, fatigue and pain, and periods of flare-up and remission. Wiener comments on the need of these people to balance the inner, physiological world with the outer world of normal existence. She describes behaviours such as covering up, pacing and the renormalising to reduced activity levels. The process of normalising starts when the person with a chronic illness begins to take control over their life. It requires active involvement of other family members. The method of 'focusing' is used as a way of placing in the background pieces of the life that don't fit into the picture of normality. This minimises the significance of the problem to those involved, although outsiders see abnormality. Constant restructuring needs to occur to cope with the likes of physical change. This then becomes the new 'normality'. Renormalising is the 'psychological acceptance of a new level of normality' (Strauss 1984, p.86). Strauss goes on to state that those who can not employ this strategy will not cope. Other behaviours employed are mirroring, covering up (pushing, pacing, and controlling information), maintaining a routine, role reversal, and eliciting help. Desensitising and making jokes are also techniques used. Participants showed use of these techniques:

1. *Mirroring.* Comparing yourself with others less fortunate enhances this psychological shift.

   > I would say that 75 per cent of the people [visiting Citizen's Advice Bureau] were worse off than me ... few people [who] came in were worse off physically than me but most were worst off financially and in other ways.

2. *Covering up.* This process makes problems less visible to others. 'Pushing' or 'super-normalising' is a way of proving continuing ability, but is often at a cost of increased fatigue or pain. It is usually followed by 'pacing' – the acceptance that activities must be dispersed.

   > Whereas before I would get on with it and do it ... now I will tell myself ... 'You're sitting down! Turn the telly on and you're sitting down'. And if I'm feeling tired I'll stay in bed.

   Clients who have problems getting up or down stairs use this technique. They plan ahead so the need to go up and down is minimised. Controlling information is another technique for covering up. Clients described not telling friends and colleagues their diagnosis and not wanting to discuss it as that imposed a focus on the disease.

   > My life has got to be round what I can do not what I can't. I don't like sitting around and discussing it ... it's not what I'd call an interesting subject.

   Covering up can lead to frustration when activity aggravates pain or fatigue.

   > I can't do the things I want to do. I mean I do them sometimes and then I regret having done them as I'm crippled with pains ... it makes me angry ... I get so frustrated with it and I take it out on everybody around the house.

3. *Maintaining a routine.* This involves all family members in doing normal things. Making the house easy to operate in is especially important with children in the house.

   > They get up at a certain time, they get ready for school, they make sure there is nothing left on the stairs in case Mummy trips on it. They make sure there are no toys or books downstairs.

4. *Eliciting help.* When covering up is no longer possible help has to be sought and a level of dependency accepted.

> I can see colours and that but as for writing, no ... we get a newspaper and my youngest will read the headlines for me. And that's nice.

It is at this stage that equipment may be accepted to assist the person to continue to carry out valued personal goals (Robinson 1988).

5. *Role reversal.* This occurs when activities have to be permanently taken over, dependency is a reality and a shift in the distribution of labour takes place. Tasks may be shared or children may carry out activities.

> ... ours are having to do things earlier which seems a bit unkind but I think it takes the pressure off the whole family.

*Conclusion*

The effects of normalisation allow for the hope of living in a family unit. Normalisation enables people to cope with the uncertainties of MS in a positive way by minimising areas of difficulty and emphasising abilities. If normalisation is practised successfully there is a risk that health and social care workers may not be aware of the important areas of difficulty for which help may be available and identify the need for assistance. Occupational therapists usually utilise a rehabilitation model which is orientated towards maximising the abilities of the person and minimising difficulties. This practice model takes into account psycho-social aspects of a person's life and should fit with the normalisation model. Time needs to be taken to understand the client and family's perspective of how they cope with a chronic illness. As part of the interview and assessment, patterns of activity of all family members and the meaning of activity need to be explored in order to understand the client's needs and offer advice on options. The occupational therapist needs to be aware that the person with MS may be utilising some of the above techniques. The use of cognitive and behavioural approaches may allow the client more ably to pursue options. If clients contact the service at an early stage, information, advice and a personal contact will enable the client to make informed choices in the future. Early information about types of adaptations and sources of financing can assist clients to start to consider their possible future needs prior to any change in functional ability. The concept of normalisation takes account of the acceptance of rearrangement of the environment and the use of equipment to assist the person with MS. However it would appear that when major structural alterations such as ramps or through floor lifts are contemplated, allowance needs to be made for the person and their family to adjust to the idea. In the words of one of the participants when speaking about his reluctance to have a wheelchair:

> ... once you've got it you think that I was stupid not to have one ... but to impart that to somebody else – I don't think you'd do that very easily. The only way you can do it is actually them to see you and really understand that it does make a difference.

For most of the participants, the design of their house presented a major barrier to their everyday living. Easier access to the home and an additional toilet downstairs would have been of considerable help to most participants. Occupational therapists need to lobby with disabled people to have houses built to a more accessible standard.


### Homeless not helpless

Despite the high visibility and media attention homelessness receives there is still considerable debate and theorising about the needs of homeless people. As the title suggests, much of that debate has been about whether a homeless person is just in need of resources such as a house to meet their needs or whether in fact they are also in need of rehabilitative support and social care. This section is based on research done on the role of the occupational therapist in the field of homelessness by the Specialist Homelessness Occupational Therapy Service in the London Borough of Tower Hamlets, and attempts to show how occupational therapists have unique skills that can empower our homeless community with some solutions (Mace and Donald 1996)

David Willetts, a member of Margaret Thatcher's policy unit in 1989, was quoted as saying homelessness 'was an example of a rise in individualism and taste for independence' (Fisher 1993). Such statements, especially from the monetarist new right, has led to the theory that homelessness is a chosen lifestyle and therefore homeless people can also choose not to be homeless, especially with the numerous resources available to them. These views have come from psycho-dynamic theories that suggest that a person, having been rejected by a 'significant other', may subconsciously choose homelessness as an escape from the harsh realities of life (Levinson 1963).

Pushing the psycho-dynamic theory further there are others who believe that homeless people are all mad, bad, sad and in desperate need of rehabilitation. The incidence of mental illness in the homeless sector is higher than that of the general population but not as high as some may think, and physical problems are often overlooked. It must be recognised that the situations in which homeless people live are often insane and that their adaptation to these circumstances is often misread as insanity. Therefore assessments of mental illness on the streets will be fraught with error and skewed diagnosis (Snow *et al.* 1988).

There is no doubt that homeless people suffer from many biopsychological and sociocultural problems. However, rehabilitation and well meaning care can not be done without the acknowledgement of homeless people's primary handicap – lack of access to adequate housing and employment (Fisher and Collins 1993).

By first looking at homelessness legislation we can start to see who the homeless are and what if any are their needs. The duties to homeless people were firmly placed in the hands of local authority housing departments (LAHD) through the 1977 Homeless Persons Act. Although this act has changed several times since its implementation, the concepts whereby a person is accepted for housing through this act still stand:

- You must be homeless or likely to be homeless within twenty-eight days.

- You must be in priority need, for example pregnant, with dependent children, vulnerable (elderly, mentally or physically ill), or in an emergency situation.

- You must be non-intentionally homeless. You are found intentionally homeless if 'you deliberately do something or fail to do something in consequence of which you cease to occupy accommodation which is or was available for your occupation and which it would have been reasonable for you to continue to occupy'.

- You must have a local connection with the authority concerned or no such connection anywhere. Recent legislation has added an 'eligible for assistance' test which means some applicants newly arrived in the country are denied assistance (Department of the Environment 1996).

If a person is found to be homeless within the definition of the new Housing Act 1996 local authorities will offer temporary housing and review the application every two years. If accepted as homeless the applicant is placed on the single housing register and competes with other people in the borough for council housing on a points system. Housing departments may also use the private rented sector to secure housing for homeless people. If found intentionally homeless and in non-priority need the applicant is given advice on alternative accommodation and voluntary sector organisations that may be able to assist. This law divides homeless people into two fairly distinct categories, the statutory homeless and non-statutory homeless.

This distinction between these two types of homeless people is vital for the occupational therapist to recognise as the two groups have different needs and would be seen in two different work environments.

The statutory homeless are more likely to be families and/or single people with physical or mental health needs or who are vulnerable in some way. Although housing needs are identified by the housing department, health or social services are often missed unless the homeless persons unit has specialists working within it. In one unit in the London Borough of Tower Hamlets, users are assessed for vulnerability by a social work team and housing needs assessments are carried out by a team of occupational therapists. The two professions work closely to provide for the user's community care needs. They co-ordinate with housing to ensure the person concerned is offered the accommodation they require and follow-up re-settlement input to ensure users manage independently in their new home. As housing suitable for the needs of disabled people is in short supply the occupational therapists must be asked to recommend adaptations in a home for the client rather than expect the applicant to wait for the appropriate accommodation to become available.

The non-statutory homeless person is more likely to be a single person or a couple without children because they are not deemed a priority under housing law. The longer a person remains homeless the more likely they are to learn the skills of coping in hostels or on the street. The conventional skills required to live in a permanent home become increasingly foreign as a person becomes more dependent on voluntary organisations for basic needs such as shelter, food, hygiene and health. In a study by the Joseph Rowntree Foundation seven out of ten single homeless people identified advice as the support they required the most to cope in their own accommodation (Bines 1994). The majority of people in this study did want their own home but felt they needed support to achieve the goal. Most homeless organisations now recognise that this functional dependency on services for basic needs deskills people. These organisations now provide life skills groups to help the transition from temporary accommodation to permanent accommodation (Mace and Mobsby 1995). These people are often seen by specialist community teams for homeless people where occupational therapists are often found working generically.

For both categories of homeless people the occupational therapist has expertise in helping the individual to attain skills in all aspects of life to live successfully in whatever environment they choose as their own. This is demonstrated clearly in the Reid and Sanderson model of occupational therapy (Sanderson and Reid 1980). This may mean teaching someone who is roofless where they can find nutritious food or how to get a good night's sleep in the street, or it may mean providing removable equipment in a bed and breakfast hotel. It may also mean assisting in the design of a wheelchair accessible property large enough for a family needing a six-bedroom house. In the London Borough of Tower Hamlets this is usually achieved by creating a large property from through joining two council flats together.

The occupational therapist in whatever area of homelessness he or she may choose to work is essentially a housing occupational therapist. However, as occupational therapists we also have generic skills to help in the adjustment of the homeless person to their environment. As specialists in housing and disability the occupational therapist can assist housing organisations in the provision of appropriate allocation of houses and resettlement skills to this sector of our population and thus reduce the number of people living in unhealthy and distressing situations.

## Culture and its impact on housing adaptations

### What is culture?

Culture is generally defined as a set of guidelines (both explicit and implicit) which individuals inherit as members of a particular society. This tells them how to view the world, how to experience it emotionally, and how to behave in it in relation to other people, to supernatural force or gods and to the natural environment. It also provides them with a way of transmitting these guidelines to the next generation – by the use of symbols, language, art and ritual. To some extent, culture can be seen as an inherited 'lens' through which individuals perceive and understand the world which they inhabit, and learn how to live within it.

### The impact of culture on activities of daily living

Cultural background therefore has an important influence on many aspects of peoples' lives, including their beliefs, behaviours, perceptions, emotions, language, religion, family structure, diet, dress, body image, concepts of space and time, and attitudes to illness, pain and other forms of misfortune – all of which have important implications for occupational therapists. Most occupational therapists consider the assessment and treatment of problems related to activities of daily living as their 'bread and butter'. Most activities of daily living are based on the person's culture – the way they dress, prepare and eat food, wash, do their toilet and so on. Religion and religious customs along with social customs can have a big impact on how a person engages in daily living tasks. These may also dictate how the housing environment is used on a day-to-day basis.

*How daily living activities relate to use of living space and housing*

One of the main distinguishing features of traditional housing from the places of origin of most minority ethnic groups is the flexible use of rooms. Compared to modern Western practices, rooms (other than bathrooms, WCs and stores) are used more interchangeably – they are less dedicated to a single activity. For example, sleeping can happen in a variety of places and not necessarily in a bedroom. There may be issues where the care of the person with disabilities, especially an elderly parent, is shared between more than one family living in different homes.

There may be segregation of the sexes in the home, especially when entertaining. This should be borne in mind when living areas are being considered for conversion into bedrooms.

*Adapting properties of clients of minority ethnic groups*

- People from many minority ethnic groups consider that proper hygiene requires washing in running water as opposed to lying in a bath or washing from a filled basin. Where showers are unavailable, some people may bathe by pouring water over the body with a jug dipped in a bucket of water while squatting in a unfilled bath. Muslims and Jews have a requirement for washing their feet and hands in running water prior to prayer. Muslims may wash their genital area with water after using the lavatory. The left hand is generally used for this purpose.

- The bed arrangements generally reflect the sleeping patterns within the whole family as well as the tradition of having extended family members to stay. There may often be a custom for children to sleep together, and it is not uncommon for a child to sleep in his/her parents' bed or have his/her bed in the parents' bedroom.

- Some of the considerations in relation to kitchen adaptations include volume and type of cooking. Many of the meals of minority ethnic groups include cooking with large amounts of fat and oil. This demands an air change rate which is very high relative to the average provision in housing and higher than the improved standards of the building regulations of 1992 (30 litres per second). There may be a need to wash large pots, and some preparation and cooking may be done at floor level.

- Non-English speaking people may have difficulties following instructions and safety manuals (of specialist equipment and adaptations) written in English. Safety instructions should be available in an appropriate language.

The above is not an exhaustive list, but five some examples of the cultural variations in the use of housing and the space inside the house. This is intended to identify some of the issues about which professionals working in the housing field should be aware. There is no substitute for asking the client relevant questions; never assume that everything applies in every case. Always check with the person concerned. It should also be remembered that cultures are never homogenous and therefore one should avoid making generalisations in explaining peoples' beliefs and behaviours.

## A brief discussion of the demographic features of the UK's minority ethnic population

The number of clients from minority ethnic groups that a therapist may come across will vary considerably. The 1991 census found that the total minority ethnic population in England and Wales was 5.9 per cent of the total (2,945,000). For the UK as a whole the figure falls to 5.5 per cent. The minority ethnic population is not evenly distributed, but is clustered in different localities, often urban. Over half of the minority ethnic population lives in the south east where it forms 9.9 per cent of the total. The major concentration of minority ethnic populations is to be found in Greater London, which has 20.2 per cent of the total. Other major concentrations are to be found in the West Midlands with 8.2 per cent, and Yorkshire and Humberside, both with 4.4 per cent. Among the UK's minority ethnic population, the largest single group is Indian, constituting 28 per cent of the minority population as a whole. The second largest population is the black Caribbean group making 17 per cent of the total ethnic population.

## An action plan – what occupational therapists can do

KNOW THE ETHNIC GROUPING OF YOUR CLIENTS

There are a number of sources of information. Business plans of local authorities and health trusts generally contain information about the local population. The 1991 census produced local base statistics which are freely available in the library or through the Stationery Office (formerly HMSO). Areas with high populations of minority ethnic groups tend to have local branches of the Council For Racial Equality (CRE). It is generally accepted that figures produced by CRE of the local population tend to be more reliable than the census figures.

KNOW YOUR CLIENTS' CULTURES

A variety of information is available about the different minority ethnic groups and their customs. Some authorities, such as Oxfordshire County Council and Oxfordshire Health; Southwark, Lambeth and Lewisham Health Commission, have produced their own fact files/profiles of minority ethnic groups living in their areas. Karmi (1996) and Meghani-Wise (1996) are some other sources of information.

TRAINING

Application of the knowledge gained about the clients' religious and social customs is essential. The therapist (and the manager!) needs to be sensitive during the assessment process and be willing to accept that locally drawn up criteria and the colour blind approach (i.e. treating everybody equally) may actually be discriminatory against clients from minority ethnic groups. The Social Services Inspectorate document *Occupational Therapy – The community contribution* (1994) made it clear that therapists need to be trained in the different customs and lifestyles of minority ethnic groups, especially in relation to disability and their need for services.

MAKE CONTACT

Consult local and national organisations that have been set up by and for specific minority ethnic groups. Publish accounts of your successes.

*Case Study*

Mrs Fatma Faik, a 74-year-old lady, was referred to the occupational therapy team for problems in negotiating stairs and hence accessing the bathroom and bedroom. The person taking the referral found that there was a toilet at ground-floor level and that the living area was a through lounge. It was suggested to the client's daughter that Mrs Faik's bed be brought downstairs and that she lived on one level on a temporary basis while the case was on the waiting list for assessment. The client was told that there would be at least a six-month wait as the case was not priority.

Mrs Faik's daughter was informed that the solution suggested was not practical as her mother was a practising Muslim and needed to wash. She was informed that according to local policy, washing was not a high priority and the client would have to wait.

Three months later, Mrs Faik was referred to the occupational therapy team, this time by the hospital occupational therapist as discharge home was imminent.

On assessment the following was found:

- Medical condition: osteoporosis, osteoarthritis, circulatory problems leading to episodes of sudden loss of consciousness.

- Accommodation: town house type property – ground floor had a through lounge, kitchen and toilet. The first floor had two bedrooms and the second floor had one bedroom and a large bathroom with bath, toilet, sink and bidet. Stair rails had been fitted but had proved to be practically useless.

- Religious customs which affect activities of daily living: the client was a practising Muslim and was required to wash hands and feet in running water prior to praying (prayers are said five times a day). The client was perching on a stool inside the bath to be able to do so. The client also needed to wash her bottom in running water after toiletting. For this she was using her bidet. The solution of living on one level was not practical as there were no washing facilities or a bidet on the ground level. The client was negotiating the stairs eight to nine times a day in spite of a number of falls (with very high risk due to osteoporosis) and on numerous occasions was unable to get out of the bath.

DISCUSSION

The low priority allocated to this case was certainly inappropriate as the client's life was at risk. The advice to refrain from doing the activity that put the client's life at risk was inappropriate. The client's culture demanded that she carry out certain rituals as a part of her daily living routine.

A disabled facilities grant (DFG) was applied for to install an additional shower and bidet downstairs. The client's life was still continually at risk while the DFG was being processed and until the work was completed.

This is one small example of some of the factors that an occupational therapist may have to take into account during daily practice.

### Conclusion

In conclusion one must realise that cultures are not static and are influenced by other human groups around them. What is true of them one year may not be true the next. There are no cook-book solutions to any of the problems that a therapist may encounter when dealing with clients from minority ethnic groups. A sensitive and open approach which places the client at the centre of the assessment and rehabilitation process is essential to enable solutions to work.

*Useful addresses*

### The Buddhist Society
58 Eccleston Square, London SW1 1PH.
Tel: 0171 834 5858.

### Confederation of Indian Organisations (UK)
5 Westminster Bridge Road, London SE1 7XW.
Tel: 0171 928 9889.

### Islamic Cultural Centre
London Central Mosque, 146 Park Road, London NW5 7RG.
Tel: 0171 724 3363.

### Jewish Care
221 Golders Green Road, London NW11 9DW.
Tel: 0181 458 3282.

### African Caribbean Community Development Unit
London Voluntary Sector Resource Centre, 356 Holloway Road,
London N7 6PN.
Tel: 0171 700 8148.

### Chinese Community Information Centre
146 Bromsgrove Street, Birmingham B5 6RG.
Tel: 0121 622 3003.

### African Welfare and Immigration Advisory Centre
200 The Grove, Stratford, London E15 1LS.
Tel: 0181 519 6935.

### Commission for Racial Equality
Elliot House, 10–12 Allington Street, London SW1E 5EH.
Tel: 0171 828 7022.

### Local Authority Race Relations Information Exchange (LARRIE)
38 Belgrave Square, London SW1X 8NZ.
Tel: 0171 259 5464.

### London Interpreting Project
20 Compton Terrace, London N1 2UN.
Tel: 0171 359 6798.


## Housing for elderly people
*Health and housing – is there a connection?*

> The connection between health and the dwellings of the population is one of the most important that exists [Florence Nightingale].

Housing still influences our health today, although evidence for this is slow to accumulate and usually applies to populations rather than to individuals. Houses should provide basic health requirements like shelter, warmth, sanitation and privacy, and badly designed or dangerously constructed homes can have a direct effect on an individual's health (Lowry 1989). The effects of housing may also be complicated by poverty, age, pre-existing illness and personal preferences. For example, an elderly person living in cold conditions is at increased risk of illness, but this may be the result of unwillingness to turn on a heater, inability to remember how to do it, or insufficient money to pay the fuel bills, rather than a specific defect in housing.

However, some of the strongest evidence for the effects of housing conditions on health concerns the effect of cold damp homes (Martin, Platt and Hunt 1987). Ideally all homes should be capable of being heated to 21° – the winter room temperature recommended by the British Geriatrics Society. The people most at risk of the effects of cold and damp often live in poor quality homes that are hard to heat and these are often those that can least afford large fuel bills.

> Since I moved into this new purpose built flat, my health has improved a lot – it's lovely to be warm all the time and I feel a lot happier.

### What are the housing needs of elderly people?

For an increasing number of people, retirement spans a period of 30 years or more. Often starting before the age of 60, some will achieve the age of 90 or more still mentally alert and physically independent. But for some this period of life will be marked by sad events, a degree of physical restriction and maybe mental frailty. Under such circumstances, many people find they have to make the very hard decision to leave their family home and live in more suitable accommodation. The key factors appear to be anxiety about declining health and isolation, a wish to be nearer relatives and a concern at coping with an existing home which is no longer secure or easily run, and too large or too expensive to maintain. Much has been learnt in designing housing specifications for elderly people since the first old peoples' housing scheme was built over 30 years ago. It demands having an appreciation for and empathy with the ageing process such as:

- the effort needed to open an outside door or a fire door
- the need for accommodation which will give privacy yet be conducive to socialising
- the possible difficulty in smelling smoke, hearing fire alarms or seeing obstacles
- a decrease in general mobility due to joint pain and muscle weakness

- that the functions of carrying, climbing, gripping, lifting, pushing and pulling will be restricted

- that changes in memory, orientation and spatial organisation will be present

- that accidents are more likely to happen because of impaired co-ordination

- that noise levels (e.g. of an internal extractor fan) and shadows (e.g. in a kitchen) can be irritating and can cause anxiety

- the need to have familiar facilities, such as a kitchen window to look out of and which can be easily opened

- that people 'lose' height with age so window heights, sockets, cupboards and so on need to be lower than standard.

### Sheltered housing

In the last 30 years, sheltered accommodation has become more commonplace as the problems associated with an ageing population become more apparent. Sheltered housing 'combines the security of group living with an environment which should ideally be designed carefully for the physical limitations of ageing' (Weal and Weal 1988, p.13). Sheltered housing categories and standards in the UK originated with government circular 82/69, (Ministry of Housing and Local Government). This circular introduced the idea of two categories of accommodation for the elderly, with mandatory minimum space standards for schemes in the public sector. It also encouraged higher standards of heating and safety measures. The two categories were defined as 'self-contained dwellings' (Part 1), and 'grouped flatlets' (Part 2). The main point of the circular was to define standards of space and design enabling elderly people to maintain an independent way of life in an environment planned for sociability where they could avoid loneliness and isolation. A decade after the implementation of the Part 1 and Part 2 schemes, the problems associated with an ageing community began to emerge. Neither scheme could cope with the amount of care needed as residents became more frail, so nursing homes (or Part 3) were the only alternative.

During the last decade it became apparent that the gap between Parts 2 and 3 was too great and that there was a stage midway between a fully independent lifestyle and a residential nursing home. To this end, the Part 2 ½, or 'extra care sheltered housing' was born and has been gaining popularity ever since.

*Determining the needs of frail, elderly people*

Before looking at how needs may be assessed and priorities decided for this client group, it is worth considering what is meant by need. Is it normative need; that is, need as defined by an expert or professional such as occupational therapist, architect or housing committee? The problem in this case is that the values and standards of the 'expert' may be different from those of the client.

Is it felt need; that is, the need which people feel and very often want but which is limited by the perceptions and knowledge of what is available? Or is it expressed need, when people request or demand what they want?

Not all felt need is automatically turned into expressed need. Lack of opportunity, motivation or assertiveness skills could all prevent the expression of felt need, particularly if frail and elderly. Expressed need may also conflict with the professional's view of normative needs (Ewles and Simnett 1987).

---

### Example

Two extra care sheltered accommodation complexes were built in Surrey within one year of each other (1989 and 1990) and have both been successful in meeting the needs of an increasingly frail group of people. However, in one complex, each bathroom contains a shower with a bathing facility available elsewhere. The other contains a bath with availability of a shower elsewhere.

Does this example reflect normative need, felt need or expressed need? The remainder of this section hopes to explore this and is based on the responses of 60 residents from extra care sheltered housing.

---

*The occupational therapist's role*

Community occupational therapists are frequently asked to advise on internal facilities needed in sheltered accommodation, particularly when new schemes are being planned. As shown in the previous example, an area of confusion lies around the design of bathrooms.

The following section uses the 'bath or shower' debate to illustrate how an occupational therapist might consider the problem holistically. The same principle can be applied to other areas of internal design such as kitchen layout. The diagram below helps to illustrate the holistic view to personal hygiene.

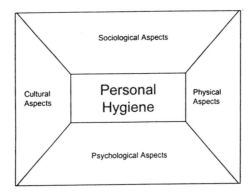

CULTURAL ASPECTS

    Cleanliness is next to Godliness. (Anon.)

Taking a bath is something now taken for granted, but in terms of modern social history, it is a very recent development. For centuries people paid little heed to bodily cleanliness, and it was only with the Victorians that the bath became established as a household object. It is against this background that our indigenous client group, the elderly of 70–90 years, grew up.

Patterns of behaviour established in early childhood often have a very strong influence on present day attitudes of elderly people and therefore should be recognised. Most people of this generation used a tin bath when they were a child and, more often than not, this was used in the scullery and the water was shared with the rest of the family, having usually been heated in a copper which was fired by wood or coal.

Bath night was something that many people remember vividly. It was usually a pleasurable activity which took place once a week, more often on a Friday or Saturday, and which was part of a whole routine for all the family. Other activities were often associated with bath night such as taking 'opening medicine' and combing hair with a fine tooth comb to rid the hair of head lice.

The British Public Baths and Wash Houses Act of 1846 introduced warm showers for the labouring classes, but it wasn't until about 1930 that the glass shower cabinet or tub screen arrived in England from the USA and could be found in some prestige bathrooms. It has been suggested that showers have bad associations for anyone over 55 years old as it reminds them of showers at school, after games lessons, with little or no privacy or comfort; or in some cases during time in National Service or in the Army where showers might have been cold and/or dirty.

    It is not surprising, therefore, that the elderly people appear to be biased more towards baths. This might well change in the future as showering becomes more the norm.

PSYCHOLOGICAL ASPECTS

From recent psychological studies, one of the most valuable indicators of adjustment in old age is self-esteem. Loss of self-esteem appears to be one of the characteristic symptoms in depression in old age and therefore maintenance of a positive attitude and a sense of being in control of one's own life are key issues in old age (Wade and Tavris 1990). In relation to bathing/showering, personality and previous background will obviously have an influence on adaptability to anything new, but if elderly people are given a sense of control and choice, physical and mental decline may be halted. It could be argued that by being offered an assisted bath, the tenant in sheltered housing is being given a clue that their physical capabilities are declining. Eventually the tenant will come to believe this and the loss of confidence will prevent him or her attempting bathing or showering again.

Maintaining self-esteem appears to be essential in order for the elderly person to remain mentally healthy. If bathing/showering makes the person 'feel good' and is a pleasurable activity which boosts self-esteem, then it deserves to be ranked as an important aspect of daily life and not just as a means to an end in terms of hygiene.

SOCIOLOGICAL ASPECTS

One of the most obvious achievements of the last few decades has been the increase in size of the elderly population. Improved standards of living and child health earlier in the century, together with better nutrition, prevention and health care, have all helped to raise life expectancy. By the third or fourth decade of the next century, a quarter or even a third of the population will be over 60. The retired population now forms about 16 per cent of the community and projections for the next 35 years suggest that the biggest expansion in numbers will take place in the oldest age groups; a 23 per cent increase in the 65–79s and a 45 per cent increase in the over-80s is expected between 1988 and 2056 (Central Statistical Office 1990). Another striking aspect of old age is that two thirds of retired people are women. By the age of 85, women outnumber men by four to one. At present, 75 per cent of those over 80 have disabilities compared with 45 per cent of elderly people generally. The most commonly reported chronic diseases in the over-65s are arthritis and joint problems followed by respiratory disease. However, studies of the functional capacity of the elderly give a more informative picture. In the OPCS General Household Survey 1986 (OPCS 1986), over 80 per cent of the 'young old' were independent in activities in daily living and the over 75s only showed a minority suffering severe functional incapacity.

From a planning perspective, therefore, bathing design should be biased towards the needs of people predominately over 80, female and who suffer from joint problems.

PHYSICAL ASPECTS

There are many therapeutic purposes ascribed to bathing. Among these are cleansing the body of pathogenic organisms, stimulation and massage of muscles, relaxation of muscles and maintenance of a sense of well-being. But, as any community occupational therapist knows, bathing is often a vexed issue. When does a 'medical' bath begin and a 'social' bath end? A recent study (Parkes 1993), involving personal interviews of 60 frail elderly people in Part 2 ½ accommodation revealed a surprisingly high percentage of non-usage of both baths and showers (16 out of 30 who had baths didn't use them: 16 out of 30 who had showers didn't use them). The reasons for non-usage were:

*Baths*

- 22 per cent had difficulty getting out.
- 6 per cent had difficulty getting in.
- 27 per cent found it difficult getting in and out.
- 17 per cent preferred other methods.
- 11 per cent were frightened of slipping
- 17 per cent other reasons.

*Showers*

- 33 per cent preferred other methods.
- 23 per cent found adjusting water temperature difficult.
- 19 per cent had a fear of slipping.
- 16 per cent were nervous about possible water overflow.
- 6 per cent found it difficult in washing body parts.
- 3 per cent other reasons.

When asked what their ideal bathroom would consist of, most suggested both bath and shower.

By looking at bathing and showering needs of the frail elderly from cultural, psychological and sociological perspectives as well as physical need, it is hoped that the subject can be seen in a context not immediately obvious to those responsible for determining design. The current population of elderly people have been brought up in a very strong hygiene culture which has remained with them throughout their lives. Personality and previous experience affect how easily people adapt to new techniques and physical impairment will also affect preference and compliance. Whether using a bath or a shower, it is rated as a very important activity for this client group, not only for the practical purpose of keeping clean, but also because it is a pleasurable activity which enhances self-esteem and has a high 'feel good' factor.

## Conclusion

This section has attempted to give an overview of both general and specific issues related to housing for elderly people. As the statistics show, we are fortunate in this country that people are living longer and healthier lives. Housing needs will need to reflect this. Maintaining independence for as long as possible is vital for an elderly person's quality of life as well as the economy of care provision. Attention to the details of design of even standard household furniture can make the difference between dependence and independence.

## Designing for people with a visual impairment

### Introduction

Many occupational therapists, housing and related staff are unaware of the needs of people with a visual impairment; neither are they aware of the simple design solutions which can aid access to and orientation within a visually impaired person's home. The purpose of this section is therefore to highlight the housing needs of blind and partially sighted people, to outline some of their design requirements, and to consider how occupational therapists can begin to develop services to respond to and meet these needs.

### Incidence of visual impairment

The Royal National Institute for the Blind (RNIB) needs survey revealed that there are approximately one million people with a registerable visual impairment in the United Kingdom, an incidence of 1 in 60 of the total population (Bruce *et al.* 1991). The survey also showed that of the one million registerable blind and partially sighted people, 750,000 were unlikely to be identified by health or social services and, as a result, may not have been receiving appropriate help or support. This includes access to mobility aids and suitable adaptations. In addition to this, it is estimated that there are 700,000 people who cannot be regarded as registerable as blind or partially sighted but whose sight is so poor that they cannot recognise a friend across a road. These figures combined increases the total visually impaired population in the United Kingdom to 1.7 million people.

However, the future incidence of visual impairment (based on the official statistics) suggests that the registerable visually impaired population is set to rise to just over 1.1 million by the turn of the century and to increase to nearly 1.4 million by 2021, the majority of whom will be over the age of 60. Indeed, there is a correlation between visual impairment and old age – as many as one in seven people over 75 are blind or partially sighted. Furthermore, a relatively high proportion of older visually impaired people also report one or more additional disabilities. The most commonly known conditions are hearing impairment and mobility difficulties, for example, brought on by arthritis. It is therefore essential for occupational therapists and other professional staff not to consider visual impairment and the disabling effects of the environment in isolation.

### Common eye conditions

The degree and character of visual impairment varies considerably from person to person. Only 5 per cent of those who are visually impaired have no sight at all. For registration purposes, the most common eye conditions recorded as causing poor sight are glaucoma, cataracts and macular degeneration. Each of these create differing functional difficulties such as a loss of sharpness across the visual field and areas of 'non-vision'.

For example:

- Glaucoma constricts a person's field of vision, resulting in tunnel vision and causing mobility problems – giving no warning of obstacles and making progress very slow. The use of tactile clues and texture can be used to provide information on oncoming hazards.

- Cataracts lead to increasingly blurred vision, features begin to merge and detail is drastically reduced. This can effect close visual tasks such as reading and cooking or seeing distant objects. Cataracts are also adversely affected by glare and therefore the use and positioning of natural and artificial lighting is important.

- Macular degeneration causes problems with central vision so that vision is distorted, making way finding extremely difficult even though peripheral vision remains. Appropriate colour contrasting can be used to give orientation and directional guidance.

In addition to the conditions described above, there are also many people who are not eligible for registration but who suffer a visual disability. Under the 1995 Disability Discrimination Act (Section 1), they too will be regarded as 'disabled' if they have 'a physical or mental impairment which has a substantial and long-term adverse effect on a person's ability to carry out normal day-to-day activities'.

## Assessing for aids and adaptations

Provision for assessing needs of people with disabilities is contained in the 1970 Chronically Sick and Disabled Persons Act (CSDP Act). The provisions are wide ranging and include an assessment for adaptations to the home, or equipment for greater safety, comfort or convenience. This should apply equally to people with a visual impairment and to people with other disabilities alike. However, there is no information to show how successful the former have been in obtaining assessments for aids and adaptations to their home using the CSDP Act.

The RNIB experience is that there is very little professional understanding and knowledge amongst occupational therapists, social workers, architects and housing staff on the specific design consideration of people with a visual impairment; consequently people with a visual impairment are not being fully assessed. At the same time, blind and partially sighted people are largely ignorant of their rights under the CSDP Act. One of the major causes for this is due to the fact that information on the procedure is not widely available in accessible formats such as large print, braille and tape.

Research for the Housing Corporation also suggests that visually impaired people are 'passive' about expressing their housing need (Cooper *et al.* 1995). On account of their visual loss, people with a visual impairment are often not aware of what products are available to enhance their vision to aid everyday living skills, or used to enable their home to be adapted to make it accessible. As a result, there is a greater reliance on family, carers and professionals to provide expert advice. This is particularly the case for visually impaired people who have lost their sight in later life.

## What proactive measures should occupational therapists adopt?

- To establish appropriate aids, adaptations or design solutions for visually impaired people, assessment forms should incorporate key trigger questions to identify the disabling effects of a visually impaired person's environment.
- Occupational therapists should liaise more closely with organisations such as RNIB Housing Service, local voluntary societies for the blind, and social services visual/sensory impairment teams. Where necessary, this could involve 'shared'

assessments where there is a need for specialist services (Lovelock *et al.* 1995).

- There is an urgent need for occupational therapists to receive visual impairment awareness training.

### Applying for disabled facilities grants

Unfortunately, the Department of the Environment does not hold information on the number of people with a visual impairment who have been granted disabled facilities grants (DFGs) and the nature of the works undertaken. However, a recent survey of 60 visually impaired people identified that a quarter (15) had made one or more alterations to their property because of their visual impairment (Tillesley 1996). The types of alterations made are outlined below:

- 5 extensions to their home
- 4 bathroom alterations
- 4 put in handrails
- 3 appliances adapted
- 2 stairs or doors widened
- 2 better lighting installed
- 2 rooms modified.

Of the 15 people who had their property adapted, 8 received a local authority grant, the remainder had used their own savings or borrowed money. It is likely that the latter is an underestimate as many visually impaired people make improvements to their accommodation without seeking advice from home improvement agencies, applying to the local authority for a grant, or involving other statutory bodies.

The 1996 Housing Grants, Construction and Regeneration Act introduced major changes to the housing grants system. Under the new Act, the DFG remains largely unchanged. Grants are still mandatory in specified cases and the upper limit remains at £20,000. During the passage of the legislation through Parliament, RNIB sought to ensure that the needs of people with a visual impairment were addressed. In particular, they tabled an amendment which would have resulted in a new criteria for a mandatory DFG, namely, for safety purposes, improved lighting systems in the dwelling of a visually impaired occupant. This was rejected by the House of Lords. However, the Government did introduce a new clause relating to safety. This covers 'making the dwelling or building safe for the disabled occupant and other persons residing with him' (Section 23(1)(b)). The Government's intention was to broaden the issue of safety so that it did not just relate to people with a visual impairment. In practice, this means that in future a DFG should be available to any disabled occupant who can demonstrate that aids and adaptations are required for reasons of safety. This can be far reaching. For example, for blind and partially sighted people, it may result not only in improved lighting but also improved tactile clues, colour contrast or signage.

### Design solutions in the home

The majority of people rely on their sight for mobility and orientation. People with a visual impairment are encouraged to develop ways of using whatever vision they have. The environment is also learned by recognising key features through touch, smell and through a process of mental mapping. The whole process can take upwards of two years and is often assisted by support of mobility officers or rehabilitation staff. The disabling impact of a visual impairment can be greatly reduced by the use of aids in the home and simple changes in interior finishes, layout and building design. Measures designed to improve access to and movement within a visually impaired persons home are outlined in RNIB's design guide (Barker *et al.* 1995). A summary checklist is provided below.

### I. LAYOUT

It is essential that the layout of a dwelling is accessible to anyone with a visual loss. This should include features such as:

- level or gently sloping approaches to the dwelling
- flush thresholds
- entrance doors that are wide enough for a visually impaired person accompanied by a sighted guide or a guide dog.

### 2. LEVELS OF LIGHT

For some eye conditions, visually impaired people need twice as much light as a sighted person. For other eye conditions, the light level may need to be decreased. As a result, people with a visual impairment need to make flexible use of existing natural and artificial light. Features that should be considered include:

- installing dimmer switches to control lighting levels

- avoiding large variations in brightness from one area to another, for example entrances should be illuminated (this could also be a safety feature)
- evenly distributing lighting throughout an area
- avoiding creating pools of intense light surrounded by darkness, for example by using spotlights or uplighters
- illuminating kitchen work surfaces (and other work areas), for example with task lighting.

### 3. COLOUR CONTRAST

Colour contrasted and tone finishes can help to enhance visibility and help visually impaired people to identify objects and avoid hazards. For example:

- there should be good contrast between doors, walls and floors, background surfaces, furniture and fillings
- the edge of each step should be highlighted with a colour contrasted, non-reflective, non-slip nosing; and switches, sockets and handrails should contrast with their background.

### 4. TEXTURE AND TACTILE CODING

The use of texture and tactile coding provides clues to aid orientation.
For example:

- landmarks/tactile coding on handrails provide information clues
- textured floor surfaces mark junctions in corridors, pathways and indicate the bottom or top of a flight of stairs
- slip resistant flooring in bathrooms and kitchens.

### 5. SIGNAGE

The use of concise, easily understood and appropriately placed signage is a valuable source of information to visually impaired people. Signs should therefore:

- be located in a logical, well-lit position
- contrast with the background surface
- be highly visible, with upper and lower case lettering and, above all, be kept to a minimum.

6. AIDS AND ADAPTATIONS

There are a wide range of products available for blind and partially sighted people. These include braille embossed or symbol embossed controls for domestic appliances such as cookers, washing machines, shower units and so on.

Many manufacturers now also supply colour contrasted equipment such as grab rails, door fittings, kitchen units and bathroom/toilet furniture. In addition, electronic and audible aids can be used to pass on essential information to people with a visual impairment. For example, an infra-red talking information system can be set to give positional details, relay instructions or warnings.

Importantly, all these products can be incorporated into the home at relatively little cost. Further information on specific aids is available from RNIB[1] Alternatively, blind and partially sighted people can sample items at local resource centres for the blind or disabled living centres.

### Conclusion

There are a number of measures that occupational therapists and related staff should implement into service delivery in order to ensure that the needs of people with a visual impairment are taken into account. These include ensuring that occupational therapy and other services are accessible and produce information about their service, application and assessment forms in accessible formats and so on. (Occupational therapists will also need to comply with the 1995 Disability Discrimination Act which came into force on 2 December 1996.) In this way, blind and partially sighted people can begin to make informed decisions about altering their disabling home environment so that their everyday needs are accommodated.

### Postscript

This chapter has been written by members of the College of Occupational Therapists Specialist Section in Housing (COTSSIH). One of the several aims of this organisation is to 'encourage research and development'. As stated in the introduction, very little research has been done to measure the outcome of the part occupational therapists play in meeting the housing needs of disabled people. More is being done and some (not mentioned here) have been used by the various contributors to this book. Blom-Cooper (1990) in his report *Occupational Therapy: An Emerging Profession in Health Care*, could not

---

1   The RNIB catalogue of products is available from RNIB customer services, PO Box 173, Peterborough PE2 6NS. Tel: 0345 023153

draw on hard data to prove the benefits of involving occupational therapists and states

> the virtual absence of experimental research designed to evaluate the effectiveness of occupational therapy practices and procedures, as well as of surveys designed to test patient response to OT services, leaves the profession unnecessarily vulnerable to challenge.

This was directed at the occupational therapy profession as a whole, but applies to occupational therapists working with housing – either adaptation of existing housing or new build housing. The Commission of Enquiry, headed by Blom-Cooper, 'did obtain a considerable volume of evidence' supporting the value of the work of occupational therapists, and concluded 'that the occupational therapist is the health professional best equipped to comprehend and meet their [disabled people] needs' (Blom-Cooper 1990, p.46). This report was published in 1990 and since then, of course, changes have occurred, most notably the rejection of the medical model by disabled people themselves, and some legislation (see Chapter 1). In 1994 the Social Services Inspectorate (SSI) and the Department of Health (DoH) produced a report – *Occupational Therapy: The Community Contribution* – which included the part of the profession which is involved in tackling the problems disabled people have with the built environment – especially their homes. The recommendations included:

- making better use of housing improvement agencies (HIAs) (see Chapter 3) to 'improve the speed and quality of supervision of contracts for housing adaptations'
- 'better communication between therapist and technical supervisor' and 'that users are consulted about follow-up arrangements and decisions agreed which are appropriate to their needs'.

More recently, studies have been carried out in:

- Nottingham – which led to the setting up of a central database of disabled people and adapted housing (Logan *et al.* 1996)
- Shropshire – which highlighted the need for 'an integrated inter-agency approach to meeting disabled people's housing needs' (Nocon and Pleace 1996)
- the north east of England looking at targetting resources to those in most urgent need (Brewis 1994)
- a county-based adaptation service and found a great variation in service delivery according to housing tenure (Adams 1996).

These have all been reported in the *British Journal of Occupational Therapy* (BJOT). What effect do they have on service delivery nationwide? Measurement of outcomes is time consuming and few community occupational therapists can put such objectives high up on their agenda. The members of COTSSIH would welcome other organisations co-operation and support in furthering research that will influence the improvement of both the quality and delivery of an adaptation service and better designed homes in new build projects.

## References

*Exploring the issues influencing the decision to adapt a home for people with multiple sclerosis*

REFERENCES

Jensen, J. (1993) *Multiple Sclerosis: A Series of Studies Exploring the Issues that Influence the Decision to Structurally Alter a Home.* (Unpublished). London: College of Occupational Therapy.

Robinson, I. (1988) 'Managing symptoms in chronic disease: Some dimensions of patients experience.' *International Journal of disability studies 10*, 3, 112–118.

Strauss *et al.* (1984) *Chronic Illness and the Quality of Life, 2nd Edition.* Chicago: Mosby.

Wiener, C. (1984) 'The burden of rheumatoid arthritis in chronic illness and quality of life.' In Strauss, C. *et al. Chronic Illness and the Quality of Life, 2nd Edition.* Chicago: Mosby.

FURTHER READING

Brooks, N. and Matson, R. (1982) 'Social-psychological adjustment to Multiple-Sclerosis. A longitudinal study.' *Social Science and Medicine 16*, 2129–2135.

Cunningham, D. (1977) *Stigma and Social Isolation: Self perceived problems of a group of Multiple Sclerosis patients. Health Services Research Unit. Report no.27.* University of Kent: Centre for Research in Social Sciences.

Devins, G., Seland, T., Klein, G. and Saary, M. (1993) 'Stability and determinants of psychosocial well-being in Multiple Sclerosis.' *Rehabilitation Psychology 38*, 1, 11–25.

Lincoln, N. (1981) 'Discrepancies between capabilities and performance of activities of daily living in multiple sclerosis patients.' *International Rehabilitation Medicine 3*, 84–88.

Peyser, J., Edwards, K. and Poser, C. (1980) 'Psychological profiles in patients with Multiple Sclerosis: A preliminary study.' *Archives of Neurology*, July, 37, 437–440.

Rao, S. (1986) 'Neuropsychology of Multiple Sclerosis: A critical review.' *Journal of Clinical and Experimental Neuropsychology 8*, 5, 503–542.

Robinson, C. (1993) 'Managing life with a chronic condition: The story of normalisation.' *Qualitative Health Research 3*, 1, 6–28.

Wineman, N. (1990) 'Adaptation Multiple Sclerosis: The role of Social Support functional disability and perceived uncertainty.' *Nursing Research*, September/October, 39, 5, 294–299.

Zeidow, P. and Pavlou, M. (1984) 'Physical disability, life stresses, and psychosocial adjustment in Multiple Sclerosis.' *The Journal of Nervous and Mental Disease 172*, 2, 80–84.

## Homeless not helpless

REFERENCES

Bines, W. (1994) *Findings – Housing Research 128.* York: Joseph Rowntree Foundation.

Fisher, K. and Collins, J. (eds) (1993) *Homeless, Healthcare and Welfare Provision.* London: Routledge.

*Homeless Persons Act 1977.* London: HMSO.

*Housing Act 1985.* London: HMSO.

*Housing Act 1996.* London: HMSO.

Levinson, B. (1963) 'The homeless man: A psychological enigma.' *Mental Hygiene 47,* 596–9.

Mace, J. and Donald, J. (1996) *Report on the Specialist Homelessness Occupational Therapy Service.* London: London Borough of Tower Hamlets, Homeless Persons Unit.

Mace, J. and Mobsby, I. (1995) *No Place Like Home.* London: Oasis Trust.

Sanderson, S. and Reid, K. (1980) *Concepts of Occupational Therapy.* Baltimore: Williams and Wilkins.

Snow, *et al.* (1988) 'On the precariousness of measuring insanity in insane contexts.' *Social Problems 33,* 5, 407–22.

## Culture and its impact on housing adaptations

REFERENCES

Karmi, C. (1996) *The Ethnic Health Handbook: A File for Health Care Professionals.* London: Blackwell Science.

Meghani-Wise, Z. (1996) 'Why this interest in minority ethnic groups?' *British Journal of Occupational Therapy 59,* 10, 485–489.

Social Services Inspectorate (1994) *Occupational Therapy: The Community Contribution.* London: HMSO.

## Housing for elderly people

REFERENCES

Central Statistical Office (1990) *Social Trends 20.* London: Harcourt Brace.

Ewles, L. and Simnett, I. (1987) *Promoting Health: A Practical Guide to Health Education.* London: Scutari Press.

Lowry, S. (1989) 'Housing and health.' *British Medical Journal.* London: British Medical Association.

Martin, C. Platt, S. and Hunt, S. (1987) 'Housing conditions and ill health.' *British Medical Journal.* London: British Medical Association.

Ministry of Housing and Local Government (19??) *Circular 82/69.* London: HMSO.

OPCS (1986) *General Household Survey.* London: OPCS.

Parkes, B. (1993) *What the Professionals Need to Know: To Bath or to Shower? The Responses of Frail Elderly People in Extra Care Sheltered Accommodation.* (Unpublished thesis.) London: College of Occupational Therapists.

Wade, C. and Tavris, C. (1990) *Psychology.* Wokingham: Addison-Wesley.

Weal, F. and Weal, F. (1988) *Housing the Elderly: Options and Design.* London: Mitchell Publishing Co. Ltd.

## Designing for people with a visual impairment

REFERENCES

Barker, P., Barrick, J. and Wilson, R. (1995) *Building Sight: A Handbook of Building and Interior Design Solutions to Include the Needs of Visually Impaired People.* London: RNIB/HMSO.

Bruce, I., McKennell, A. and Walker, E. (1991) *RNIB Needs Survey.* London: HMSO.

*Chronically Sick and Disabled Persons Act 1970.* London: HMSO.

Cooper, S., Sharpe, K., Barrick, J. and Crowther, N. (1995) *The Housing Needs of People With a Visual Impairment.* London: The Housing Corporation.

*Disability Discrimination Act 1995.* London: HMSO.

*Housing Grants, Construction and Regeneration Act 1996.* London: HMSO.

Lovelock, R., Powell, J. and Craggs, S. (1995) *Shared Territory: Assessing the Social Support Needs of Visually Impaired People.* York: Joseph Rowntree Foundation.

Tillesley (1996) *RNIB (Blind in Britain Survey).* Peterborough: RNIB.

## Postscript

Adams, J. (1996) 'Adapting for community care, Part 1 and 2.' *British Journal of Occupational Therapy 59,* 3 and *59,* 4.

Blom Cooper, L. (1990) *Occupational Therapy: An Emerging Profession in Health Care.* Report of a Commission of Enquiry. London: Duckworth.

Brewis, C. (1994) 'Targetting the resources of housing adaptations for people with disabilities.' *British Journal of Occupational Therapy 60,* 3, 123–128.

Logan, P.A., Batchvarova, M. and Read, C. (1997) 'A study of the housing needs of disabled applicants to the Nottingham City Council Housing Department and the problems faced by local housing providers in meeting these needs.' *British Journal of Occupational Therapy 60,* 3, 129–131.

Nocon, A. and Pleace, N. (1997) '"Until disabled people get consulted…": The role of occupational therapy in meeting housing needs.' *British Journal of Occupational Therapy 60,* 3, 115–122.

Social Services Inspectorate/Department of Health (1993) *Occupational Therapy: The Community Contribution.* London: HMSO.

# The Contributors

**Ian Bradford** is community care advisor for Care and Repair (England), the national co-ordinating body for home improvement agencies. These are non-profit making organisations helping older and disabled people to organise repairs and adaptations to their homes. A significant part of Ian's work concerns the role of HIAs in helping disabled people achieve successful adaptations to their homes. Ian is an affiliate member of COTSSIH.

**Ruth Bull**, BA (Hons) Dip COT, has been practising since 1970. She was an occupational therapist in housing in the London Borough of Waltham Forest from 1983–1989, and then occupational therapy manager with housing lead. She has been manager of community care assessment services for people with physical/ sensory disability in the London Borough of Redbridge, and is currently Adult Resources Manager with Southend on Sea Borough Council, Social Services Department.

**Trevor Dodd**, DipCOT SROT, is housing senior occupational therapist in the housing disability team, Greenwich Council, London. He works on major adaptations, rehousing and access advice on new build schemes.

**Christine Galbraith** worked as senior occupational therapist, Lewisham Community Team, with responsibility for developing and implementing care in the community for adults with learning disabilities specialising in housing design and models for support.

**Jan Jensen** MSc (Health Psychology) DipOT (NZ) is a community occupational therapist with Kent Occupational Therapy Bureau.

**Jennifer Mace**, DipOT (NZ) SROT carries out research and development into occupational therapy and homelessness with the London Borough of Tower Hamlets, and is studying for an MSc in Health and Social Services Policy at the London School of Economics.

**Zeenat Meghani-Wise** BSc MSc SROT was formerly an independent practitioner in occupational therapy in London and is now living in Georgia, USA.

**Madeline Middle** Dip COT, SROT, is the disabled persons housing adviser for the Disabled Persons Housing Service, Walbrook Housing Association, Derby. She was previously senior occupational therapist in the disability team, Leicestershire Social Services Department.

**Brenda Parkes** BSc (Hons) (Occupational Therapy), SROT is a community occupational therapist with Suffolk County Council.

**Jackie Parsons** Dip COT SROT qualified as an occupational therapist in 1980. Her experience is mainly in community work and most recently as manager of Sheffield Disability Housing Service.

**Jeremy Porteus** BA (Hons), PGDip Law and Soc. was manager of the RNIB Housing Service.

**Veronica J. Watts**, DipCOT SROT, as senior community occupational therapist (housing) in the London Borough of Lewisham, assisted the housing department with their responsibilities for the design, assessment and allocation of housing suitable for disabled people.

# Subject Index

# Name Index